Hidden Rhythms

Eviatar Zerubavel

Hidden Rhythms
Schedules and Calendars in Social Life

University of California Press
Berkeley, Los Angeles, London

University of California Press
Berkeley and Los Angeles

University of California Press Ltd.
London

First published by the University of Chicago Press 1981
First California Paperback Edition 1985
ISBN 0-520-05609-4

Printed in the United States of America
1 2 3 4 5 6 7 8 9

To Noga, my starlight

Contents

Introduction

The present volume is intended as an introduction to a new area of investigation—the sociology of time. It has a two-fold purpose and is, therefore, essentially written for two distinct audiences. On the one hand, it aims at introducing the field of the sociology *of time* and is addressed to sociologists. On the other hand, it also aims at introducing the field of the *sociology* of time and is, thus, addressed to readers who are interested in the topic of time in general. The entire book has been written with this twofold purpose in mind.

My first task in writing this volume is to sensitize sociologists to temporality and, thus, to contribute to the development of a new field of interest and investigation within the discipline of sociology. While time is definitely one of the most central dimensions of the social world, it has so far been relatively neglected by sociologists, who have dealt with it—if at all—only as an aspect of other phenomena, such as social change or leisure, and hardly ever as a topic in its own right. This may be partly explained by the fact that time is an ever-present constituent of social life and, as such, tends to be taken for granted and ignored as a special focus of attention. And yet, precisely because time is such a major parameter of the social world, its significant role in social life can no longer be ignored. By bringing into focus some of the main themes underlying the temporal patterning of social life, I intend to demonstrate to sociologists that time ought to become a special topic of sociological concern. I first attempted to accomplish that in my earlier book, *Patterns of Time in Hospital Life,* where I offered a close look into the social foundations of the temporal patterning of hospital life.[1] The primary focus of the book was the temporal organization of social life in general, and it was mainly a matter of circumstance that I chose to study it in a hospital rather than anywhere else. I tried to make it clear from the outset that, "though the study took place *in* a hospital, it was never intended as a study *of* the hospital, since its analytical focus was clearly the temporal structure of social organization, rather than hospital life."[2]

However, as I was soon to learn, the way authors define their work and the way it is perceived by others are two entirely different things. Despite the fact that I had done my best to point out that a study done in a hospital is not necessarily a study of the hospital, my book has nevertheless been often perceived as a study of hospital life, and I myself as a sociologist of medicine!

It is a universal fact of life that, upon encountering novel, unfamiliar experience, people nevertheless tend to try and fit it into rather familiar conceptual categories. Since, at the present moment, no such field as the "sociology of time" seems to exist, it is only natural that my study would be cognitively pushed into well-established conceptual slots. It was, therefore, hardly surprising that the first category by which the Library of Congress decided to index the book for cataloguing purposes was "hospitals—sociological aspects"! Along the same lines, it was also quite typical that when I presented parts of my study at sociological conferences, I had to do that in sessions devoted to the sociology of medicine and the sociology of work.

The problem of *Patterns of Time,* as far as introducing the field of sociology of time is concerned, is that, even though it gives the reader a general sense of the potential depth of the field, it does not provide him or her with a clear sense of its potential scope. By deciding to concentrate on one particular institution, I managed to demonstrate how a sociologist might go about analyzing in depth the temporal organization of hospital life. What I did not demonstrate, however, was the applicability of my analysis to the investigation of the temporal organization of so many other domains of social life.

Therefore, in the present volume, I intend to complement my

previous work by deliberately focusing around a wide variety of substantive areas and topics. Thus, I shall be dealing with substantive areas as varied from one another as religion, cognition, ideology, group identity, and work, and with cultural contexts as different from one another as the medieval Benedictine monasteries, Revolutionary France, Orthodox Judaism, and the modern hospital. (Along the same lines, I shall also be moving from discussing cognitive patterns and cultural values to analyzing actual behavior routines, as well as from the microscopic level of interpersonal relations to the macroscopic level of societal symbols, according to my analytical purposes.) I have deliberately chosen this methodological approach in order to show the reader that the main focus of the book is not any one of those substantive areas or topics, but, rather, the unifying analytical theme of temporality. Thus, this is clearly not a book about either cognition, symbolism, ideology, religion, or work. Rather, it is a sociological exploration of *time*. I firmly believe that it is precisely the substantive variety of the discussions in this volume that would be most suggestive of the potentially rich scope of the field of the sociology of time.

I should add that some of the ideas presented in this volume have already been published—albeit in a more rudimentary form—in various sociological journals.[3] Here again, however, I was publishing separate articles that were dealing with different substantive topics— the French Revolution, the organization of modern professional commitments, and the social organization of life in the monastery— and were obviously perceived as separate from one another. It was impossible to convey the thematic unity of a number of articles that appeared in separate journals and were not necessarily read by the same readers. Hence my motivation to publish all my separately published and unpublished investigations of the temporal aspects of social life in the form of a single publication that would capture their unity and would have to be viewed as a whole.

As I pointed out earlier, this volume is not addressed to sociologists alone. My second major purpose in writing it has been to demonstrate to those who are interested in time in general that this topic, which has so far got considerable attention from philosophers, physicists, biologists, psychologists, and economists, can also be approached from yet a novel, relatively neglected analytical angle—the sociological perspective.

In order to highlight the specific contributions of a sociological perspective to the study of temporality, I have decided to deliberately avoid time-related topics such as historical change or biological rhythms, which have traditionally been explored by other disciplines. Whereas physicists and biologists, for example, have traditionally been concerned with temporal orders which regulate the motions of bodies or the lives of organisms, respectively, I intend to restrict my concern to an entirely different temporal order—the *sociotemporal order,* which regulates the lives of *social* entities such as families, professional groups, religious communities, complex organizations, or even entire nations.

This order is clearly distinct from other temporal orders. Whereas the physiotemporal and biotemporal orders, for example, are natural and, thus, inevitable, the sociotemporal order is essentially a socially constructed artifact which rests upon rather arbitrary social conventions. Consequently, while the physical and biological approaches to temporality have tended to emphasize the objective qualities of time, the sociological approach would be more likely to highlight its subjective qualities, the meanings that people attach to it. Obviously, this is also true of much of the psychological concern with temporality. However, whereas the psychology of time is essentially concerned with the way in which the individual perceives time, the sociological perspective would be more likely to emphasize the way time is perceived and handled by collectivities.

Having established what I believe ought to be the distinctive direction of the sociology of time and its major concerns, let me now discuss briefly the specific contributions of each of the chapters of the present volume to this field.

The first chapter centers around temporal regularity, a phenomenon that involves the structuring of social life by forcing activities into fairly rigid temporal patterns. I shall explore four major forms of temporal regularity by trying to unveil regular patterns of associating social events and activities with (*a*) rigid sequential structures, (*b*) fixed durations, (*c*) standard temporal locations, and (*d*) uniform rates of recurrence, stressing the fact that these often constitute binding normative prescriptions. The chapter also examines the cognitive dimension of temporal regularity. After all, as a result of the highly regular temporal profile of so many social events, it is often possible to tell the time by simply referring to our social environment. I shall focus particularly on people's responses to "pathological" situations, where things take place at times other than their usual ones, since they might tell us a lot about the "normal," temporally regular world in which we live.

Probably most responsible for the establishment and maintenance of temporal regularity in our daily lives is the schedule. Undoubtedly one of the institutions most characteristic of Western civilization, the schedule originally evolved in the medieval Benedictine monasteries, and the second chapter first explores, within the context of Benedictine monasticism, the genesis of the particular sort of temporal regularity which is associated with the schedule. The effective use of the schedule has also benefited from the invention of the mechanical clock, and the examination of the temporal organization of Benedictine monastic life also provides us with better insight into why it was also through the Benedictine monasteries that this timepiece was first introduced to the West. The chapter then proceeds to identify some of the fundamental principles that underlie any modern schedule and to examine the relation between schedules and modern life in general. After discussing the conventional basis of the schedule and the arbitrariness of so many regular temporal patterns, it considers both the constraints and loss of spontaneity involved in leading a scheduled life and the advantages of introducing routine, orderliness, and structure into life. It then proceeds to examine notable implications of the introduction of the schedule to the West, such as the development of a utilitarian philosophy of time and an abstract conception of temporality. Finally, the intricate relations between schedules and social solidarity are considered.

The relations between temporal arrangements and group formation are further explored in the third chapter, which revolves around the ways in which various groups throughout history have used their calendars for solidifying in-group sentiments as well as establishing intergroup boundaries to separate group members from "outsiders." The cases of the Sabbath, the Lord's Day, Easter, and the Dead Sea Sect and Mohammedan calendars will all be examined as part of a general discussion of the role of calendars in promoting social segregation. However, I shall also discuss the proliferation of the Gregorian calendar and the Christian Era as an attempt to establish no less than an international temporal reference framework, allowing for an almost universally valid standardization of time reckoning and dating. Finally, I shall also examine the symbolic functions of calendrical systems through an in-depth analysis of the French Republican calendrical reform of 1793, since this reform—undoubtedly the most radical attempt in modern history to have challenged the standard temporal reference framework that prevails in the world to this day—was deliberately meant to reflect as well as promote certain cultural values. The discussion will center around the variety of ways in which the reformers managed to design the new calendar so that it would symbolically represent some of the main themes of the spirit of the French Revolution.

The discussion of the symbolic function of calendrical systems indicates that people clearly view time not only as a physico-mathematical entity, but also as an entity which is imbued with meaning. The fourth chapter sheds some light on the way in which time functions as a context for anchoring the meaning of social acts and situations within the particular domain of religion. One of the fundamental essences of many religious systems is the necessity of achieving a total separation of the sacred and profane domains so as to maintain the conceptual distinction—and, thus, prevent any moral confusion—between them. Time plays a central role in facilitating the dichotomization of the universe into sacred and profane domains which are mutually exclusive, since it allows man to establish in a clear-cut manner and with minimum ambiguity whether something "belongs" within one sphere of life or another. The chapter examines the temporal segregation of the sacred from the profane by exploring the various ways in which Jews have traditionally managed to substantiate and accentuate the fundamental cognitive distinction between the Sabbath and the regular weekdays, periods of time that are entirely identical from a purely quantitative standpoint. The chapter also explores the ways in which the Sabbath and the regular weekdays are actually separated from one another as well as the means by which passage from one to the other is made possible, demonstrating that the very same temporal boundaries which serve to separate the sacred from the profane domain also serve to allow the transition between them.

In the final chapter, I shall demonstrate how, as a most effective principle of differentiation, time serves to keep apart not only the sacred and profane domains, but also the private and public spheres of life. With the increasing functional and structural differentiation within individuals' webs of social affiliations and the growing bureaucratic split between "person" and "role," maintaining the partiality of the involvement of modern individuals in each of the various social roles they occupy has become a necessity. Time is a major organizational principle which facilitates the institutionalization of privacy as well as the "segmentation" of modern individuals along the lines of their various social involvements. By providing some fairly rigid boundaries that segregate the private and public spheres of life from one another and to which the association of person and role is confined, time has become indispensable to the regulation of the social accessibility of modern individuals as well as to the maintenance of the partiality of each of their various social involvements. Following an examination of the temporal structure of social accessibility in general, I shall proceed to demonstrate that time constitutes a major dimension of social organization along which professional commitments are defined in modern society and that the temporal rigidity of modern work schedules is one of the key structural characteristics of modern social organization. I shall conclude the chapter by comparing the temporal structure of the professional commitments of physicians with that of nurses, and of high-ranking officials with that of low-ranking personnel, demonstrating that the degree of temporal rigidity or flexibility in defining professional commitments can help us to identify and differentiate various occupational roles and professional ethics, as well as to distinguish among various status rankings within a stratification system.

A general note regarding this work as a whole. This volume obviously presents a rather biased picture of the temporal organization of social life. Certainly not all social life is temporally structured in a rigid manner. There are a lot of people who conduct their everyday life without using calendars and schedules, wearing a watch, or respecting deadlines, who are often late to appointments, and who sometimes forget what day it is. I am by no means oblivious to all of the above. On the contrary, I deliberately try to ignore them, for heuristic purposes.

Following Max Weber,[4] I firmly believe that deliberate *one-sidedness* not only should not be regarded as obstructive, but also ought to be hailed as a methodological virtue. I think that one of the great strengths of classic sociological works such as those of Emile Durkheim, Georg Simmel, Sigmund Freud, Max Weber, and Karl Marx is the fact that, rather than try to portray the world "as it is" (whatever that means), they chose to deliberately concentrate in the most biased, one-sided fashion only on selected aspects of social reality and ignore others.

As Weber himself pointed out, however, scholars ought to have the necessary discipline to tell their readers where their biases lie. I therefore wish now to lay out before the reader the nature of my one-sidedness in the process of writing this volume, as I see it.

Like Weber and Simmel, I tend to believe that one of the most essential characteristics of modern life is the "rationalistic" character of modern culture.[5] Hence my decision to focus my concerns exclusively around the introduction of the "rational"—precise, punctual, calculable, standard, bureaucratic, rigid, invariant, finely coordinated, and routine—into our lives. I have done that deliberately so as to concentrate on what I believe to be *highly rationalized temporal orders*.

This involved, for one thing, a decision to deliberately ignore all nonrational or irrational manifestations of the temporal organization of social life—waiting, latecoming, spontaneity, and so on. It also accounts for the fact that the process of picking my substantive topics was by no means random. On the contrary, it was strategically designed—in a most selective manner—to dramatize the features of what I consider to be highly rationalized temporal orders. This is how I came to choose only those domains of social life as well as those cultural contexts where the rigid organization of time can be seen at its most extreme form—the Benedictine monastery, Revolutionary France, Orthodox Judaism, and the bureaucratic hospital—

to be the contexts of my discussions. I have done that deliberately so as to highlight the *rational elements of temporal organization.*

Despite the generally impersonal ethos of much of contemporary sociological research, I have always been motivated to study what is also of considerable personal concern and significance to me. Unlike many sociologists I know, I happen to regard the fact that I study human beings rather than stars, rocks, bacteria, or fish not as an inherent obstacle, but, rather, as one of the true fascinations of being a sociologist. For me, doing sociology has always implied further harmony between my professional life and my personal life. The present volume has a lot of personal significance, mainly because it touches some of the most serious problems I face in my own life.

One such problem is that of social accessibility. While I have always prided myself on being accessible to meaningful others in my life, I also cherish privacy and strongly dislike having acquaintances or neighbors drop by without notice when I least expect them. The very same ambivalence regarding accessibility also characterizes my general attitude toward the temporal organization of professional commitments. On the one hand, I have always had great difficulty understanding bureaucrats who leave their office precisely at 5:00 P.M. and refuse to be associated with their professional self beyond their "regular" hours. On the other hand, I have always felt a particularly strong distaste toward "greedy" institutions[6] which would swallow their employees if they could. Working on the fifth chapter of this volume, therefore, provided me with a most unusual opportunity to wrestle sociologically with a problem that has always intrigued me personally.

The same is true of the discussion, in the second chapter, of the clash between spontaneity and routine. When discussing the medieval Benedictine monk, I was actually addressing a most personal problem, namely, being constantly torn between the need to organize my life through the adherence to schedules and a gut-level love of spontaneity! In my own life, I have always oscillated between the two. On the one hand, I consider myself a spontaneous person who has a strong dislike for routine and prefers to conduct his life according to his whim. On the other hand, I have always known that only through order and discipline—which necessarily entail the introduction of deadlines and various forms of time management—can I accomplish projects such as completing a book. Working on the second chapter of this volume, therefore, was very significant to me not only as a sociologist wrestling with a sociological problem, but also as a person attempting to solve the ever-present existential conflict between striving for spontaneity and leading a relatively structured life.

Finally, I would like to take this opportunity to thank a number of friends and colleagues who, each in his or her own special way, helped me significantly throughout the process of writing this book.

Three persons in particular influenced my decision to write the book and helped me shape its general direction. My wife, Yael Zerubavel, was the first one to encourage me to assemble my various —published and unpublished—ideas regarding temporality and present them as a whole. She was the first critical audience for many beginnings—some of which were dropped right away and others which did evolve into coherent ideas—and later reviewed early drafts of the manuscript. At the early stage when I was still uncertain whether I had a book or just a collection of separate essays, I also got much support and some very useful suggestions from Renée Fox and Kai Erikson, particularly regarding the interrelations of the various chapters as parts of a whole.

Charles Lidz provided me with much sociological feedback at a time when I was working in a department of psychiatry. I am very grateful for his many patient readings of early drafts of most of the chapters of the book.

However, as I pointed out earlier, this volume is my very first attempt to address a scholarly piece of mine to an audience wider than the academic sociological community. This is how my friend Linda John came to play such an important role as a critical reader of the manuscript. It was she who provided me with the necessary feedback from someone other than a professional sociologist. Her critical reading of early drafts of the manuscript was most important to me at the stage of trying to extend beyond the academia as my exclusive audience.

I would like to thank various colleagues—particularly Rose Coser, John R. Hall, Samuel Heilman, Joshua Lederberg, and Joel

Telles—who provided me with various suggestions regarding many ideas presented here. I am also greatly indebted to my friends Lin Ehrenpreis, Diane Enerson, Alan Meisel, and Amos Yoran, who helped me significantly by reading and commenting on parts of the manuscript.

Last, I would like to express my deep gratitude to Barry Schwartz, not only for his most valuable comments on a number of early drafts of various chapters, but, even more significantly, for being my primary partner in the intellectual exchange around the sociology of time as a focal area of interest.

One

Temporal Regularity

The world in which we live is a fairly structured place. Even the most casual glance at our environment would already reveal a certain degree of orderliness. One of the fundamental parameters of this orderliness is time—there are numerous temporal patterns around us.

At the basis of any structure and order there is usually some regularity. At the basis of the temporal structure of the world, we, therefore, ought to expect to find some temporal regularity. The search for such regularity is the main focus of the present chapter.

Let me first delineate the major dimensions of the temporal profile of any situation or event.[1] One fundamental parameter of situations and events is their *sequential structure,* which tells us in what order they take place. A second major parameter, their *duration,* tells us how long they last. A third parameter, their *temporal location,* tells us when they take place, whereas a fourth parameter, their *rate of recurrence,* tells us how often they do.

In my search for temporal patterns, I shall thus try to identify four major forms of temporal regularity—rigid sequential structures, fixed durations, standard temporal locations, and uniform rates of recurrence. In other words, I shall be primarily concerned with the rigidification of the sequential ordering of situations and events, their duration, their temporal location, and their rate of recurrence.

There are many forms of temporal patterns. Basically, however, they all fall into one of the following categories: physiotemporal patterns, biotemporal patterns, and sociotemporal patterns.

Physiotemporal patterns lie within the research domains

of the physicist and the astronomer. They essentially involve temporal regularities such as the following: the predictable fact that lightnings always precede thunders, rather than follow them; the predictable duration of the flight of projectiles, as calculated by ballisticians; the predictable time of day at which the sun rises on any particular day of the year; the predictable period during which a particular planet completes a revolution around the sun or a rotation on its own axis; and so on.

Whereas the physiotemporal order regulates the movement of physical bodies, it is the biotemporal order that is primarily responsible for regulating the lives and daily functioning of organisms. Biotemporal patterns lie within the research domain of the biologist and involve temporal regularities such as the following: the predictable sequential relations among the stages of being a larva, a cocoon, and a mature insect; the relatively fixed duration of pregnancy periods; the fairly predictable temporal location of puberty within the life cycle; the fairly uniform circadian rhythms that govern the body's temperature; and so on.

The present chapter revolves around the *sociotemporal order,* which regulates the structure and dynamics of social life. I am primarily concerned, therefore, with *sociotemporal patterns,* which essentially involve the temporal rigidification of *social* situations, activities, and events. Such patterns clearly lie within the research domain of the sociologist. Unfortunately, unlike the physical sciences and the life sciences, sociology has so far paid relatively little attention, if any, to the phenomenon of temporal regularity. (This is not necessarily true of the other social sciences. Consider, for example, the traditional anthropological concern with seasonal cycles or the study of business cycles in economics.) And yet, this phenomenon is probably one of the fundamental parameters of any social order. It is definitely among the main characteristics of modern social life, one of the key phenomena that provide it with an unmistakable structure. As Lewis Mumford put it, "The first characteristic of modern machine civilization is its temporal regularity."[2]

Rigid Sequential Structures

Rigid sequential structures are the most obvious and conspicuous form of temporal regularity. It is in the nature of many events, activities, and situations that they cannot all take place simultaneously and must, therefore, be temporally segregated from one another in terms of "before" and "after." The sequential order in accordance with which they are arranged may sometimes be purely random. However, it is very often the case that it is rigid, to the point of irreversibility.

As Peter Berger and Thomas Luckmann have pointed out, sequential rigidity is inherent to the everyday life world:

> I cannot reverse at will the sequences imposed by [the temporal structure of everyday life]—"first things first" is an essential element of my knowledge of everyday life. Thus, I cannot take a certain examination before I have passed through certain educational programs, I cannot practice my profession before I have taken this examination, and so on.[3]

Usually, sequential rigidity is a normative prescription and not a mere empirical coincidence. It is identifiable already at the level of short ceremonial events such as weddings, funerals, military parades, religious services, classical music concerts, and official banquets. However, it is also built into entire life careers. Consider, for example, the common prohibition of procreation prior to marriage or the sequential order of various rites of passage, which is hardly ever flexible and reversible! In between those two extremes, note also the rigid sequential structure of "career timetables,"[4] academic curricula, and various bureaucratic routines and procedures. I should add that sequential rigidity is by no means characteristic of formal organizational life alone. As will soon become apparent from the discussion of courtship norms, it prevails in the more informal domains of social life as well.

Some irreversibilities are determined by nature or are inevitable from a logical or technical standpoint. It is natural imperatives that force farmers, for example, to plow their fields before, rather than after, sowing, or that make it impossible for anyone to become an infant after one has already aged. It is a logical-definitional necessity that compels track-meet organizers to schedule finals after, rather than before, heats. Likewise, it is a technical constraint that forces us to eat only after—and not before—cooking.

However, it is a mere artificial convention that underlies our custom of serving soup before, rather than after, serving meat.[5] (The

Pennsylvania Dutch tradition of serving all dishes simultaneously ought to remind us that the institutionalization of temporally segregated "courses" in meals is in itself purely conventional!) Similarly, even though the sequential rigidity of many routine bureaucratic procedures is usually based upon sound organizational rationales, it is by no means natural and inevitable. Under various circumstances, the sequential structure of these procedures may very well be altered. Given the symbolic significance of temporal priority in general,[6] it is only natural that many socially based irreversibilities are purely symbolic in nature. This is quite evident in the case of the sequential rigidity that is built into weddings, commencement ceremonies, and even formal introductions and patterns of name ordering among authors of scientific papers.[7]

A cross-specific comparison of courtship rituals highlights the fundamental distinction between naturally based and socially based sequential rigidity, and serves to demonstrate where nature ends and social convention begins. The courtship ceremonies of water salamanders or sticklebacks, for example, generally consist of biologically determined "reaction chains" wherein each link in the chain functions as a necessary "releaser" of the mate's next move.[8] Ritualized fanning by the male, for instance, is indispensable for "releasing" the female's entrance to the nest and must, therefore, precede it.

A substantial amount of sequential rigidity is built into human courtship rituals as well. Consider, for example, the temporal relations among stages such as "necking," "petting," and actual sexual intercourse. There may be some variability in the duration of these stages or in their temporal location vis-à-vis the first date, the onset of "going steady," the engagement, and the wedding.[9] And yet, the irreversibility of their sequential ordering vis-à-vis one another is quite well established. In other words, there are generally agreed-upon norms regarding which stage in the courtship ritual ought to precede or follow others.[10] According to Ray Birdwhistell, it is quite easy

> to delineate some twenty-four steps between the initial tactile contact between the young male and female and the coitional act. These steps and countersteps had a coercive order. For instance, a boy taking the girl's hand must await a counterpressure on his

hand before beginning the finger intertwine. The move and countermove, ideally, must take place before he "casually" and tentatively puts his arm around her shoulders. And each of these contacts should take place before the initial kiss.[11]

Those who deviate from the prescribed norm of proper sequence are commonly referred to as being "fast" or "slow." Note that, within the context of courtship, these terms refer primarily to sequential ordering, rather than to duration:

> The boy or girl is called "slow" or "fast" in terms of the appropriate ordering of the steps, not in terms of the length of time taken at each stage. Skipping steps or reversing their order is "fast." Insistence on ignoring the prompting to move to the next step is "slow."[12]

The considerable normative significance of the notions of "fast" and "slow" is quite evident from the negative sanctions that are usually attached to each of those deviations from the prescribed norm of "proper sequence." It also accounts for the overwhelming feeling of "bad taste" which often accompanies the act of deviating from that norm.

And yet, this sequential rigidity is, to a large extent, conventional and by no means inevitable. A "move" or "step" such as the initial kiss does not really *have* to be preceded by a finger intertwine in order to be carried out. Furthermore, in various sexual relationships it is omitted altogether! The "proper sequences" which underlie popular normative notions such as "too fast" or "too slow" in human courtship are of an almost purely nonbiological, symbolic significance. It is hardly surprising, therefore, that they often vary not only across cultures, but also across historical periods as well as age-groups within cultures.

Fixed Durations

A second facet of the temporal regularity which prevails in modern life is the fact that numerous events are associated with relatively fixed durations on a regular basis. In a way, as I shall demonstrate in the next chapter, most of the timetables and schedules we use would not have been possible were it not for the durational rigidification of so many events and activities in our daily life. As Alvin Toffler has pointed out, "In adult behavior, virtually all we do, from mailing an envelope to making love, is premised upon certain spoken or unspoken assumptions about duration."[13] Thus, most college training programs, for example, are rigidly forced into four-year periods, many therapeutic sessions are defined as fifty-minute "hours," and various warranties expire six months from the date of purchase. Even our music has been characterized, in contradistinction to non-Western music, as durationally rigid.[14]

Durational rigidity is often technologically or biologically determined. Consider, for example, the duration of a Paris-Rome flight or a pregnancy period. The durational rigidity of "determinate time tracks"[15] such as jail sentences, military service, presidential terms, vacations, classes in school, and appointments, however, is almost entirely conventional. Its conventional basis is quite evident from the fact that the durations of these "time tracks" are usually defined in terms of "rounded off" time periods, such as fifteen years (jail sentences), two weeks (vacations), or thirty minutes (appointments). They are also essentially alterable, as might be indicated by practices such as cutting down various training programs during wartime or extending an appointment by an extra couple of minutes.

And yet, despite the fairly obvious conventionality of their association to events, the fixed durations of the latter are very often commonly regarded as intrinsic to them. For example, even though it has never been stated anywhere that entertainment events ought to last about two hours, the fact that they generally do would probably lead most of us to feel cheated if a movie or a concert for which we had bought a full-price ticket lasted only ten minutes! This notion of "only" suggests that we have fairly well defined ideas of what the "proper" durations of events are, and even though these are hardly ever formally and explicitly specified, they are nevertheless regarded as normatively binding. Consider, for example, the symbolic overtones of acts such as leaving "too early" or, on the other hand, staying "too long." (The same is also true of behavior patterns such as being engaged for "too long" without getting married.) The notion of "overstaying"[16] is particularly interesting. That even very close friends are sometimes said to have stayed "too long" seems to indicate that normative notions—and, consequently, actual patterns—

of durational rigidity do exist even in the relatively unstructured realm of informal relations.

Standard Temporal Locations

Durational rigidity is closely related to a third facet of temporal regularity, namely, the standardization of the temporal location of numerous events and activities in our daily life. The fact that a particular class is to last an hour, for example, is quite inseparable from the fact that it is routinely scheduled for 2:00 P.M. and another class is routinely scheduled for 3:00 P.M. in the same room. (The standardization of the temporal location of activities and events is very often also related to the rigidification of their sequential structure. If local television news, for example, is routinely scheduled for 6:00 P.M. and national news for 6:30 P.M., the former will necessarily always precede the latter.)

The standardization of temporal location presupposes *scheduling,* a typically Western phenomenon which involves moving away "from the natural or casual sense of time toward a sense of time as schedule."[17] Unlike many non-Western civilizations, where events and activities are temporally located in a relatively spontaneous manner, we tend to "schedule" them, that is, routinely fix them at particular prearranged, and often standard, points in time—at particular hours, on particular days of the week, in particular parts of the year, or even in particular periods within one's life career. Whereas, in many non-Western civilizations, it is human activity that regulates the calendar,[18] in the modern West it is the calendar (along with the schedule) that regulates human activity!

In general, most of our routine daily activities are scheduled in a fairly rigid manner for particular times of the day and for particular days of the week. Thus, we usually eat not necessarily when we are hungry, but, rather, during officially designated eating periods such as "lunchtime" or "dinner time." Similarly, we usually go to bed not necessarily when we get tired, but, rather, when it gets "late." Cleaning one's home is another activity which typically takes place not necessarily when things get dirty, but, rather, on particular days of the week that are designated as "cleaning days" in a standard fashion.

Consider also the temporally rigid structure of work, a phenomenon which will be further explored in the last chapter. As Wilbert Moore has pointed out,

> For the primitive food gatherer or peasant cultivator time as such is not economically valued. He pursues a particular task or set of tasks steadily, except as he is interrupted by darkness or fatigue, until the work is completed, and then may spend a variable period "doing nothing" until the next endeavor is started.[19]

We, on the other hand, usually go to work not necessarily when we feel like it or when there is an urgent necessity, but, rather, at certain normatively prescribed standard hours. Furthermore, even our hours of rest are determined by "the rigid requirements of the urban schedule."[20] We usually rest not necessarily when we are tired, but, rather, during officially designated rest periods such as lunch breaks and weekends.

The association of social activities and events with some standard temporal locations is by no means a mere empirical coincidence. Very often it is a normative prescription as well. After all, children do not necessarily go to bed at a certain standard hour because they want to, but, rather, because they *have* to. Fixing the temporal location of events entails a broadly conceived norm of "punctuality," which involves assigning a deviant character to the acts of being "early" or "late." Being late for work, for example, might entail some loss in one's social reputation. In various social circles, the same is also true of men and—even more so—women who are "late" in getting married. On the other hand—yet for precisely the same reason—one would be particularly careful about keeping one's children from launching their drinking, smoking, or sexual careers "too early." Both cases indicate some deep respect for the norms of "proper" timing that derive from what Julius Roth has identified as "career timetables."[21]

Generally speaking, we have relatively fixed notions of what constitutes "the proper time." It is almost inconceivable, for example, that an event such as a dance would be scheduled for the morning (even on non-working days). However, we ought to realize that the basis for locating—or abstaining from locating—certain activities and events at particular time periods is, very often, purely conventional. To appreciate the fundamental difference between naturally determined and socially based standard temporal locations of activities and events, contrast, for example, the reasons for sowing in the spring or hunting during the daytime with the reasons which underlie routines such as going to church on Sunday or to college around the age of eighteen. As Murray Wax has noted,

> societies that live according to casual time recognize adolescence by the appearance of the appropriate social and physiological manifestations. . . . societies that perceive time as a schedule grant this status according to time-serving—so many years of school or training.[22]

The artificial nature of social scheduling is also evident from the sheer fact that so many events in our daily life are scheduled for "rounded off" times such as "on the hour." A dinner that is scheduled for 8:19 P.M., for example, is almost inconceivable. Note also how we teach our children, especially during the summer, that bedtime is determined by the clock alone and that it may very well be "late" even when there is still light outside. It should be pointed out, in this regard, that we probably would have never felt the need to invent daylight saving time were it not for the fact that our standard wake-up time is dictated by the clock rather than by the sun! The conventionality of the standard temporal locations of so many activities and events in our life is even more evident when contrasted with the way in which the same events and activities are temporally located not only in other civilizations, but also in the worlds of some segments of our own society which are not as strictly governed by the clock and the schedule—presocialized infants, the retired aged, the unemployed,[23] and bohemia.

Uniform Rates of Recurrence

In the particular case of recurrent activity patterns, the standardization of the temporal location of activities and events also entails uniform rates of recurrence, that is, some fairly rigid *rhythmicity*. That a particular seminar is routinely scheduled for Wednesdays necessarily implies also that it is being held regularly on a weekly basis. That Christmas always falls on 25 December necessarily implies also that it is celebrated regularly on an annual basis. Along the same lines, official meetings and conferences that are routinely scheduled for 2:00 P.M. or for the first day of the month essentially recur regularly on a daily or monthly basis, respectively. Such periodic patterns are regular not only in a social sense, as when families space their reunions in accordance with routines such as "every wedding or funeral," but also in a strictly mathematical sense, as when the reunion takes place "every Memorial Day" (that is, every year). In other words, in such periodic patterns, the time intervals during which sequences of recurring successions of social activities are completed are mathematically equal.

The sociological concern with periodic recurrence is analogous to the concern, in the physical and life sciences, with regularly recurrent patterns such as the revolution of the earth around the sun and its rotation on its own axis, or the various rhythms in accordance with which sleep, hunger, ovulation, and body temperature are temporally structured. It began with Emile Durkheim's, Henri Hubert's, and Marcel Mauss's pioneer explorations of the "rhythm of collective life," and was further consolidated by Pitirim Sorokin's analyses of "sociocultural rhythms and periodicities." Since then, sociologists have identified various *"social cycles"*—classic examples of which are the day, the week, and the year—that are responsible for the rhythmic structure of social life.[24]

The rhythmicity imposed on social life by the temporal spacing of numerous recurrent activities and events at mathematically regular intervals is by no means characteristic of formal organization alone, and is identifiable not only at the macrosocial level, as the above-mentioned studies and works might suggest. It is also possible to identify uniform rates of recurrence of periodic activities at the microsocial level and within relatively unstructured domains such as that of informal relations. Furthermore, these are not only empirical patterns, but actual normative prescriptions as well. The normative overtones of notions such as "too often" or "hardly ever" suggest that even the temporal spacing of visits, telephone calls, and letters exchanged among friends—a most useful indicator of what Durkheim considered to be the "moral density" of social relations[25] —is by no means "casual" and is quite often governed by some regular "proper" tempi.[26]

As Sorokin so convincingly demonstrated, many of the rhythms that govern social life are entirely conventional.[27] Most striking in this regard is the rhythmicity associated with time units such as the hour or the week. Given the artificial basis of those time units, such rhythmicity is obviously artificial as well. Consider, for example, the temporal organization of the administration of medications in hospitals.[28] Despite its strong biological basis, the fact that medication times are routinely spaced at regular "rounded off" intervals such as four or six hours—rather than, say, at intervals of five hours and thirty eight minutes—is indicative of its conventionality. Even more suggestive of the fact that we are actually dealing here with a sociotemporal phenomenon rather than with physiotemporal or biotemporal patterns are temporal regularities that are associated with the seven-day week, a cycle which is undoubtedly a purely conventional artifact. As I shall demonstrate in the fourth chapter, this cycle, which governs and regulates so much of our everyday life, actually represents man's first successful attempt to establish a social rhythmicity that is based upon an entirely artificial regularity.

Let us turn now to the daily, monthly, and annual rhythms of social life. First of all, we ought to remember that the calendar day, month, and year are slightly modified versions—and, therefore, only approximations—of their original astronomical models. Furthermore, even if they did precisely correspond to them in actuality, it is still social convention alone that ties the temporal structure of news broadcasts to the daily cycle, the temporal organization of business activity to the monthly cycle, and the professional mobility of young physicians to the annual cycle.

Much of our social life is temporally structured in accordance with "mechanical time," which is quite independent of "the rhythm of man's organic impulses and needs."[29] In other words, we are increasingly detaching ourselves from "organic and functional periodicity," which is dictated by nature, and replacing it by "mechanical periodicity," which is dictated by the schedule, the calendar, and the clock.[30] To fully appreciate the artificial basis of social rhythmicity, note that, not only is it so often quite independent of natural rhythmicity, but it sometimes even conflicts with it. It is certainly not an awareness of our internal biological rhythmicity, for example, that leads us to work for five days and then rest for two. Such discrepancies between organic and mechanical periodicity obviously entail certain risks. As Kevin Lynch has pointed out, "As men free themselves from submission to the external cycles of nature, relying more often on self-created and variable social cycles, they increasingly risk internal disruption."[31] Note for example, that our bodies are internally regulated by natural rhythms that are called "circadian rhythms" because they correspond only very roughly to our twenty-four-hour calendar days. And yet, we routinely impose on them a twenty-four-hour rhythmicity, which derives from the organization of our life in accordance with daily schedules that adhere to clock time, which involves twenty-four-hour cycles. That we are so often sleepy upon getting up yet wide awake around bedtime may well be the price we have to pay for that. Furthermore, according to Lewis Mumford,

> a population trained to keep to a mechanical time routine at whatever sacrifice to health, convenience, and organic felicity may well suffer from the strain of that discipline and find life impossible without the most strenuous compensations. The fact that sexual intercourse in a modern city is limited, for workers in all grades and departments, to the fatigued hours of the day may add to the efficiency of the working life only by a too-heavy sacrifice in personal and organic relations.[32]

Temporal Regularity—the Cognitive Dimension

The temporal regularity of our social world has some very significant cognitive implications. In allowing us to have certain expectations regarding the temporal structure of our environment, it certainly helps us considerably to develop some sense of orderliness. By providing us with a highly reliable repertoire of what is expected, likely, or unlikely to take place within certain temporal boundaries, it adds a strong touch of predictability to the world around us, thus enhancing our cognitive well-being. Temporal irregularity, on the other hand, contributes considerably to the development of a strong sense of uncertainty. As Bruno Bettelheim has noted, regarding life in the concentration camp, "Thus the endless 'anonymity' of time was another factor destructive to personality, while the ability to organize time was a strengthening influence. It permitted some initiative, some planning."[33] Dorothy Nelkin has noted the very same phenomenon with regard to migrant labor.[34]

Consider, for example, the case of durational rigidity. As Alvin Toffler has pointed out,

> Man's perception of time is closely linked with his internal rhythms. But his responses to time are culturally conditioned. Part of this conditioning consists of building up within the child a series of expectations about the duration of events, processes or relationships. Indeed, one of the most important forms of knowledge that we impart to a child is a knowledge of how long things last. This knowledge is taught in subtle, informal and often unconscious ways. Yet without a rich set of socially appropriate durational expectancies, no individual could function success-fully. . . . The child soon learns that "mealtime" is neither a one-minute nor a five-hour affair, but that it ordinarily lasts from fifteen minutes to an hour. He learns that going to a movie lasts two to four hours, but that a visit with the pediatrician seldom lasts more than one. He learns that the school day ordinarily lasts six hours.[35]

Much of the predictability which is built into modern life depends on such "durational expectancies."[36] Only on the basis of my knowledge that an appointment I have scheduled for 9:15 will not last more than forty-five minutes can I be certain that I shall be able to make a class which is scheduled for 10:00!

The cognitive indispensability of temporal regularity is generally true not only of durational rigidity. Much of our daily planning presupposes certain expectations regarding the regularity of the temporal location and the rate of recurrence of events. Railroads, airlines, radio, and television, for example, could not have functioned as effectively were it not for the invention of the timetable, one of the most conspicuous products of temporal regularity. Along the same lines, it would have probably also been much more difficult for us to budget our expenses were we to be uncertain as to how often we would get paid.

In general, it would have been almost impossible to plan our lives were we to be totally in the dark as to what might take place when, how often, in what order, and how long. In order to appreciate the extent to which temporal regularity enhances predictability—and thus planning in general—note also the considerable efforts made by people who regard themselves as potential targets for kidnapers and assassins to avoid, as much as possible, any temporally regular life patterns. They know that they cannot afford to have too many routines, since these might provide those who follow them with clear expectations upon which to base their planning. On the other hand —and yet for the very same reason—temporal regularity helps us to attain some peace of mind regarding our environment. As Elijah Anderson, for example, has noted with respect to social groups that are formed around bars, "When group members see a person going to work every day and coming to Jelly's at a regular time, they can begin to place some trust in him."[37]

It is a well-known fact that regular physiotemporal and biotemporal patterns provide us with such a high degree of predictability that we can use our natural environment in itself as a fairly reliable clock or calendar. It is quite easy, for example, to tell the time of day by reference to the position of the sun in the sky. In a similar fashion, many of us can easily tell the season—if not the actual month—by referring to the temperature, the color of the leaves, the birds and animals around, the flowers that blossom, or even our allergy symptoms. Societies that use lunar or lunisolar calendars can also tell the approximate date by the phase of the moon.

Is this not true of regular *socio*temporal patterns as well? Given its considerable temporal regularity, cannot social life in itself function as a clock or a calendar which is as reliable as any natural clock or calendar? I believe that it can and that, indeed, it very often actually does. One of the implications of the highly regular temporal profile of so many social events is that we carry in our minds a sort of "temporal map" which consists of all our expectations regarding the sequential order, duration, temporal location, and rate of recurrence of events in our everyday life. Given this "map," it is quite often relatively easy to tell the time by simply referring to our social environment!

Let us examine first one particular social environment which highlights many of the characteristics of what I would like to call "clockwork environments"—the hospital. Much of the daily life within that environment is systematically structured in accordance with the clock and the calendar.[38] Most of the activities and events in hospital life—admissions, discharges, tests, operations, the administration of medications, meals, rounds, conferences, clinic appointments, family visits, and so on—are systematically regulated by fairly rigid schedules. As I shall show in the last chapter, it is also schedules that define the temporal boundaries of staff's presence at the hospital, as well as those of their professional duties and responsibilities there.

Given all this, it should come as no surprise that, within the hospital environment, people can often tell the time, without referring to a clock, by simply observing what goes on around them at any given moment. When patients are served lunch, for example, they know that it must be around noon. Along the same lines, they can usually tell the approximate time of day by routine daily events such as the doctors' morning round, the administration of medications, the arrival of newspapers, the departure of visitors, and so on. All this presupposes, and would have been impossible without, the temporally rigid structuring of hospital life.

As we shall see in chapter 5, most occupational roles in bureaucratic organizations such as the modern hospital are "activated" only within certain temporal boundaries. This also has some very interesting cognitive implications. Those familiar with hospital routines know, for example, that they are most likely to find particular nurses in the hospital only within the temporal boundaries of their shifts, or that they are quite unlikely to find particular physicians there beyond a certain hour, unless it happens to be their night on duty. These temporally regular patterns of staff's presence at the hospital are taken for granted not only by other staff members, their friends, and their families, but by patients as well. Several years ago, when doing fieldwork in a hospital ward, I once engaged in a conversation with a particular patient around 1:00 A.M. Two days later, around noon, he asked me how come he had not seen me there on the following night. Although prior to that first night he had always seen me there only during the daytime, he probably must have assumed that, like nurses (with whom he used to see me), I had gone to nights. Being accustomed to the temporally regular structure of staff's presence on his ward, it probably did not even occur to him that my own presence there might have been temporally irregular (as it actually was)!

In short, hospital staff members are often associated—in the minds of other staff members as well as patients—not only with particular occupational roles, but also with the particular "time slots"[39] they cover. The temporal aspects of the role of "night nurse," for example, are by no means secondary to its occupational aspects.

In fact, for all practical purposes, night nurses are relevant *as nurses* only within the boundaries of the coverage time slot which is defined as "night." That hospital staff are very often referred to, and even introduced, in terms such as "the evening nurse," "the night resident," or "the day people" is indicative of the centrality of the time slot within which they work in the hospital to their relevance to others within that social milieu. Those who work permanently on a particular shift may even be identified by that time slot as if they were inseparable from it. I once heard a nurse referring to an evening nursing technician as "the 4-to-12 Bill"! (Quite similarly, in my daughter's nursery school, children who do not stay for the afternoon program and, thus, leave regularly at 1:00 P.M. are generally referred to, by the other children, as "one o'clock kids.")

Within this context, it is not hard to see how hospital staff get to function as timepieces. Many a patient can tell the approximate time of day by simply noting which staff members are around. The actual presence of a particular evening nurse on their unit, for example, might indicate to patients that the day shift has already ended or is about to end, that is, that it is approximately 4:00 P.M. In Dalton Trumbo's *Johnny Got His Gun,* a blind and deaf patient miraculously manages to keep track of the passage of time by learning to distinguish among the vibrations of the footsteps of the various nurses on his ward, as well as by noting when certain events such as the changing of his bedclothes take place.[40] Such cognitive adjustment presupposes the overall temporal regularity of that social milieu.

I have used the particular example of hospital life because it highlights some of the major characteristics of "clockwork environments" in general. However, the hospital is obviously only one of many such environments. Consider, for example, the railroad world. As Henry David Thoreau reflected, upon the introduction of the railway system to New England,

> I watch the passage of the morning cars with the same feeling
> that I do the rising of the sun, which is hardly more regular . . . .
> The startings and arrivals of the cars are now the epochs in the
> village day. They go and come with such regularity and precision,
> and their whistle can be heard so far, that the farmers set their
> clocks by them, and thus one well-conducted institution regulates
> a whole country.[41]

Generally speaking, most of us are able to tell the approximate time of day without having to refer to our watches or to clocks. We do that by simply attending to various cues in our social environment, such as particular television programs, the arrival of mail, rush-hour traffic jams, and so on. Given the highly regular temporal structuring of our social life, we tend to use such cues as fairly reliable timepieces.

Even more indicative of the considerable temporal regularity of our social world is the way in which we can tell what day it is without referring to a calendar. Here we are definitely within the realm of *socio*temporality, since the weekly cycle is a purely conventional artifact. We very often use our natural environment in order to tell what season or time of day it is. However, only our *social* environment can be of any help to us when we try to figure out what day it is.

As F. H. Colson pointed out, counting the days of the week is a form of time reckoning which is not anchored in nature and, thus, "if once lost by a single lapse would be lost forever."[42] This problem has always intrigued the Jews, who—as we shall see in the fourth chapter—were the first to have regulated their entire social life in accordance with the weekly cycle. In the Talmud, there is a lengthy discussion about what a Jew ought to do in case of losing count of the days of the week.[43] There is also a Talmudic story about seven maidens given by the Persian king Ahasuerus to his Jewish queen Esther, to help her keep count of the days of the week.[44] The terrible panic of a Jew who lost count of the days of the week is nicely depicted in Sholem Asch's short story "Losing Count of the Days."[45]

Jews have bequeathed such fears to non-Jewish Sabbatarians as well. Making sure that he would never lose count of the days of the week was one of Robinson Crusoe's first concerns:

After I had been there about Ten or Twelve days, it came into my Thoughts, that I should lose my Reckoning of Time for want of Books and Pen and Ink, and should even forget the Sabbath Days from the working Days; but to prevent this I cut it with my Knife upon a large Post, in Capital Letters, and making it into a great Cross I set it up on the Shore where I first landed, viz. *I came on Shore here on the 30th of* Sept. 1659. Upon the Sides of this square Post I cut every Day a Notch with my Knife, and every seventh Notch was as long again as the rest, and every first Day of the Month as long again as that long one, and thus I kept my Kalander, or weekly, monthly, and yearly Reckoning of Time.[46]

Such measures were necessary only because Robinson Crusoe was far away from civilization. That applies also to the hypothetical subject of the Talmudic discussion about losing count of the days of the week. Likewise, both Queen Esther and the hero of Asch's story were Jews who tried to adhere to the weekly cycle of Jewish religious life in a purely non-Jewish environment. When in their own "normal" environment, Jews never have any problem knowing what day it is. For example, as Mark Zborowski and Elizabeth Herzog noted, given the fact that, in Jewish communities, most of the cleaning work takes place toward the Sabbath, it is said that, "By the smell of the street water. . . . you can tell what day of the week it is."[47]

Today such a state of affairs is by no means characteristic of Jewish communities alone. F. H. Colson made this very clear:

> How do we ourselves remember the days of the week? The obvious answer is that something happens on one or more of them. If by some means or other we lose count in the course of the week, Sunday is unmistakable, even if personally we have no religious feeling about the day. So, too, school half-holiday or early-closing days force themselves on the notice of those who are not directly affected by them. But if nothing happens it is very doubtful whether a week-sequence could maintain, much less establish, itself.[48]

In occurring regularly in accordance with the weekly cycle, numerous events in our everyday life also function as cues which help us figure out what day it is. A nice example of that is provided by Hans Christian Andersen in his children's story "The Roses and the Sparrows":

> On Sunday mornings early the young wife came out, gathered a handful of the most beautiful roses, and put them in a glass of water, which she placed on a side table. "I see now that it is Sunday," said the husband as he kissed his little wife.[49]

Along the same lines, consider also the following social events: a political meeting that is held routinely on Mondays; a television program that is shown regularly on Tuesdays; a sociology seminar that meets regularly on Wednesdays; a piano lesson that is routinely scheduled for Thursdays; a telephone call from a friend who regularly calls on Fridays; a volleyball game that is regularly held on Saturdays; a family dinner that always takes place on Sundays; and so on. Such events help to orient us within the weekly cycle. Whenever I wake up to the sound of a garbage truck, I know immediately that it is Tuesday, because that is the regular garbage pick-up day. Likewise, on Wednesday mornings, I know that it is Wednesday, because I remember all the time that I have to teach later in the day.

One of the major contentions of cognitive psychology is that man essentially perceives objects as some sort of "figures" against some "ground."[50] Maurice Merleau-Ponty even went so far as to claim that assigning meaning is essentially an act of differentiating figure from ground, since the ground actually constitutes the context within which the meaning of the figure is anchored.[51] (This is also why the same figure might have entirely different meanings when placed against different grounds.) Any interpretive process of "defining a situation" essentially presupposes a solid, reliable ground, against which the situation can be perceived and assigned some meaning. A "groundless" figure or situation cannot be defined in any way which would make sense and is, therefore, totally meaningless.

The notion of "ground" has been incorporated into sociological theory through Harold Garfinkel's phenomenological explorations of the "normalcy" of the world of everyday life.[52] The centrality of this notion to Garfinkel's theory is quite evident from his constant use of concepts such as "routine grounds" and "background expectancies," both of which highlight the intricate relationship between regular, routine patterns and expectations. Garfinkel has demonstrated that the "normalcy" of our everyday life—which is the basis of all our expectations from our social environment—essentially presupposes a process of taking for granted some background features of familiar environments. These "background expectancies," against which all social situations are perceived, are the basis of all our standards regarding what is "normal." Our everyday life would not have been possible had we not internalized a certain interpretive order. Obviously, we are usually unaware of this order, because we tend to take it for granted.

I would like to demonstrate now that the taken-for-grantedness of our "normal environments" is actually restricted to certain time periods and does not transcend their boundaries. In other words, I claim that time constitutes one of the major parameters of any ground against which figures are perceived, and that, as a result of this, determining whether a certain situation or event is "normal" or not depends, to a large extent, on its temporal profile. In short, I wish to bring into focus the *temporal anchoring of normalcy,* that is, to demonstrate that *the "normalcy" of our everyday life world is temporally situated.*

Any meaningful definition of a situation presupposes some "sensible" configuration (gestalt) of figure and ground. We would, therefore, expect that perceiving any "groundless" figure would not make any sense. Given our strong basic need to "make sense"— a need which has been repeatedly emphasized by Garfinkel and his students as well as by cognitive psychologists[53]—we would also expect it to be cognitively intolerable. If time, indeed, constitutes one of the major parameters of any ground against which we perceive figures, we should not be surprised to find out that, in situations whereby a figure is unaccompanied by a temporal ground, we have a strong need to establish the latter. Without it, it is much more difficult to perceive the figure in a way which would "make sense."

To appreciate our strong cognitive need to associate social "figures" with some temporal grounds, consider the following instance. Once, upon arriving at a colleague's office, I was asked by her secretary, who had never seen me before, "Are you her four o'clock appointment?" By asking this "orientational" question, the secretary tried to establish some temporal ground against which she might perceive me—an otherwise "groundless" figure—in a way which would make better "sense" to her. Consider also an instance whereby a nurse, upon arriving at the emergency room around midnight to begin her night shift, asked the first intern she saw there, "Are you leaving soon or do you stay here all night?" Usually in that service, around midnight, two interns would be present—one would leave an hour later, around 1:00 A.M., while the other would stay there for the rest of the night. We should view the nurse's question as an attempt to establish in her own mind which of the two interns was working on the night shift that particular day. In other words, it was an attempt to place him in the temporal map in her mind.

Far more cognitively disturbing than groundless figures, however, are figures which are perceived against some ground other than their "normal" ground. Without its "normal" ground, it is far more difficult to perceive a figure in a way which would "make sense." Consider, for example, our quite common inability to recognize on the street persons that we encounter almost every day on the elevator or at the cafeteria of the building where we work. This is what psychologists call a "bad gestalt."

The above case is an example of an incongruity between a figure and its spatial ground. However, that any incongruity between figures and grounds is cognitively disturbing also applies to temporal grounds. The presence of so many people and other objects in our social environment passes as "normal" and is unnoticeable only within certain temporal boundaries. Outside those boundaries, it is by no means taken for granted. Thus, it is only around the months of November, December, and January that the presence of Christmas trees and Santa Clauses passes as "normal," and it is only around rush hours that we take long traffic jams for granted. Furthermore, even though most of us are present at our working place on a regular daily basis, our presence there at any time outside the boundaries of what is commonly defined as our working hours would not be taken for granted and would not pass as "normal."

The temporal regularity of our everyday life world is definitely among the major background expectancies which are at the basis of the "normalcy" of our social environment. The fairly regular temporal structure of our social life is responsible for the establishment of some solid temporal ground against which the occurrence of certain events and the presence of particular persons and objects pass as "normal" and unnoticeable. The unexpected occurrence of events and presence of persons and objects outside their usual temporal niches tend to disrupt the implicit, taken-for-granted figure-ground configuration which our "normal environment" presupposes. (This is obviously much less so in social environments that are more loosely structured from a temporal standpoint.) It results in a chaotic incongruity between figure and ground, which entails the loss of a meaningful way of anchoring our cognitive experiences. I should add that our intolerance toward *temporal anomalies* not only reflects the fairly rigid temporal structure of our social life, but also helps to sustain it.

A most useful way of demonstrating the existence of a certain phenomenon is to examine the implications and consequences of its absence. As Benjamin Lee Whorf suggested,

> if a rule has absolutely no exceptions, it is not recognized as a rule or as anything else; it is then part of the background of experience of which we tend to remain unconscious. Never having experienced anything in contrast to it, we cannot isolate it and formulate it as a rule until we so enlarge our experience and expand our base of reference that we encounter an interruption of its regularity. The situation is somewhat analogous to that of not missing the water till the well runs dry, or not realizing that we need air till we are choking.[54]

The obvious methodological implication of this is that investigating the "pathological" might help us to discover, unveil, or simply bring into focus the "normal," which we usually take for granted and—therefore—tend to ignore. This methodological principle was applied in a most successful fashion by Durkheim, who explored the phenomena of criminality and suicide only for the purpose of bringing social solidarity into focus. Likewise, it was Sigmund Freud's general concern with the "normal" personality that led him to study psychopathological parapraxes. Along the same lines, it is Gregory Bateson's general concern with the normal way of framing experience that has led him to study the way schizophrenics reason, and it is Garfinkel's general concern with commonsensical reasoning that has led him to examine misunderstandings in social interaction.[55]

In a similar manner, a useful way of sensitizing ourselves to the existence of temporal regularity would be to examine the consequences of its absence. Therefore, in order to solidify my argument regarding the prevalence of temporal regularity in our social life, I shall try to shed light on the disturbing cognitive implications of temporal *ir*regularity. I shall focus particularly on "pathological" situations which involve some cognitive incongruity between social figures and temporal grounds. People's responses to such anomalous situations might tell us a lot about the "normal," temporally regular world in which we live.

A key element to look for in such situations is surprise. It serves as evidence of the existence of prior expectations, and these, in turn, are indicative of some anticipated regularity. Given the temporally regular patterns that—even though we usually take them for granted and, therefore, ignore—regulate much of our social life, it is quite understandable that we would have certain expectations regarding the duration, sequential ordering, temporal location, and rate of recurrence of many events in our environment. Consider, for example, hypothetical situations such as when what we usually regard as an appetizer is served only after the main dish, when guests who have been invited over for the evening leave after "only" ten minutes without giving any account whatsoever, or when a mere acquaintance keeps calling us every other day. Our obvious surprise on such occasions would be indicative of the existence of some prior expectations regarding the temporal profile of social situations and events. Such expectations, in turn, are indicative of the temporal regularity of "normal" social life.

Very often, when we perceive a certain figure against its "normal" temporal ground, we may not even notice it, because the entire gestalt passes as "normal." However, we would most likely become somewhat surprised, if not actually alarmed, were we to perceive the very same figure against a "wrong" temporal ground. As Erving Goffman has pointed out,

> Points of access can easily become points of alarm. When the doorbell rings at midday, housewives may feel a slight alarm, not having expected any calls. During off-call times for the telephone (say before nine in the morning and after ten at night for adult members of the middle-class) a phone ringing may cause alarm.[56]

Something of this sort happens to the hero of Trumbo's *Johnny Got His Gun,* which I mentioned earlier:

> And then *an astonishing thing happened.* One day toward the middle of the year the nurse gave him a completely fresh change of bed linen when he had received a change only the day before. This had never happened before. Every third day he was changed no sooner and no later. Yet here everything was upset and for two days in a row he was getting the change. *He felt all in a hub-bub.*[57]

It is certainly not the nature of the event itself that causes the alarm in such situations. After all, what can be a more trivial event than the ringing of a telephone or the changing of bed linen? What seems to cause the alarm is clearly the peculiar, other than "normal" temporal context of the event. In the Northern Hemisphere, for example, we would most likely be intrigued by a snow blizzard in August, not because snow blizzards in general are so unusual, but, rather, because the association of snow with the month of August as a temporal ground is so unusual. Along the same lines, we would most likely be surprised to see a child going to school on Saturday, not because the act itself is so strange, but, rather, because of its unusual temporal location.

Note also that,

> although one ordinarily thinks of alarming signs as occurrences, the absence of an expected sign can serve the same function. A parent who fails to receive a telephone call from a child can be alarmed by the non-ringing of the bell.[58]

Given the fairly reliable temporal regularity of our social environment, we tend to build up certain expectations. If these expectations are not met, we are alarmed. Thus, we would most likely be surprised, if not alarmed, were we to arrive at our local grocery store on a regular weekday around 11:00 A.M. and find it closed. We would most probably experience a similar bewilderment if friends who always call us on our birthday suddenly did not call; if, upon arriving at a regular weekly seminar, we saw an empty room; if we were to turn on the television at the regular news time and the news was not on the air; and so on.

When people encounter cognitively disturbing situations in which there is some incongruity between a figure and its temporal ground —that is, when a figure is seen out of context—it is not at all unusual that they fail to even perceive the figure, because the entire gestalt simply does not "make sense." This obviously happens more often to those of us who, in the course of a regular day or week, get to see a great number of people, and each of them nearly always at the same time. (When such patterns of temporal regularity are established, we tend to relate to people and identify them primarily in terms of particular time slots—as students in our Wednesday evening class, as those who commute with us on the 8:26 train every

morning, and so on. In an outpatient hospital clinic, I once heard a
secretary telling a resident, "Your three o'clock is here.") In the
same way that we sometimes fail to recognize, upon seeing them on
the street, people that we see almost every day in the cafeteria of the
building where we work, we sometimes also fail to recognize, upon
seeing them in the evening, people whom we usually see only during
the day. A clinician once admitted to me that she sometimes fails to
recognize patients when she encounters them at the lobby of her
clinic at times other than those of their scheduled appointments with
her. The crucial variable here is obviously time, since that lobby is
the only *place* where she ever sees them.

Another typical response to situations where there is some cognitive incongruity between figure and ground is to refer to some external point which might help to anchor the unfamiliar situation
within a more "reasonable" context where it would hopefully "make
more sense." Many of those who listened to Orson Welles's historic
radio broadcast of *The War of the Worlds,* for example, typically
looked out of their windows or turned to other stations in order to
check whether the broadcast was real.[59] This is also true when the
ground in question is a temporal one. At the onset of the October
1973 War, for example, many Israelis, upon hearing the sound of
cars in the streets, immediately turned on their radios, because the
configuration of that sound and the temporal ground of Yom Kip-
pur, which is typically dominated by almost utter silence outdoors,
was cognitively incongruous and, therefore, alarmed them.

Consider also the following incident, which I once observed in a
hospital. On one particular ward, the attending physician used to
routinely arrive at the unit only for his daily conference with his
house staff around 10:00 A.M. That conference always followed the
routine morning rounds, which the house staff usually completed
around 9:30 A.M. One day, the morning round was still not over a
few minutes past 10:00, when the resident and the intern saw their
attending physician arriving at the unit. Both of them manifested
the very same reaction: they immediately glanced at their watches,
so as to "solve" the cognitive incongruity that had been created
by the temporal coincidence of the morning round and the arrival of
the attending physician, two events which were "normally" segregated in time.

During my fieldwork at the hospital, I also noticed numerous instances in which doctors and nurses glanced at the clock whenever they saw one of their colleagues arriving at work or leaving for the day. In part, this was done in order to make sure that the situation "made sense" from a temporal standpoint. When faced with a cognitive incongruity between a figure and its temporal ground, most of us would probably glance at our watches so as to check whether our identification of that ground was, indeed, correct.

Another typical response to such situations is to ask a question, the answer to which might hopefully help to anchor them within a more meaningful and "sensible" context. Consider for example, the following instance. On her first day coming from a long rotation of night work, a nurse was seen in the early afternoon by a colleague from a different unit. The latter was very surprised to see her, since, for the entire previous month, she had related to her only as a "night person." Her immediate response was to ask her, "Are you on days now?" When hospital staff members are seen on the hospital grounds at times other than their usual coverage time slots, they are usually asked by others, "What are you doing here?" That question is actually an elliptical form of the question "What are you doing here *now*?" since those who ask it are not at all surprised to see their colleagues at the hospital. Indeed, they usually see them only there! Rather, they are surprised to see them there *at that particular time,* which is outside the temporal boundaries of their "normal," taken-for-granted presence at the hospital. During my fieldwork, I heard the question "What are you doing here?" numerous times, in instances such as the following: when an intern came in to the hospital on his day off to pick up his paycheck; when a clerical supervisor came in unexpectedly on a Saturday morning; when a day nurse who had stayed overtime for the evening was seen around midnight by the very same night nurse whom she had relieved earlier that morning; when an intern was still working an hour past the official end of her night shift; and so on. When I first came in to the hospital on a weekend or late at night, I too was asked that question. To appreciate the extent to which "normalcy" is temporally situated, note also an instance in which a nurse asked an intern who was passing through her unit what he was doing there. She probably never asked him that same question only two months before that, when he spent a full one-month rotation on that unit!

Most fascinating, however, is the way people resolve cognitive incongruities between figures and temporal grounds by treating the figure as fixed and adjusting the ground so as to fit it. The following instance is a classic example of such a response. A part-time secretary who worked in my department on a regular Monday-Wednesday-Friday routine once came in on a Thursday to do some personal typing. Such an unusual configuration of figure and temporal ground apparently confused one of my colleagues, who was quite surprised to see her. As he himself admitted to me later, he managed to resolve the cognitive disturbance caused by that only by way of convincing himself that it was probably Wednesday rather than Thursday! The logic he applied must have been, "If it's Lucy, this must be Wednesday."

As I pointed out earlier, whereas the day and the year are essentially based on natural cycles, the week is most clearly a purely artificial cycle. This implies, first of all, that only in our *social,* man-made environment can we find any clues which might help us in figuring out what day it is. We can quite easily tell whether it is morning or evening, summer or winter, by simply referring to our natural surroundings. Nothing in our natural environment, however, can provide us with any clues as to whether it is Monday or Friday. The conventionality of the weekly cycle also implies that, while we are very unlikely to make any gross errors in reckoning the time of day or the season, it is quite easy for us to err in identifying a man-made temporal ground such as the day of the week, as my colleague obviously did.

This theme was used by the Jewish writer Chaim Nachman Bialik as the central focus of his humorous short story, "The Short Friday."[60] In this story, a rabbi is caught on Sabbath Eve in the woods, far away from his village. Despite the Jewish prohibition of traveling during the Sabbath, he decides to travel on until he reaches the closest inn, and spends the night on a bench there. The innkeeper, who had gone to sleep prior to the rabbi's arrival, is totally confused when he finds him there in the morning: "At first Feivka thought this must be illusion and some devil's hocus-pocus. . . . It seemed to Feivka that he must be crazy. . . . Am I drunk or mad? . . . There must be a mistake here."[61] Given the fact that Jews— and especially rabbis—would not normally travel during the Sabbath, Feivka is obviously bewildered at having perceived a most unusual gestalt, a rabbi who must have traveled on Sabbath Eve (since he certainly was not there when the Sabbath entered). It is definitely neither the figure nor its temporal ground by itself that confuses him. Rather, it is the configuration of both of them *together*. And, indeed, he wonders to himself, "Sabbath—*and* the rabbi?"

Interestingly enough, the innkeeper's solution to this cognitively disturbing and intolerable incongruity is identical to that of my aforementioned colleague. Firmly maintaining that no rabbi would normally travel during the Sabbath, yet being unable to ignore the presence of the figure (that is, the rabbi), he assumes that he probably must have made a mistake in identifying its temporal ground. If the rabbi is here, it certainly cannot be Saturday. "Fancy getting mixed up as to the days of the week," he thinks to himself, assuming that the rabbi who is lying asleep on his bench certainly must be a more reliable calendar than his own memory.

Assuming, then, that it is not Saturday after all, Feivka becomes worried that the rabbi will find out that he almost observed the Sabbath on the wrong day. He therefore decides to transform their immediate environment so that it will look like a regular weekday (which he now assumes it is). While people cannot transform their natural environment so that—outdoors, at least—nighttime will appear as daytime and wintertime as summertime, they can transform their sociocultural environment so that the Sabbath will appear as a regular weekday. (In his film *36 Hours*, George Seaton has suggested that man can deliberately transform his social environment even to the point of making the 1940s appear as the 1950s.)

As we shall see in the fourth chapter, Jews have always made particular efforts to make the Sabbath appear clearly distinct from the regular weekdays. Anyone who is familiar with the Jewish culture can actually "see" the Sabbath: "Only by putting your head inside the door, they say, just by sniffing the atmosphere of the house, you can tell whether it is Sabbath or weekday."[62] Given this, Feivka first tries to remove from the environment everything that might be evidence of the Sabbath. He explicitly instructs his wife, "Don't keep as much as a sign of it."

The moment Feivka realized what had happened, he dashed off to remove all signs of Sabbath from the house before the rabbi woke up and caught him. To begin with, he put away the brass candlesticks, the remains of the Sabbath meal, and the white tablecloth. . . . And straightway the whole appearance of the house was transformed. Sabbath departed and weekday arrived.[63]

Cultural items such as brass candlesticks, the white tablecloth, and certain food simply had to be removed, since their presence would certainly indicate to any Jew, in the most unambiguous manner, that it was Saturday.

Not only does Feivka make the Sabbath leave, he also makes the weekday arrive. That is accomplished by performing acts that would never take place during the Sabbath. Thus, he starts up the fire, stokes up the samovar with fuel so that it will begin to hum, arranges for the sound of hammer and ax to be heard by having his hostler chop wood and fix things with nails, orders his daughter to start peeling potatoes, and winds his phylacteries around his arm while repeating the morning prayers to their ordinary weekday tune. To any Jew, any one of these components of the newly transformed environment would indicate, in the most unambiguous manner, that it is actually an ordinary weekday, that it simply cannot be Saturday. The message of these acts is so clear that any verbal explanation is totally unnecessary. When the rabbi finally wakes up, the entire communication between him and the innkeeper is nonverbal and consists of the visible and audible cues that he picks up—as Feivka intended it to be—from his environment!

Feivka's operation is quite successful. He manages to transform the environment so that the Sabbath actually appears as an ordinary weekday. As far as the rabbi can tell from looking at his surroundings, it is definitely not Saturday:

And where was the Sabbath? There was no sign or memory of the Sabbath! Peasants, a weekday crowd. And a samovar was boiling just over there.[64]

All this makes the rabbi feel, very much like Feivka felt a couple of hours earlier, quite bewildered. He is faced with a delicate cognitive incongruity that leaves him rather confused. On the one hand, he remembers very well that when he went to sleep it was still Friday night. On the other hand, his entire surrounding environment indicates to him quite clearly that it is not Saturday, but, rather, an ordinary weekday. The entire gestalt simply does not "make any sense" to him.

Ironically enough, he arrives at a solution which is identical to the one arrived at earlier by the innkeeper. He decides not to rely on his memory as a basis for identifying the temporal ground of the figure that he perceives:

> in that case I went on sleeping through the Sabbath and the night of the departure of the Sabbath.[65]

The irony, of course, lies in the fact that the rabbi is totally unaware that it was his own presence at the inn that was responsible for the entire confusion in the first place! It is also ironical that, while it is actually Saturday, both Feivka and the rabbi mistake it for some other day, and yet each one of them has a different day in mind. While the rabbi concludes that he must have overslept through the entire Sabbath and that it is already Sunday, the innkeeper must conclude that it is some other day, both because of the availability of Gentile labor and because he knows that he has not celebrated the Sabbath yet.

Let me reiterate a point I made earlier with respect to Robinson Crusoe, Queen Esther, and the hero of Asch's story. All this could have happened only in a setting such as Feivka's inn—an isolated Jewish enclave surrounded by an overwhelming Gentile environment. Feivka's transformation of his environment would not have been as easy and successful—nor would he or the rabbi have encountered such confusion in the first place—were the entire story to take place in an exclusively Jewish environment. And, indeed, the entire confusion is resolved and everything becomes clear at the end of the story, in an extremely comic scene in which the rabbi arrives—in his coach—at his own village, at the very moment that his followers begin to leave the synagogue for a traditional leisurely Sabbath stroll in the street!

It is quite ironical that the environment which the rabbi prefers to his own memory as a reliable source of reference is essentially a totally fabricated environment. That, of course, would not have been possible were the weekly cycle to be anchored in nature. The story highlights the *social* context within which much of our temporal reference is anchored. The above confusion is inherent to cycles such as the week, where one must rely exclusively on sociocultural cues. It would certainly not have arisen with regard to cycles such as the day or the year, which are anchored in nature.

Two

The Schedule

The first major institution that man invented in order to establish and maintain temporal regularity was the calendar. The calendar is primarily responsible for the creation of most of the temporally regular patterns through which nearly all societies, social institutions, and social groups manage to introduce some orderliness into their lives. They do that mainly by regulating the temporal location and the rate of recurrence of socially significant collective events. As Durkheim pointed out, "A calendar expresses the rhythm of the collective activities, while at the same time its function is to assure their regularity."[1]

However, while the calendar has been primarily responsible for the establishment and maintenance of temporal regularity on an annual, monthly, and even weekly basis, it certainly cannot promote temporal regularity at the level of relatively microscopic temporal units such as the day and the hour. That level of temporal regularity, which is so uniquely characteristic of modern life, has become possible only with the invention of another institution—the schedule.

The establishment of temporal regularity at a daily level is quite an old idea. As early as two thousand years ago, Jewish rabbis were already regulating individuals' lives as well as communal life through a strict daily schedule of religious services. However, it is in the medieval Benedictine monasteries that we find what most probably constituted the original model for all modern Western schedules. The earliest instance, in the West, of a rigid schedule that imposed temporal regularity not only on a weekly or daily basis, but at the level of the hour as well, is none other than the medieval Benedictine "table of hours"—the *hora-*

rium. Therefore, it is in the medieval Benedictine monasteries that we ought to look for the genesis and source of diffusion of the particular type of temporal regularity that is so characteristic of modern life, as well as of one of the most fundamental sociocultural institutions in the modern West.

In order to appreciate the sociohistorical significance of the monastic horarium, we must first realize how central a role the Benedictine order played in the intellectual and economic shaping of the modern West. Aiming at the complete "ordering" of Christian life, the Benedictines came to be a major factor in promoting the rationalization of life in the West.[2]

Of particular significance here was the temporal regularity introduced by the Benedictines. As Harold A. Innis pointed out, "The spread of monasticism and the use of bells to mark the periods of the day and the place of religious services introduced regularity in the life of the West."[3] It is because of the rigid temporal patterning of monastic life that the monasteries are said to have "helped to give the human enterprise the regular collective beat and rhythm of the machine."[4] It is because "his time is scheduled" that the monk has been depicted by Reinhard Bendix as "the first 'professional' of Western civilization."[5]

The common folk characterization of the monk is humorously rendered in a famous French song:

Frère Jacques, Frère Jacques,
Dormez-vous, Dormez-vous?
Sonnez les matines, Sonnez les matines,
Din, din, don, Din, din, don.

The notion of temporal regularity has become almost synonymous with monasticism. In the sentence "The public school routine was still monastic in its severity," for example,[6] the word "monastic" is used as an adjective which is suggestive of the rigidity of a schedule. This is hardly surprising, since, as Dom David Knowles, one of the foremost authorities on medieval monasticism, pointed out, "The life within the monastery is a common life of absolute regularity. . . . of unvarying routine."[7] The rigid temporal patterning of life is among the fundamental essences of Western monasticism. Its principal canon, *The Rule of Saint Benedict,* regards it as one of the necessary foundations of a desirable social order and devotes several chapters exclusively to the horarium. Most scholarly works on Western monasticism regard the horarium as a key to a better understanding of the structure and meaning of everyday life in the monastery.

I shall therefore begin my exploration of the schedule by examining the Benedictine horarium. Admittedly, it probably differed in its details from most modern schedules. And yet, it was most probably the original model for all of them and can serve as an ideal-typical example of a generic schedule. An analytical examination of its essential features would therefore be most useful for shedding light on the fundamental principles which underlie any modern schedule.

The Benedictine Horarium

Much of the life of a Christian person is structured along the annual cycle, so it is quite understandable that this cycle helped introduce some rhythmicity into the monastery. An annual rhythm of liturgical activity, for example, was established through seasonal variations such as the following:

> From the sacred feast of Easter until Pentecost, let *Alleluia* be said always both with the psalms and with the responsories. From Pentecost until the beginning of Lent, let it be said every night at Matins with the second six psalms only. On every Sunday out of Lent, let *Alleluia* be said with the canticles of Matins, and with the psalms of Lauds, Prime, Terce, Sext, and None; but let Vespers then have an antiphon. The responsories are never to be said with *Alleluia*, except from Easter to Pentecost.[8]

Seasonal variations were also implied by the fact that Saint Benedict established for his order separate horaria for the summer and for the winter, and even three separate ones with respect to mealtimes.[9] Finally, there were also various routine activities such as bathing, bloodletting, head shaving, and mattress refilling, which were performed on a regular basis a fixed number of times during the year.[10]

Another cycle that helped introduce some rhythmicity into the Benedictine monasteries was the week. A weekly rhythm of liturgical activity, for example, was established through variations made in accordance with the day of the week:

> After this let two other psalms be said according to custom: that
> is, on Monday the fifth and thirty-fifth; on Tuesday the forty-
> second and fifty-sixth; on Wednesday the sixty-third and sixty-
> fourth; on Thursday the eighty-seventh and eighty-ninth; on
> Friday the seventy-fifth and ninety-first; and on Saturday the
> hundred and forty-second and the canticle from Deuteronomy.[11]

Furthermore, mealtimes and wake-up time also varied in accordance with the day of the week, and even feet and beer jugs were to be washed on a weekly basis.[12] To appreciate the weekly "beat" of monastic life, note also that the reading of the full cycle of 150 psalms began every Sunday, as did the rotations of kitchen service and of reading to the community during meals.[13]

Most characteristic of life in the Benedictine monasteries, how-ever, was the pervasiveness of a daily rhythm of activity. By having their location fixed at particular times of the day on a regular basis, almost all events and activities in monastic life recurred at twenty-four-hour intervals. Consider, for example, the following instruc-tions from *The Rule of Saint Benedict:*

> The brethren . . . must be occupied at stated hours in manual
> labor, and again at other hours in sacred reading. To this end we
> think that the times for each may be determined in the following
> manner. . . . the brethren shall start work in the morning and from
> the first hour until almost the fourth do the tasks that have to be
> done. From the fourth hour until about the sixth let them apply
> themselves to reading. After the sixth hour, having left the table,
> let them rest on their beds in perfect silence.[14]

In his attempts to establish temporal regularity in the monastery, Saint Benedict even went as far as to impose an artificial temporal order on organic activities which would have otherwise been regu-lated by natural temporal patterns of their own:

> the brethren shall rise at the eighth hour of the night, so that their
> sleep may extend for a moderate space beyond midnight. . . . let
> the hour of rising be so arranged that there be a short interval
> after Matins, in which the brethren may go out for the necessities
> of nature.[15]

From the feast of Easter until Pentecost let the brethren dine at the sixth hour and sup in the evening. From Pentecost throughout the summer . . . let them fast on Wednesdays and Fridays until the ninth hour; on the other days let them dine at the sixth hour.[16]

Most pervasive, however, was the daily rhythm of liturgical activity, which was the direct result of fixing the celebration of the eight Divine Offices (Matins, Lauds, Prime, Terce, Sext, None, Vespers, and Compline), whose liturgical significance by far exceeded that of any other services, at particular hours. The *Rule* was particularly strict in dictating to monks when these Offices ought to be celebrated.[17] Moreover, it was at those eight points during the day that the monastery bells rang. Thus, those eight *canonical hours* actually functioned as "landmarks" punctuating the daily cycle of the monastery.

It has been argued by Mumford that orderly punctual life in the West first took shape in the monasteries.[18] And, indeed, the temporal rigidity of monastic life definitely presupposed *punctuality*. No wonder that the duty of "indicating the hour for the Work of God" was entrusted to the abbot himself or to some other "careful brother."[19] The Divine Offices simply *had* to begin at the "appointed hours." Hence also the condemnation of any delay: "As soon as the signal for the Divine Office has been heard, let them abandon what they have in hand and assemble with the greatest speed."[20] Given the centrality of punctuality to life in the Benedictine monasteries, it became necessary to define the act of being "on time" in a manner that would preclude any ambiguities. And, indeed, Saint Benedict actually managed to do that long before any precise timekeeping devices were invented. As early as the sixth century, he put forward quite explicitly the following definition of *latecoming:* arriving at Matins after the Gloria of the ninety-fourth psalm, at any other Divine Office after the Gloria of the first psalm that followed the verse, and at meals after the verse.[21]

Note the use of terms such as "the *proper* time" or "the *appointed* hours" in the *Rule.*[22] It is indicative of the Benedictine sanctification of punctuality by elevating it from the merely practical domain to the moral domain. Adherence to the horarium was actually regarded as involving ascetic obedience. Abandoning everything at the precise moment the bells rang was seen as a commendable manifestation of

a total surrender of one's self. It is within this context that the Benedictine moral condemnation of latecoming as a grave sin ought to
be understood. Latecomers were actually punished by being placed
apart from the community and had to do penance as well.[23]

However, Saint Benedict seems to have been a most realistic plan-
ner, and, in order to ensure that the monastic sociotemporal order
would not collapse that easily, he built into it some possible channels of minor deviation. He was somewhat lenient, for example,
regarding wake-up time during the summer, and allowed that "the
lessons from the book be not read, on account of the shortness of
the nights."[24] Along the same lines, the Matins service was to be
celebrated in full on Sundays, "unless (which God forbid) they be
late in rising, so that the lessons and responsories have to be short-
ened."[25] Finally, also taking into consideration the possibility that not
all monks would actually arrive on time for the Lauds service, Saint
Benedict advocated the following: "Let the sixty-sixth psalm be
said without an antiphon and somewhat slowly, as on Sunday, in
order that all may assemble in time for the fiftieth."[26]

The centrality of an institution such as the canonical hours suggests the particular significance of the *hour* in monastic life. So do
the names of both the monastic daily schedule (*horarium*) and the
first mechanical clock (*horologium*), which, as we shall soon see,
was indispensable for its implementation. Both names were derived
from "*hora*," which was the Latin word for "hour." Furthermore,
no less than half of the Divine Offices—Prime, Terce, Sext, and None
—were even named after the particular hours at which they were
celebrated (the first, the third, the sixth, and the ninth, respectively).
The use of phrases such as "the rest of the Hour" in the *Rule* also
suggests that the hour constituted the standard unit of duration of
various events in monastic life.[27] (It should be noted, however, that
the hour had had a considerable religious significance long before
Benedictine times. According to the ancient astrological doctrine of
"chronocratories," time was segmented into "planetary hours," each
of which was associated with a particular planet which was believed
to be its "controller.")[28]

The unit of time to which the *Rule* refers as "hour," however, was
slightly different from the modern hour. In medieval Europe, the
use of hours of standard length was restricted to theoretical and

technical purposes.[29] Otherwise, until the end of the fourteenth century, everyday life was temporally organized in accordance with the ancient Egyptian-Roman method of time reckoning and time measurement, whereby the intervals between sunrise and sunset and vice versa were each divided into twelve equal parts called "*horae temporales*." The length of these "hours" was a function of the length of daylight and, therefore, varied across seasons. Thus, day "hours" were longer than night "hours" during the summer, but shorter during the winter. Only on the two equinoxes were all hours of a standard length.

One of the most obvious consequences of this was that the canonical hours did not always fall on the same time of day. The location of "the ninth hour" within the daily cycle, for example, would vary from one season to another. Furthermore, since the length of the unit "hour" varied across seasons, the Divine Offices could not be spaced at the same regular intervals throughout the year. In other words, the most critical daily events would vary constantly both in their duration and in their absolute location within the daily cycle.

All this made it rather difficult to live in accordance with a rigid daily schedule. The variant horaria established by Saint Benedict for the summer and for the winter, as well as for the mealtimes,[30] could help the awkward situation only in part. An effective use of such a rigid and complex daily schedule as the one mandated by the *Rule* called for a standardization of the length of hours as well as of their temporal location within the daily cycle. It is within this context that we can most fully understand the second tremendous contribution of the Benedictine order to the development of temporal regularity in the West—the introduction of the mechanical clock.

The etymological affinity between the first mechanical clock (the *horologium*) and the first rigid daily schedule (the *horarium*) is not coincidental. Rather, it suggests some very close functional affinity between the two. It was the invention of the mechanical clock that actually made it possible for man to use the schedule effectively. The mechanical clock was the first timepiece ever to be paced at a uniform rate and whose use was not restricted to certain temperatures or lighting conditions. (The effective use of the water clock and the sundial, for example, was always hindered by below-freezing temperatures and by cloudy skies, respectively.) The mechanical clock, therefore, made it possible for man to transform the traditional seasonally based "hours" into durationally uniform ones, as the effective use of the schedule required. Thus, even if we do not go as far as to claim, like Mumford, that the clock "is the key-machine of the modern industrial age,"[31] it is hard not to appreciate its unique social role in modern Western civilization, at least as far as the maintenance of temporal regularity is concerned.

Given the centrality of temporal regularity to monastic life, which accounts for why regular timekeeping and promptitude in ringing the bells were so essential to the Benedictines, it is quite understandable that the monastery would be the obvious door through which the clock could most easily be introduced to the West. It is not surprising, therefore, that the earliest wheel- and weight-driven clocks, as well as the first clocks to have applied the escapement mechanism, were all introduced to the West through the monasteries.[32] They functioned primarily as alarms that indicated to the sacristan when to strike the monastery bells and give the signal for the monks to assemble for their Divine Offices. This intimate historical association between the clock and the bell is still preserved today in the clock's English name, which derives from the medieval Latin word for bell—"*clocca*." To further appreciate the close affinity between the first mechanical clock and religious services, note that, in the Greek Orthodox Church, the word "*horologium*" or "*horologion*" refers to the breviary itself!

The invention of the mechanical clock entailed an unprecedented convergence of the functions of time measurement and time reckoning in one and the same timepiece. Prior to that, people used timepieces such as the sandglass exclusively for time measurement and timepieces such as the sundial exclusively for time reckoning. The clock can be used, and is actually used, for both purposes. On some occasions, we may look at our watch just in order to know what time it is. However, when we look at it upon putting a thermometer in our mouth or placing a casserole in the oven, we are primarily concerned with the position of the minute and second hands and may not even notice what time it indicates.

And yet, when the clock was first introduced to the West, its primary function was not to measure duration, but only to indicate the time of day, so that the sacristan would know when to ring the bells.

In fact, the early monastery clocks did not even have minute and second hands. They were essentially "horologia," whose only function was to "tell the hour." Interestingly enough, in various languages such as French, Spanish, and Hebrew, the question "What hour is it?" is still the most common form of asking the time.

Nevertheless, one of the inevitable consequences of the standardization of the temporal location of events and activities in monastic life was their durational rigidification as well. While the horarium specified only the times at which daily events were to begin, the fact that these times were fixed also entailed the durational rigidification of these events. The duration of a particular reading session, for example, was limited to—and could not be stretched beyond— the period between the time that marked its beginning and the time that marked the beginning of the following scheduled event. Likewise, if supper was scheduled for 5:45 P.M. and the beginning of the Vespers service for 6:10 P.M., monks could clearly not spend more than twenty-five minutes at the supper table.

Not only did the standardization of the temporal location of events and activities in monastic life entail a standardization of their duration and rate of recurrence; it also involved a rigidification of their sequential structure. The sequential arrangement of the various Divine Offices in an irreversible order is a perfect case in point. The celebration of the Compline service, for example, could never precede that of the Terce or Vespers services, on any given day.

Yet even more impressive a manifestation of this fourth aspect of temporal regularity was the sequential rigidity which characterized the internal ordering of the various structural slots *within* each Office. As many as five chapters of the *Rule* actually consist of detailed prescriptions regarding the sequential organization of each Divine Office.[33] The following passage, for example, is quite typical:

> When the six psalms and the versicle have been chanted . . .
> then let there be read from the book, as we said before, four
> lessons with their responsories. . . . After these lessons let there
> follow in order another six psalms with antiphons, like the
> previous ones, and a versicle. After these again let four more
> lessons be read with their responsories. . . . After these let there
> be three canticles from the book of the prophets. . . . Then, when

the versicle has been said and the abbot has given the blessing,
let another four lessons be read from the New Testament. . . .
When the fourth responsory is finished, let the abbot begin the
hymn *Te Deum Laudamus.* When that has been said, the abbot
shall read the lesson from the book of the Gospels, all standing
with fear and reverence. That having been read, let all answer
Amen, and then let the abbot follow with the hymn *Te decet laus,*
and the blessing having been given let them begin Lauds.[34]

Unlike the Benedictine monks, most of us do not lead the sort
of life in which almost every moment is accounted for by a schedule.
Furthermore, unless we happen to be inmates of a total institution,
the schedules we use do not govern and regulate practically every
aspect of our lives, as the monastic horarium did.

And yet, even though the Benedictine horarium clearly differed
to a large extent from most modern schedules, it nevertheless constituted the original model for all of them as well as an ideal-typical
example of a generic schedule. A thorough analysis of its most essential features would, therefore, be most useful for us, because it
would help us identify the fundamental principles that underlie any
modern schedule.

Schedules—The Conventional Dimension

One of the most significant characteristics of almost any schedule
is its conventionality. The Benedictine horarium was no exception—
many of the temporal regularities that were dictated by it were essentially based upon social convention alone. As I have shown in the
previous chapter, such patterns ought to be distinguished from
temporal patterns that are determined by nature. To appreciate the
fundamental difference between the two, contrast, for example, the
reasons for skiing in the winter or for sunbathing during the daytime
with those underlying monastic routines such as reading the eighty-
seventh psalm on Thursday or saying the Alleluia with the responsories only between Easter and Pentecost.

The largely conventional character of the horarium is most
clearly evident from the fact that even purely biological activities
were structured, in the monastery, in accordance with sociotemporal, rather than biotemporal, considerations. For example, it was

a socially based, normative imperative, rather than any natural imperative, that compelled monks to wake up every day as early as 1:30 A.M. Furthermore, such a temporal pattern would have strongly violated any daily schedule which might have taken into consideration, or been dictated by, physical and biological factors. It could have been justified only by a socially based ascetic philosophy of renunciation of the flesh.

The standardization of the rate of recurrence of periodic events and activities in monastic life was also largely conventional. The artificial basis of the weekly cycle is quite obvious, since there is absolutely nothing in nature that would suggest the inevitability of a seven-day rhythmicity. As for the day and the year—it is true that they originally derived from purely natural periodicities such as the rotation of the earth on its axis and its revolution around the sun, yet their selection as cornerstones of the monastic temporal order was in itself a matter of convention. Unlike the annual work/rest cycle of hunters, for example, which is inherently related to natural periodic phenomena such as seasonal variations in the availability of game, associating the saying of Alleluia with an annual rhythm was entirely conventional. Similarly, it was not natural inevitability, but social convention alone, that tied the spacing of Vespers services to the daily cycle. Along the same lines, there is nothing in nature that would compel monks to shave their heads on an annual basis.

All this was also true of the rigidity of the sequential ordering of events and activities in monastic life as well as of their duration. The rules that prescribed how monks ought to structure their day and which Office, psalm, hymn, or responsory ought to precede or follow which were purely artificial. Likewise, the duration of most monastic daily activities and events was not intrinsic to them, and the patterns of associating a particular activity such as reading, eating, or meditating with a particular fixed duration usually rested on social convention alone. This is also evident from the fact that these durations usually derived from an artificial unit of time such as the hour. The replacement of seasonally variable "hours" which derived from nature by durationally uniform hours that are anchored in clock time alone was just one further step in the evolution from a naturally based temporal order to an artificial and conventional one.

Admitting that most schedules are mere artifacts is probably much easier when we analyze the monastic horarium than when we examine our own schedules! We usually tend to forget, for example, that patterns such as going to work at 9:00 A.M., resting in accordance with a seven-day rhythm, or structuring classes in fifty-minute time blocks are actually not necessitated by nature but are, rather, matters of social convention alone, as are so many other patterns pertaining to when we do things, how often, how long, and in what order. We normally overlook the overwhelming fact that conventionality is one of the fundamental characteristics of the sociotemporal order, in contradistinction to the physiotemporal and biotemporal orders.[35] In fact, most of us are usually not even aware that there is any fundamental difference among those orders.

Interestingly enough, even though the sociotemporal order is based, to a large extent, on purely arbitrary social convention, it is nevertheless usually perceived by people as given, inevitable, and unalterable. One of the implications of standardizing the temporal location of events and activities in monastic life was that it most probably came to be regarded as intrinsic to them, as if particular time periods were the inevitable "containers" of those events and activities. The act of saying the fifty-sixth psalm, for example, must have appeared to monks as inseparable from its temporal locus—Tuesday morning. The perceived inseparability of events and activities from their standard temporal locations was also manifested in the fact that half of the Divine Offices were even named after the hour at which they were supposed to take place. The use of such phrases as "its proper time," "the appointed hours," or "unreasonable hours" in the *Rule*[36] must have also contributed to make the association between events and activities and their conventional temporal loci appear to monks as God-given—natural, inevitable, and absolutely unalterable.

Man's tendency to treat social conventions as if they were natural and inevitable has intrigued sociologists ever since Karl Marx's classic discussion of the "fetishism of commodities" and Georg Lukács's examination of the phenomenon of "reification."[37] The phantom objectivity of the social world has been depicted more recently by Berger and Luckmann:

Reification is the apprehension of human phenomena as if they were things, that is, in non-human or possibly supra-human terms. Another way of saying this is that reification is the apprehension of the products of human activity *as if* they were something else than human products—such as facts of nature, results of cosmic laws, or manifestations of divine will. Reification implies that man is capable of forgetting his own authorship of the human world. . . . The reified world is, by definition, a dehumanized world. It is experienced by man as a strange facticity. . . . The objectivity of the social world means that it confronts man as something outside of himself.[38]

Given our tendency to reify the social world, it is not surprising that most of us are totally unaware of the conventional basis of our schedules. For the nonsociologist, sociotemporal patterns are essentially indistinguishable from temporal patterns that derive from nature. Peter Beagle has nicely expressed this in his novel *The Last Unicorn*:

When I was alive, I believed—as you do—that time was at least as real and solid as myself, and probably more so. I said "one o'clock" as though I could see it, and "Monday" as though I could find it on the map. . . . Like everyone else, I lived in a house bricked up with seconds and minutes, weekends and New Year's Days, and I never went outside until I died, because there was no other door. Now I know that I could have walked through the walls.[39]

It is in the nature of "social facts" such as the temporal regularities that derive from the schedule that they are generally seen as natural and inevitable. As Durkheim pointed out, even though they may actually be no more than mere artifacts, "social facts" are generally treated as "external to the individual, and endowed with a power of coercion, by reason of which they control him."[40] Thus, as we shall soon see, despite its obvious conventional basis, the schedule is in no way less compelling and binding than temporal patterns that derive from nature. Very much like the latter, it can impose itself on individuals and constrain them quite independently of their will. This is how it came to be perceived as natural and inevitable, and why we usually resist quite passionately any attempts to make changes in it. As I shall demonstrate in the next chapter, this is also true of the other major social institution that is responsible for establishing and maintaining temporal regularity—the calendar.

Routine and Spontaneity

What becomes quite clear now from all the above is that our growing independence of nature has by no means entailed total independence of all temporal determinants of our activities. Despite the fact that we have abandoned the traditional seasonally based rural life-style and have constantly attempted to defy the night, the summer, and the winter by inventing technological facilities such as artificial lighting, refrigeration, and mechanical heating systems, we have not fully liberated ourselves from all temporal constraints. As far as the temporal patterning of our life is concerned, we have only replaced natural control with social control.

One of the most significant consequences of the invention of the schedule has been the consolidation of the element of routine in our daily life. As I shall show later, this has been a great blessing for social organization as well as for our personal lives. And yet, as a principle of organizing human life, routine is essentially antithetical to spontaneity. Thus, the very same institution that is responsible for much of the orderliness and predictability of our daily life is, almost by definition, also responsible for robbing the latter of much of its spontaneous flavor.

Consider, for example, the implications of rigidifying the duration of activities. Being spontaneous definitely entails being engaged in one's activities *for as long as one desires,* and, as the military routine which compels soldiers in basic training to complete eating their meals within a fixed number of minutes clearly suggests, having control over the duration of a person's activities is one of the obvious manifestations of social control in general. While durational rigidity has some strong symbolic associations with strictness and orderliness, durational flexibility is intimately associated with spontaneity. It was quite typical of the late 1960s, for example, that rock concerts used to last much longer than conventional concerts, with their organizers deliberately refusing to adhere to an arbitrary, externally imposed durational rigidification of artistic events and experiences. It is also interesting to contrast, in this respect, the durational profiles of organized jazz performances with those of spontaneous "jam sessions" which involve the very same musicians. The constraining aspect of durational rigidity must also be felt by speakers who are expected to talk for a given amount of time, regardless of whether they might have much more—not to mention much less—to present. Finally, consider also the institution of the *deadline*. That durational rigidity necessarily involves a considerable loss of spontaneity must be an experience shared by every university professor coming up for tenure, as well as by every writer and composer who has had to face the problem of adapting his or her own rhythms of creativity to publishers' deadlines. Most of us are probably also all too familiar with situations whereby superiors impose deadlines on the work of their subordinates for the sheer purpose of displaying their social power.

The rigidification of the sequential order of activities and events presents a similar case in point, since being spontaneous also entails doing things *in the order that one prefers to do them.* Every child who is told that he can have his candy only after he finishes eating his dinner and every player who learns that she cannot make a move before her turn must face the fact that sequential rigidity inevitably involves a considerable loss of spontaneity. Consider also the moral codes that forbid couples to experience sexual intimacy before going through an official wedding ceremony, as well as those bureaucratic procedures which keep patients from being seen by a doctor before going through a long process of filling out forms of all sorts.

To appreciate the intimate relationship between temporal regularity and social control, consider also the rigidification of the rate of recurrence of events and activities. I have already noted that the calendar not only expresses the rhythm of social life, but also is actually responsible for the creation of social periodicities by assuring the regular recurrence of socially significant periodical events such as feasts, ceremonies, holidays, and religious services. It is therefore not surprising that gaining control over the calendar has always been essential for attaining social control in general. As we shall see in the next chapter, two of the most radical social upheavals in modern history, namely, the French and Bolshevik revolutions, actually involved serious attempts to introduce some dramatic changes in the weekly rhythm of collective life.

The rigidification of the rate of recurrence of events and activities robs them of much of their otherwise possible spontaneous character, since being spontaneous also entails doing things *at the rate that one desires*. Consider, for example, the loss of spontaneity that is necessarily involved in the calendrical arrangement of sentimentally significant celebrations such as holidays in accordance with a rigid annual rhythm. (Along the same lines, contrast also the experience of getting a "non-scheduled," spontaneous present with that of getting annual birthday presents.) It obviously would have been impossible to regularly synchronize the sentiments of a large number of people on the basis of spontaneity alone. And yet, calendars are known to create emotional rhythms that affect large collectivities.[41] Furthermore, an extreme case such as the calendrical arrangement of the Israeli mournful National Memorial Day and festive Independence Day immediately next to each other serves as a useful reminder that it is actually possible, with the calendar, to "steer" the collective mood of an entire society, at the sound of a siren, from one extreme emotional state to its diametrical opposite! (Note, however, that both days of commemoration were introduced only about thirty years ago and that the events they commemorate probably still bear much personal significance to many Israelis. It is quite possible that the emotions that they involve will not be as diametrically opposed to one another for future generations as they certainly still are toady.)[42] Finally, to further appreciate the considerable loss of spontaneity involved in establishing rigid rhythms of activity, consider also some of the possible effects of the publication of the Kinsey Report on human sexual behavior, which included statistical data on the average frequency of sexual intercourse among married couples. . . .

The inevitable conflict between routine and spontaneity can also be seen in the case of the standardization of the temporal location of events and activities, since being spontaneous also entails doing things *whenever one feels like doing them*. To appreciate the considerable price we must pay for introducing orderliness and predictability into our lives, consider, for example, the following couple of portrayals of modern life:

> let the white-collar man consider how his days are spent. Would he not sometimes like to lie abed for an extra hour, after a hard day or a gay night? And dare he thus disrupt the regime of home and office? It might be pleasant to get out of doors an hour early on a fine spring morning. Without pre-arrangement? To rouse the household by the 7 o'clock news; to breakfast an hour early, before the newspaper, and the milk for the cereal, are due on the doorstep? To any normal family, this would seem eccentricity bordering on dottiness. *People do not get up because they have woken duly refreshed, and feel like doing so, but because it is getting-up time....* At least an extra cup of coffee, another cigarette, just this one morning? Preposterous notion; the whole day would run fifteen minutes late.[43]

> From the moment of waking, the rhythm of the day is punctuated by the clock. Irrespective of strain or fatigue, despite reluctance or apathy, the household rises close to its set hour. Tardiness in rising is penalized by extra haste in eating breakfast or in walking to catch the train: in the long run, it may even mean the loss of a job or of advancement in business.... As the scale of industrial organization grows, the punctuality and regularity of the mechanical régime tend to increase with it: the time-clock enters automatically to regulate the entrance and the exit of the worker, while the irregular worker—tempted by the trout in spring streams or ducks on salt meadows—finds that these impulses are as unfavorably treated as habitual drunkenness: if he would retain them, he must remain attached to the less routinized provinces of agriculture.[44]

The loss of spontaneity that is involved in our adherence to schedules is particularly salient with regard to the standardization of the temporal location of purely biological activities. After all, most of us get up, eat, and go to sleep not necessarily when we feel like it, but, rather, in accordance with a schedule. Consider also the social conventions that force individuals' need to rest into particular parts of the weekly cycle and their sexual activity into particular phases of their menstrual cycle. In all these instances, *the establishment of routine is accomplished only at the expense of spontaneity.*

The replacement of the individual's internal biological clock by the conventional daily schedule of his or her social environment is a process which usually begins right at the very first days of infancy and is manifested by phenomena such as nursing babies by the clock rather than by demand. As Durkheim himself pointed out, it is definitely one of the most conspicuous accomplishments of primary socialization.[45] Only later in their life, through a symbolic process that is deliberately meant to reflect their maturation, are children gradually promoted to a later bedtime and, eventually, to the attainment of complete control over it.[46] As for the daily conflicts between parents and children over bedtime and mealtimes—they are most indicative of the coercion involved in establishing routine at the expense of spontaneity.

The coercive aspect of establishing sociotemporal regularity was noted as far back as two thousand years ago by the Roman poet Plautus:

> The gods confound the man who first found out
> How to distinguish hours—confound him, too,
> Who in this place set up a sun-dial,
> To cut and hack my days so wretchedly
> Into small pieces! When I was a boy,
> My belly was my sun-dial—one more sure,
> Truer, and more exact than any of them.
> This dial told when 'twas proper time
> To go to dinner, when I ought to eat;
> But now-a-days, why even when I have,
> I can't fall to unless the sun gives leave.
> The town's so full of these confounded dials....[47]

The oppressive implications of sociotemporal regularity have since been noted time and again, whether by critics of standard retirement age, advocates of flexible work schedules, or opponents of the government's imposition of daylight saving time. As the chief propagator of sociotemporal regularity, the schedule has been denounced as a tyrannical oppressor that regiments individuals' lives and is representative of the infantile submission to repressive toilet training.[48] The clock, too, has been portrayed as having had "a more radical influence than any other machine, in that it was the means by which the regularization and regimentation of life necessary for an exploiting system of industry could best be attained."[49] That many people, when they are on vacation, often display a strong defiance of social constraints by deliberately refusing to wear a watch ought to be understood within this context.

Whether it is imposed on individuals from without or within, the schedule obviously represents an interference with one's spontaneous wishes regarding when to do things, how often, how long, and in what order. The rigid planning that it involves often does not leave much room for improvisation. The prearranged balance among our activities in terms of time entails a general rigidification of the proportions of our involvement in each of them. Even if we prefer playing with our children to working, our daily schedules simply do not allow that.

The Benedictine horarium was admittedly an extreme example of rigidifying the temporal structure of life and establishing orderliness at the expense of spontaneity. Given the "total" character of monastic life, it can be argued that monks were reduced, symbolically as well as in actual practice, to the level of children, whose entire lives are scheduled for them. And yet, the question may be asked, Is the average modern individual that far from the restrictions of childhood?

Schedules and Planning

So far I have emphasized only the "negative" dimension of scheduling, focusing exclusively on the oppressive aspect of establishing routine at the expense of spontaneity. However, in order to understand how the schedule has nonetheless come to play such an important role in modern life, let us now examine some of its more "positive" aspects.

The indispensability of scheduling to social organization is quite obvious. If all of us were to behave spontaneously, we would probably not have any form of social organization. Social life requires some coordination among individuals, and the schedule is certainly a major facilitator of such coordination. No social event could ever take place if every individual were to have a say in deciding when it ought to begin. Along the same lines, most social enterprises would have been impossible were it not for the durational rigidification of tasks in accordance with some deadlines.

However, while the indispensability of scheduling to social organization is obvious, how are we to account for the apparent indispensability of schedules to the individual himself? It is quite clear that we have developed a sort of addiction to rigid temporal constraints, to the point of actually missing them when they are absent and submitting ourselves to them even when no one coerces us to do so. Most of us seem to feel quite uncomfortable in situations in which we are not provided with any external temporal constraints and tend to impose on ourselves some of our own creation. That we so often rigidify the duration of our activities by submitting ourselves to self-imposed deadlines and that some of us adhere to fairly rigid schedules even when we are on vacation are perfect cases in point.

As demonstrated in the previous chapter, one of the most obvious psychological benefits of temporal regularity is the minimization of the element of uncertainty in our lives. By providing life with a definite structure, schedules certainly help to make the world around us far more predictable. As such, they are clearly indispensable for any form of planning.

Furthermore, by providing the world with some structure, the rigid scheduling of our activities also constitutes a most adequate solution to the problem of how we ought to order our lives. The same element that robs my life of a considerable degree of spontaneity, namely, routine, also introduces much orderliness and structure into it by providing me with some safeguards against a state of normlessness.

In their search for structure and orderliness, many people are quite grateful that society can provide them with some constraints, since self-imposed discipline is rather difficult to attain.[50] Every constraining order is at least somewhat attractive to many of us, since it provides us with the discipline that we need yet find so difficult to impose on ourselves. (This might explain the attraction of some people to the "total institution,"[51] an extreme version of social organization of which the monastery serves as a perfect example.) Much of our adherence to schedules ought to be understood within this context. While it may very well represent an infantile aspect of human nature, is it not also true that many of us wish to be like children at times?

Along the same lines, note also that every constraining order entails some element of convenience, since the submission to compelling external forces also implies freedom from constantly having to make decisions. The very rigidity of the schedule entails a considerable amount of freedom for its users, since it relieves them from constantly having to consider when to do things, how often, for how long, and in what order. To return to the example of the monastery—despite all the constraint that the horarium imposed on monks, it nevertheless also allowed them more freedom, as does a secretary who schedules an executive's entire working day for him. It provided monks with all the normative standards and prescriptions which were necessary for relieving them from the burden of having to make by themselves decisions such as what to do next, when to go to work, how long to meditate, or how often to wash themselves. Without the schedule, most of us would have to address ourselves to question after question of that sort.

One of the main goals of Saint Benedict was to provide his followers with a highly systematic method of conducting a perfect life. A major aspect of this perfection was the achievement of a delicate equilibrium among the individual's involvements in the various domains of life. Monks were supposed to devote most of their daily life to only three major activities: study, work, and prayer. Furthermore, they were also expected to achieve and maintain a perfect balance among those activities.

The indispensability of the horarium for the individual monk must also be understood within this context. Time is definitely one of the most effective principles that can help the individual organize and regulate the allocation of his resources and could certainly help monks maintain a desired equilibrium among their involvements in the various domains of their lives. Adherence to the horarium guaranteed that some time would be allotted for everything a monk was supposed to do—and only for those things—without him ever having to worry about that.

This also accounts for much of the fascination of the modern West with the schedule. Modern life typically involves a most complex system of numerous daily activities, events, and commitments that require a lot of regulation and coordination. It is only the effective temporal organization of our daily life, which the schedule makes possible, that allows us to get to do everything that we want and need to do, only that, and in the desired proportions.

This involves, first of all, a temporal segregation of one's activities, which helps them avoid interfering with one another. (The segregative function of time will be further examined in chapters 4 and 5.) As Talcott Parsons pointed out,

> The fact that there is a time for each of many different activities ... keeps the claims of each from interfering with those of the others. In fact *a society so complex as ours probably could not function without relatively rigid time scheduling.*[52]

The schedule allows people to separate their various involvements in life from one another and, thus, also to be much more comfortably involved in each of them without feeling so much competition from their involvements in the others. For example, it is much easier for me to be involved in playing soccer without feeling that I do that at the expense of doing my homework if my schedule designates special time slots for both activities. An effective temporal organization of one's activities thus certainly helps to relieve one from much of the pressure that a modern individual typically experiences.

Modern Western civilization is also typically characterized by a strong cultural emphasis on efficiency, which, as we shall soon see, goes hand in hand with a utilitarian conception of time. That involves a strong condemnation of "time wasting," which necessarily entails a devaluation of "dispensable" and "unnecessary" activities. Hence the need that so many of us feel to minimize our involvement in such "time wasting" activities.

Scheduling, which entails the modern art of effective time management, helps us to function more efficiently by encouraging the development of a certain sense of priority as well as allowing the systematic, routine elimination of all involvements that just "stand in our way." A rigid scheduling of our days and weeks simply does not leave any room (that is, time) for involvements that we consider "dispensable." It was the introduction of the horarium that enabled monks to free themselves from the vanities of this world and to concentrate solely on those activities essential for their salvation. Along the same lines, a most adequate solution to the problem of wasting one's time on watching too much television or talking too much on the telephone is to introduce a strict daily or weekly schedule that precludes those activities altogether.

Scheduling one's life effectively also allows one to be involved in activities that would have otherwise been left out of it. By allowing some special time for certain activities, the schedule makes sure that we get to do them. Excuses like "I just did not get to do it" or "I just cannot find any time for it," which are so commonly heard in our society, would simply not be possible within the ideal monastic world. If the activity in question was regarded as necessary, the horarium would certainly allot some time to it. While so many of us complain that we simply do not find the time to read, no Benedictine monk could ever use that excuse for not reading, since reading time was built into the horarium in a most rigid manner. If I faithfully adhere to a daily schedule that includes thirty minutes of doing yoga, there is simply no way I can ever claim that I just did not get to do it.

Finally, the schedule also allows us to allocate our involvements in the various domains of life in desirable proportions, which makes the above-mentioned balance among them possible. Time is definitely one of the principles that can best allow us to establish and organize priority in our lives as well as to symbolically display it. Take, for example, the rate of recurrence of social events. All other things being equal, the friends whom I see more often than others are usually also those whom I enjoy more. Consider also duration, which is even more widely used for displaying the proportional significance of some involvement vis-à-vis another. The number of hours a week students spend in studying mathematics vis-à-vis history, for example, is certainly indicative of the relative significance of the two subjects within the school curriculum.

It is quite difficult to imagine any principle that would be more useful and helpful than time in organizing our lives in this respect, which brings us to the modern art of time budgeting. With the help of the schedule, good time managers can go quite far in approximating a perfect equilibrium among their involvements in the various domains of their lives. If listening to music is more important to me than reading the newspaper, for example, I can certainly make sure, by using a schedule, that I do not allow the latter as much time as I do the former. Along the same lines, if I carry on a busy social life, I can make sure that the amount of time I spend with my different friends reflects their relative significance to me, in much the same way that busy executives do not allow their low-priority appointments to be as long as their top-priority ones.

The Utilitarian Philosophy of Time

The notion that one can allocate and budget one's time presupposes a certain philosophy of what time is. After all, these concepts definitely have some very clear economic overtones. And indeed, from the very start, the evolution of the schedule in the West has always been embedded within a pronouncedly economic philosophy of time.

The basic assumptions underlying the Benedictine utilitarian orientation toward time were already laid out by Saint Benedict himself in the prologue to the *Rule*: "And if we could escape the pains of hell and reach eternal life, then must we—*while there is still time,* while we are in this body and can fulfill all these things by the light of this life—*hasten to do now* what may profit us for eternity."[53] In line with the traditional Christian rejection of the ancient myth of the "eternal return"—a typically cyclical conception of temporality which will be further discussed in the fourth chapter—the Benedictines viewed time as unidirectional and irreversible. Regarding it as irrecoverable, they treated it as a scarce resource that ought to be optimally utilized.

While utilitarianism is typically regarded by most economists as an absolute truth, it may also be seen as a socially based ethical doctrine. It is interesting to note that, whereas many economists totally ignore the moral dimension of utilitarianism, Saint Benedict chose to provide the utilitarian orientation toward temporality with an extrapractical basis, by legitimizing his demand for an optimal use of time on purely moral grounds. Quite typically, he condemned monks of being "lukewarm" and "very slothful in their sacred service" for needing an entire week to do what "our holy fathers strenuously fulfilled in a single day."[54] Note also the rationale he gave for requiring that his followers sleep with their clothes on: "Being clothed they will thus always be ready, and rising at the signal *without any delay* may hasten to forestall one another to the Work of God."[55]

Saint Benedict also required his followers to be occupied at all times so as to avoid idleness, which he condemned as no less than an "enemy of the soul."[56] His particular intolerance toward any "unaccounted for" time periods is most clearly evident in the case of the definition of the interval between the end of the Matins service and the beginning of Lauds. This period was to be particularly short, only long enough to allow monks time to "go out for the necessities of nature." Moreover, during the winter, when the nights were long and Matins was concluded long before dawn—prior to which Lauds could not begin—it was to be devoted to study.[57]

The Benedictine order bequeathed its utilitarian philosophy of time to Western civilization at large. In the fourteenth century, we find some of the leading writers of the Renaissance publishing discourses with titles such as "Of Leisure and the Loss of Time," "What Reasons Lead Us to Conserve and to Keep an Account of Time," and "How Great a Vice It Is to Delay Doing Good Works," and with messages such as the following: "and think that *time passed can never be regained*. Be diligent and provident in all your affairs, and keep from laziness as from the Devil himself or from any other enemy if you want to arrive at success."[58]

And yet, it was the Protestant Reformation that carried the spirit of this particular Benedictine legacy into modern times.[59] No wonder that Calvin's Geneva became the mecca of watchmakers and that the British developed such an obsession with horology. After all, it was the Puritans who maintained that time is irrecoverable and—as a scarce resource—should therefore be optimally utilized: "Remember still that the Time of this short uncertain life is all that ever you shall have, for your preparation for your endless life. When this is spent, whether well or ill, you shall have no more."[60] It was also the Puritans who regarded activities such as "excess of sleep," "needless gluttony," "idle talk," "inordinate adorning of the body," "reading of vain books," and "vain ungoverned and sinful thought" as nothing less than morally condemnable "thieves."[61]

These themes, which are so characteristic of the Protestant Ethic, have been fully incorporated into the modern Spirit of Capitalism.

An *activity cult,* whereby people are expected to maximize their "active" time and to minimize any "empty, unaccounted-for" time periods, is quite evident from some of the now classic guiding maxims of one of the leading propagators of this spirit, Benjamin Franklin:

> Remember that *time* is money. He that can earn ten shillings a day by his labour, and goes abroad, or sits idle, one half of that day, though he spends but sixpence during his diversion or idleness, ought not to reckon *that* the only expense; he has really spent, or rather thrown away, five shillings besides.[62]
>
> He that idly loses five shillings' worth of time, loses five shillings, and might as prudently throw five shillings into the sea.[63]

The use of the concept "five shillings' worth of time" is particularly interesting. It implies that, within the context of the modern Spirit of Capitalism, time has come to be viewed as a commodity. The popular use of colloquialisms such as "spending," "wasting," "saving," "investing," "allocating," and "budgeting" with regard to time is quite indicative of this trend. Note also that, in line with an economic philosophy whereby time is central to any cost-benefit analysis, time units and monetary units have become convertible into one another. Consider, for example, the manner in which we tie prices to the duration of consumption, as in the case of radio and television air time, rent, or long-distance telephone calls. Note also the formulas that courts use when allowing one to choose between paying a certain amount of money as fine and doing a certain amount of time in jail.

The prevalence of the utilitarian conception of time as a commodity is most evident within the industrial domain.[64] There, time is viewed as an entity that can literally be bought and sold.[65] Consider, for example, the institution of the *time wage*. As work is increasingly being measured by units such as "man hours," more and more employees are getting paid by units of time such as the hour, the day, the week, the month, or the year, rather than by the amount or the quality of the work they do. The introduction of time cards which record employees' starting and quitting times is indicative of the fact that the boundaries of the professional commitments of the modern individual are increasingly defined in a most rigid manner by time, a phenomenon which will be further discussed in chapter 5.

It is also in the industrial domain that man's attempts to optimally utilize time are most evident. Industrialization is primarily responsible for our almost cultic attitude toward efficiency. This attitude manifests itself in a variety of forms, such as the rise of the time-management consultant, the growing appreciation of speed as one of the major qualifications of employees, the institutionalization of the deadline, and the popular application of time-and-motion studies, the obvious goal of which is to speed up the production process by cutting down on the duration of activities.

And yet, the utilitarian orientation toward time in the modern West is by no means restricted to the industrial domain alone. As Sebastian de Grazia has demonstrated, it is quite characteristic of the modern conception of leisure as well.[66] According to Staffan Linder, "time famine" is a general modern disease which manifests itself in the speeding up of activities ranging from eating and lovemaking to religious sermons and cultural pursuits.[67] As he has pointed out,

> Those who complain that girls these days are "easy" fail to understand that in a hectic age girls must accelerate to save time, both for themselves and for their male friends. It would be inconceivable, for reasons of time, that a modern young lady should require her presumptive lover . . . to appear for one hundred evenings and wait outside her door, to be admitted in the hundred-and-first.[68]

The rise of the "quickie" as a modern institution must also be understood within this context.

Jet airliners, computers, microwave ovens, speed-reading techniques, scientific abstracts, instant food, Polaroid cameras, and even intelligence tests are all products of the modern Western preoccupation with time saving and speed. The rise of the fast-food eatery, our extremely negative attitude toward waiting, and the business-like character of so many social encounters today are all manifestations of the growing acceleration of the tempo of life in the West. The hectic pace of our so-called leisure time is quite evident from comparing the length of our entertainment events with that of ancient Roman gladiatorial games, Japanese Kabuki shows, or Spanish bullfights. Even our artistic preferences are indicative of our strong attraction toward "activity density" (that is, toward a high volume of activity per any given time unit). Many Westerners, for example, find Japanese movies rather boring, because they typically put very little emphasis on action. Along the same lines, the pornographic film industry seems to operate under the assumption that audiences generally prefer a dozen short, "compact" lovemaking scenes to a couple of long ones.

Many people today are becoming specialists in the fairly sophisticated art of "killing time," which involves "filling" otherwise "empty" and unaccounted-for time intervals such as riding on the subway or waiting in a lobby with "fillers"—with newspapers and magazines, crossword puzzles, and even business letters. They also try to defy the traditional zero-sum relationship among the durations of different activities—whereby time can be spent on one activity only at the expense of the time spent on another—by carrying on several activities simultaneously. The way many doctors today manage to see several patients within the very same period of time (albeit in several different rooms) is most suggestive of this pattern, which Linder has termed "simultaneous consumption."[69] Consider also such common combinations as doing business while having lunch, listening to music while driving, watching television while eating dinner or talking over the telephone, and so on. (I have also met a number of people who, by constantly turning the knob or the remote-control button, even manage to "watch" several television programs on different channels, all at the same time.) The rise of background music (or Muzak) as an institution ought to be understood within this context. As Walter Kerr, a pronounced critic of utilitarianism, has pointed out,

It is a commonplace joke that recording companies have now
nearly exhausted a certain kind of album title: we have had
Music to Read By, Music to Make Love By, Music to Sleep By,
and, as one humorist has had it, Music to Listen to Music By.
What is interesting about these titles is that they so candidly
describe the position of the popular arts in our time. They admit
at the outset that no one is expected to sit down, for heaven's

sake, and attend to the music. It is understood that, while the music is playing, everyone within earshot is going to be busy doing something else, and it is merely suggested that, if no one minds, it might be pleasant to have a whisper coming over your shoulder while you go on doing the things you must do. We have not yet got around to the business of advertising a novel as a Book to Cook By or a television show as a Show to Mend Furniture By. But that is simply an oversight; we have the novels and the shows.[70]

The inevitable price we must pay by applying the principle of simultaneous consumption to our social life as well is quite obvious. According to Linder,

> People have a surprising liking for large banquets, conventions and cocktail parties. One explanation for this may be that it seems a highly efficient way of exploiting the time allocated to social intercourse. One meets a lot of people at once. One devotes oneself to the simultaneous consumption of food and people. To be the only guests to dinner is normally considered less flattering than to be invited with many others. In a way, it should be the other way round. Perhaps it is not flattering because it suggests that your time is at such a low price that you are content to meet a couple of people at a time. Efforts to economize one's time in this way lead in due course to one's *having numerous acquaintances and no friends.*[71]

Time as an Abstract Quantity

The economic-utilitarian philosophy of time presupposes a particular way of viewing temporality, namely, from a quantitative perspective. It reflects, as well as promotes, a *quantitative view of time,* which involves a definition of time as an entity which is segmentable into various quantities of duration and, therefore, is countable and measurable. According to Lukács, one of the most significant consequences of the modern phenomenon of the fetishism of commodities is that

> time sheds its qualitative, variable, flowing nature; it freezes into an exactly delimited, quantifiable continuum filled with quantifiable "things."[72]

(Nevertheless, as we shall see in chapters 4 and 5, this perspective still coexists today with a qualitative view of time.)

The quantitative view of time is most evident in the case of schedules and time budgets. The main reason why rigidifying the duration of activities in our daily life is so necessary in an age of schedules is that the expected duration of events is of primary concern in any process of scheduling. From a logical viewpoint, it is very often the case that the act of locating an event between 2:30 P.M and 3:15 P.M., for example, is only secondary to the act of defining it as a "forty-five minute event." In a way, the process of scheduling as we know it would not have been possible were it not for some notion of *"time slots,"* which are defined essentially as quantities of duration and into which we "fit" durationally rigid activities and events.[73]

As Whorf pointed out, Western time units are

> objectified as counted *quantities,* especially as lengths, made up
> of units as a length can be visibly marked off into inches. A
> "length of time" is envisioned as a row of similar units, like a
> row of bottles.[74]

As quantities, these units are interrelated as multiples of one another. Thus, the week is defined as a precise multiple of the day and the minute is defined as a fraction of the hour, which, in turn, is defined as a fraction of the day. Furthermore, even the units "day," "month," and "year," which originally derived from some natural cycles, no longer correspond precisely to those cycles, and their definition as units of time is essentially a mathematical one.

As quantities of duration, all those units of time are also treated as divisible, as is quite evident from acts such as "splitting up" a twenty-one-day annual vacation into two or three shorter "blocks" of time that are taken off independently of one another. They are also treated as addable, as the use of plurals in "they stayed for ten days" or in "it took me six weeks to complete it" might indicate. In fact, modern scheduling procedures often presuppose our ability to add up quantities of duration and subtract them from fixed points in time.[75] After all, this is how we usually decide the time for which to set our alarm clocks on regular working days, for example. A satirical portrayal of such scheduling procedures is provided by C. Northcote Parkinson:

> the punctual person has substituted a process of subtraction for the simpler process of addition. The important meeting is at 11:45. Punctual Peter takes that as his fixed point and works backward. He must leave his office at 11:40, check his briefcase and contents at 11:30, give instruction to his deputy at 11:25, having transferred incoming telephone calls at 11:23. That leaves time to see Marty (allow ten minutes) at—say, 11:10; and Mac (allow fifteen minutes for a Scotsman) at 10:55. There are two important telephone calls to make, six and three minutes, so it is best to start dialing at 10:45. Allow fifteen minutes for reading the report and estimate (Item 4 on the agenda), so bring the file in at 10:30.[76]

As quantities of duration, our time units are uniform, that is, *standard*. We call a certain period of time a "year," whether it begins on 1 January (the civil New Year's Day), the first week of September (the beginning of the academic year), or 25 November (my birthday), because it is *always of the same length*. Similarly, unlike the ancient Egyptian-Roman "hour," whose length varied across seasons as well as across latitudes, the modern "hour" is always of the same standard length, whether its measurement begins at 6:22 A.M. or at 11:18 P.M., during the winter or during the summer, in Finland or in Sudan.

I have argued earlier that we are able to treat our time units as standard quantities of duration mainly because we can measure them against a timepiece that is paced at a uniform rate. It is thus the clock, whose introduction to the West cannot be separated from the evolution of the schedule there, that allows the particular notion of temporality which has become so characteristic of Western civilization. It is *clock time* that is at the basis of the modern Western notion of duration and that allows the durational rigidity that is so typical of modern life.

One of the most significant consequences of the introduction of the clock—and, with it, the quantitative view of duration—to the West has been the evolution of an *abstract* conception of time there. As Marshall McLuhan has noted, great cultural changes occurred in the West when it was found possible to fix time as something that happens between two points. From this application of visual, abstract, and uniform units came our Western feeling for time as duration.[77]

The clock allows us to remove ourselves one step further away from nature. Whereas a time unit such as the solar tropical year, for example, is essentially anchored in nature—being defined as the period between two successive passages of the sun through the spring equinox—units such as the hour and the minute are purely abstract, since they exist only within clock time. Like language, clock time is a symbolic system whose elementary units, like words, have no intrinsic value of their own. Whatever meaning they might have can derive only from the system of which they are a part, since, if it were not for this system, they would not even exist.

In other words, the modern Western time units are purely abstract entities, totally dissociated from nature and "separated from the rhythms of human experience."[78] They are utterly removed from, and not anchored within, any concrete context of events. In Irving Hallowell's words, "Time assumes for us an autonomous character and we are free to manipulate temporal concepts instrumentally, without constant reference to specific events."[79]

The full historical significance of the Benedictine invention of a schedule which was based entirely on a mechanical timepiece ought to be appreciated within this context. Prior to the introduction of the mechanical clock, various societies had been very precise and rigid with regard to the timing of particularly significant social events. Their precision, however, was essentially tied to nature, having been basically linked to purely astronomical phenomena such as sunrise and sunset, equinoxes and solstices, and special arrangements of stellar constellations. With the single exception of the ancient Jews, who—as we shall see in the fourth chapter—had partially dissociated their social calendar from nature when they invented the seven-day week, the Benedictines were clearly the first ones to have established a rigid temporal regularity that was not directly geared in any way to nature.

The abstract conception of temporality allows us to make a fundamental conceptual distinction between "gross time" (or passing time) and "net time" (or measured time), and to entirely dissociate the latter from the former. This is quite evident from the manner in which we so often add up chunks of time which are not even juxtaposed in actual reality. Note, for example, how we accumulate sick leave, or how we refer to someone as having had "seventy-five hours" of psychoanalysis. Consider also the way in which we add up working days, as in "It will take three business days to repair it," which obviously excludes weekends and holidays. That measured time can be entirely dissociated from passing time is also evident from the way time is measured in chess or in basketball, whereby breaks and "time out" periods are not counted. The distinction between "gross time" and "net time" also helps us to understand why some people finish "six-semester training programs" in three years while others, who also take summer courses, manage to do that in two years. That time can be "frozen" for the purpose of measuring it is also evident from the way some universities stop counting the years toward coming up for tenure when one is on special leave.

The abstract conception of time is at the basis of the modern notion of duration, which is essentially what we measure when we use the stopwatch, the parking meter, or the egg timer. It is also responsible for the introduction of timed records to running and swimming,[80] along with the modern distinction between being a champion, which involves beating others, and being a record holder, which involves "beating" the best previously recorded clock time. (It enables us to compare, for example, a mile run that took place on a summer evening in 1966 in Oslo with another mile run that took place on a winter afternoon twelve years later in Sydney.) It also allows us to solve various linear programming problems, as might be indicated by the use of the critical-path method in operations research, for example.

Finally, the abstract conception of time is also responsible for the fact that we so often treat time slots that are durationally equivalent to one another as if they were actually interchangeable. Consider, for example, our ability to "move" a one-hour class or appointment from one day to another. Note also the quite common practice of switching shifts in organizations that operate around the clock. It certainly presupposes a notion that, if I do not work my eight hours today, I can still work "them" on some other day, as if those were still the same eight hours! The very same notion is also at the basis of the practice of granting "compensatory time" to employees who work overtime.

The interchangeability of time periods is inherent to the quantitative view of time in the West and is quite antithetical to the traditional qualitative conception of temporality. President Roosevelt's act of "moving" Thanksgiving Day from the last Thursday of November to the third Thursday in November, for example, would have been utterly inconceivable within a traditional conception of time, wherein holidays certainly cannot be arbitrarily "moved." To appreciate the intimate relationship between the interchangeability of time periods and a pronouncedly rational social order, note also the abolition of the weekend in some utopian societies.[81]

Schedules and Social Solidarity

One of the main characteristics of life in the Benedictine monasteries was the prevalence of one particular pattern of temporal coordination there—*temporal symmetry*.[82] What made the activities of the individual monks communal was the sheer fact that they were carried out *simultaneously*. Not only was every monk required to do certain things at certain times, but he was expected to do them *together* with all the rest of his community. All members of a monastic community would engage in the same activity—whether it was reading, eating, meditating, working, praying, studying, or going to bed—*at the same time*.

Thus, standard bedtime, mealtimes, or the canonical hours were actually "social facts" that applied to each particular member of the monastic social system only because they applied first to that system as a whole. From a logical standpoint, the fact that a monk would retire at 6:30 P.M., for example, was only secondary to the fact that that was actually the time at which his entire community would retire. In this respect, it can be argued that all individuals' schedules were essentially designed as duplicates of one another.

Given all this, it was necessary to synchronize the activities of entire monastic communities in the most precise manner. This explains Saint Benedict's particular emphasis on punctuality. Furthermore, it justifies the claim that the earliest role of the clock was "the synchronization of human tasks."[83] (It is interesting to note, in this respect, that the widespread use of the wristwatch many centuries later was also associated originally with the need to synchronize the movements of military units during the Boer War and World War I.)[84]

Temporal symmetry, which involves synchronizing the activities of different individuals, is actually one of the fundamental principles of social organization. Being "in sync" with one another is at the basis of some of the most simple social activities, from dancing and sexually climaxing together to participating in religious rituals, as well as of the "mutual tuning-in relationship," which, according to Alfred Schutz, is the very essence of musical performance.[85] Hence the centrality of the notion of being "together" among jazz musicians, for example.[86] In fact, the most distinctive characteristic of Western music, namely, harmony, would not have been possible were it not for the establishment of temporal symmetry.

Temporal symmetry undoubtedly contributed to a sense of "togetherness" in monastic life. It added to the element of similitude among the different monks and, thus, helped to form a strong basis for what Durkheim called "mechanical solidarity."[87] To appreciate the prevalence of temporal symmetry in monastic life and its contribution to the formation of mechanical solidarity there, note also that a most common method of punishing monks was to segregate their activities temporally from those of the rest of their community, as by having them eat their meals three hours after them, rather than together with them.[88]

Along with the schedule, we have also inherited from the Benedictines the adherence to temporal symmetry as a formal pattern of organizing our lives. In other words, we have developed a tendency to do many things in our lives at the same time as everyone else.[89] Yevgeny Zamyatin, Lewis Mumford, and Lawrence Wright offer the following portrayals of this phenomenon:

> Every morning, with six-wheeled precision, at the same hour and the same moment, we—millions of us—get up as one. At the same hour, in million-headed unison, we start work; and in million-headed unison we end it. And, fused into a single million-headed body, at the same second, designated by the Table [of

Hours], we lift our spoons to our mouths. At the same second, we
come out for our walk, go to the auditorium, go to the hall for
Taylor exercises, fall asleep.[90]

Breakfast, lunch, dinner, occur at regular hours and are of
definitely limited duration: a million people perform these
functions within a very narrow band of time, and only minor
provisions are made for those who would have food outside this
regular schedule.[91]

Nine tenths of [the working force], despite some attempt to
stagger office hours, start homeward within the same 90 minutes,
queuing for buses in vacuous resignation, squeezing in indecent
intimacy in the Underground, rather than linger awhile in park or
café; for who will await the roomy 6:30 if he can just find standing
room in the 5:45?[92]

The almost complete identity between personal and collective schedules and rhythms has already caused great problems to urban de-
signers. It is solely responsible for the unbearably congested peak
periods around rush hours in the streets and in the public trans-
portation systems, around mealtimes at restaurants, and during
weekends and holidays on the road and on the beaches. Note also
the implications of temporal symmetry as a way of life on the consumption of energy (electricity, heating gas, and so on).

The mechanical solidarity within the monastery was also en-
hanced by the fact that, by adhering to the horarium, monks definitely put themselves out of phase with the rest of society. Consider,
for example, the Benedictine bedtime and wake-up time. In having
to wake up in the middle of the night and to go to bed early in the
evening, monks were essentially required to disregard some of the
fundamental conventions of the "outside world" and put themselves
out of phase with it.

They could defy that world only because they were provided with
a self-subsistent alternative world (with which they willingly identified, unlike prisoners, for example). The "total institution"[93] is
an ideal setting within which unusual or innovative social orders may
incubate and develop quite independently of the surrounding social
environment. It was the "total" character of monastic life that made
it possible for Saint Benedict to introduce such a unique sociotemporal order into the Benedictine monasteries.

In being responsible for putting them out of phase with society at large, the horarium again contributed to the formation of mechanical solidarity among monks. It helped to establish powerful inter-group boundaries which distinguished, as well as separated, members of the monastic order from "outsiders." It is well known that boundaries which distinguish and separate group members from "outsiders" also serve to solidify in-group sentiments.

We are now in a better position to appreciate the powerful function of sociotemporal orders in solidifying in-group sentiments and fostering mechanical solidarity. The case of the Benedictines is quite similar to that of night workers, who develop among themselves strong "mechanical" ties around the sheer fact that they live and work out of phase with the society at large.[94] (The same holds for many military units as well.) It is generally true that sharing a common schedule—or, for that matter, calendar, as we shall see in the next chapter—definitely helps to solidify in-group sentiments.[95] *A temporal order that is commonly shared by a social group and is unique to it to the extent that it distinguishes and separates group members from "outsiders" contributes to the establishment of inter-group boundaries and constitutes a powerful basis for mechanical solidarity within the group.*

And yet, if Saint Benedict indeed meant the schedule to function as a solidifier of "mechanical" ties, history then certainly gave his invention a most interesting twist. The very institution he introduced in order to foster mechanical solidarity has also evolved into becoming one of the cornerstones of what Durkheim called "organic solidarity." Not only is it able to promote the basis of the former, namely, interpersonal similitude, but it has become one of the most effective facilitators of the basis of the latter, namely, intragroup complementary differentiation. This could not have happened, however, had Saint Benedict's original model of a schedule not undergone some fundamental modifications.

Temporal symmetry was the pattern of temporal coordination most suitable for a predominantly "mechanical" social order, since it helped to emphasize the element of interpersonal similitude. Mechanical solidarity is essentially antithetical to individualism and, therefore, usually involves an attempt to establish similitude by stripping individuals of their individuality. In Benedictine monasticism, this was accomplished through similar clothes and haircuts, as well as through the application of principles of social organization such as temporal symmetry.

A predominantly "organic" social order, which is far more characteristic of modern Western civilization, cherishes individualism and, therefore, emphasizes interpersonal differentiation.[96] In order to meet the particular demands that are inherent to such a social order, some patterns of temporal coordination other than temporal symmetry have become necessary. The schedule has managed to meet this challenge as well, by allowing for a particular pattern of temporal coordination that facilitates the establishment and maintenance of interpersonal differentiation—*temporal complementarity*.[97] We must appreciate this second solidifying function of the schedule in order to account for the fact that it has survived to this day. Only then can we understand Georg Simmel's claim that it is precisely the variety of the relationships and daily affairs of modern individuals and the differentiation of their interests that accounts for the fact that "the technique of metropolitan life is unimaginable without the most punctual integration of all activities and mutual relations into a stable and impersonal time schedule."[98]

This definitely calls for a number of different—albeit interdependent—schedules, as well as for a number of different levels of temporal coordination.[99] In the predominantly "mechanical" monastic communities, where there was very little social differentiation, the existence of a single common schedule was possible, necessary, and sufficient. Such situation is impossible within a modern form of social organization. Unlike the Benedictine monks, whose schedules were essentially duplicates of one another, modern individuals must have their own unique personal schedules, which are deliberately designed to complement those of others. Parts of one's schedule are obviously going to be shared by others who belong to the same social circles. Otherwise, family dinners, church services, work conferences, seminars, and basketball games, for example, would not be possible. Almost all modern enterprises require at least some element of temporal symmetry, which implies some degree of sharing a common schedule. However, since each modern individual also represents a unique intersection of social circles,[100] some parts of his or her schedule are inevitably always unique to him or her.

The result is a *temporal division of labor*, whereby group members participate in one and the same temporal order, yet differently from one another. *The temporal coordination of complementary differences among them enhances their interdependence and, thus, functions as a most powerful basis for a strong organic solidarity within the group.* The organization of rotations, shifts, night duties, calls, and vacations among hospital staff is a perfect case in point.[101]

The introduction of flexible working hours exemplifies the way in which individualism may be promoted by the establishment of some temporal differentiation among individuals. It basically involves staggering individuals' living patterns, which essentially entails some temporal coordination among them. It is hard to envision how that could have been accomplished without the schedule, which allows for deliberate temporal complementarity.

Had the schedule not met the modern demands for social differentiation and individuation, it probably would not have survived to this day. Its particular strength and indispensability to modern social organization lies in its ability to contribute to the establishment and maintenance of both major constituents of social solidarity. It is this unique ability of the schedule to enhance both interpersonal similitude and intragroup complementary differentiation—and, thus, both mechanical and organic solidarity—at the same time that accounts for the fact that it has survived to this day and has become one of the institutional cornerstones of social life in the modern world.

Three

The Calendar

Calendars and Group Identity

As demonstrated in the previous chapter, temporal arrangements are closely interlinked with group formation. A temporal order that is commonly shared by a group of people and is unique to them functions both as a unifier and as a separator. On the one hand, by highlighting and accentuating the similitude among group members vis-à-vis others, it helps to solidify in-group sentiments and, thus, constitutes a most powerful basis for "mechanical" solidarity within the group. On the other hand, it clearly contributes to the establishment of intergroup boundaries that distinguish and separate group members from "outsiders." We have already explored the relationship between temporality and group identity with respect to schedules and small groups. Let us now examine it with respect to calendars and societies.

One particular social group that has traditionally put much emphasis on its distinction for "outsiders" is the Jewish people. Let us begin, therefore, with a discussion of the various calendrical means by which Jews have managed throughout history to solidify their in-group sentiments and separate themselves from non-Jews.

As Max Weber pointed out, one of the most important "differentiating commandments" that have been responsible for the actual segregation of Jews from non-Jews is the observance of the Sabbath.[1] Jews have traditionally maintained that it is *only they* who share the obligation to observe the Sabbath, and it is quite typical that, at the expiration of this holy day, as we shall see in the next chapter, they bless God for distinguishing between Israel and the other nations. That several rabbinical authorities even went as far as to condemn non-Jews who observed the Sabbath as offenders who tried to put themselves between God and Israel[2] ought to be understood within the context of the traditional Jewish belief that God actually gave the holy day to the Jews alone:

> Moreover also I gave them My sabbaths, to be a sign between Me and them, that they might know that I am the Lord that sanctify them.[3]

> And He said unto us: "Behold, I will separate unto Myself a people from among all the peoples, and these shall keep the Sabbath day, and I will sanctify them unto Myself as My people, and will bless them."[4]

The Jews' claim to the Sabbath as their own possession is also manifested in their ritual metaphorical depiction of the holy day as a bride and Israel as its groom.[5] Within a monogamous universe, this can only mean that the Sabbath "belongs" exclusively to the Jews.

The actual observance of the Sabbath has thus served a most significant symbolic function throughout history, namely, reflecting the fundamental need of Jews to distinguish themselves from their Gentile environment and emphasize their uniqueness as a group.[6] As such, it has helped to solidify the "mechanical" ties among the Jewish people. By observing the Sabbath, Jews have managed to mark themselves off as an entity that is quite distinct from the Gentiles around them.

Not only has the observance of the Sabbath served a symbolic function of expressing and reflecting particularistic Jewish sentiments, but it has served a far more practical function, namely, actually segregating Jews from—and keeping them from assimilating into—their Gentile environment. It is within this context that we ought to view the decree of Nehemiah, the governor of Judah in the fifth century B.C., to close the gates of Jerusalem during the Sabbath so as to prevent any Jewish-Gentile transactions.[7] The fact that Jews have persistently maintained their practice of resting on Saturday even though, for many centuries, they have lived among Gentiles who rest on Sunday (in the Christian world) or who regard

Friday as their holy day (the Moslems) obviously helped to actually segregate them from their surrounding social environment. In Europe, for example, Jews and Christians were kept from having any social contacts with one another on no less than two out of the seven days of the week (Saturday and Sunday)!

This explains why it was particularly during the period of Exile—when Jews were forced to live as a minority surrounded by a Gentile environment—that the Sabbath grew to be such an important institution in Jewish life.[8] It also explains its recent decline in modern Israel, an almost entirely Jewish society! That within the American Reform movement, which tries to play down the significance of the distinctions between Jews and Gentiles, some congregations have already gone as far as to "move" the Sabbath from Saturday to Sunday, the Christian Lord's Day, also ought to be understood within this context.

Ironically, the Christian ecclesiastical week originally derived from the Jewish week, and the Christian practice of resting on Sunday, which the Jews have continuously tried to ignore, was originally a reaction against the Jewish practice of resting on Saturday! The story of the origin of the Christian Lord's Day is most useful for highlighting the need of social groups to distinguish themselves from other groups by calendrical means.

From its very early days, the Church made every possible attempt to accentuate its dissociation from Judaism, the faith out of which it had sprung. Choosing one particular day of the week as a day on which they would congregate on a regular basis was among the very first things the early Christians did as a group.[9] Whether they chose Sunday to be the Lord's Day (*dies Dominica*) because they adopted the Mithraist cult of the sun—with which Sunday was associated—or because they actually believed it to be the day on which Christ had risen from the dead is quite irrelevant to our discussion. The main thing is that they deliberately chose a day other than Saturday, the traditional Jewish holy day. In order to distinguish and dissociate themselves from non-Christian Jews, they chose to assemble on a day other than the one on which the latter used to assemble. In short, they wanted to have a day "distinctively their own."[10] Establishing Sunday as the Lord's Day was definitely one of the most significant sociopolitical moves made by the early Christians. It was a deliberate attempt to accentuate a social distinction by means of applying a calendrical distinction. (I would like to speculate here that it was for precisely the same reason—namely, to distinguish and segregate Moslems from both Jews and Christians— that Mohammed chose Friday as the holy day of the week for the followers of the Islamic faith. It is noteworthy in this regard that two of the three days of the week that are regarded by Islam as unfortunate and evil are none other than Saturday and Sunday.)[11]

While the early Christians "moved" the Sabbath from Saturday to Sunday, they did not alter the basic fact that the week is a seven-day cycle. However, a number of attempts have been made throughout history to establish—for purely political or cultural purposes— a new weekly cycle of a different length altogether. Two of the most notable anticlerical movements in modern history—the French and the Bolshevik revolutions—made serious attempts to replace the seven-day week, which was highly associated with Christianity, by new weekly rhythms of collective life. As we shall soon see, the French Revolution brought with it an entirely new weekly cycle, the ten-day *décade,* and replaced Sunday by *Décadi*, a new rest day which was observed every ten days. This presented people with both practical and cognitive difficulties in keeping up with the ecclesiastical seven-day cycle and was certainly meant to disrupt church-attending practices. A similar anticlerical measure was applied by Joseph Stalin when he introduced a five-day, and then a six-day, weekly cycle between 1929 and 1940.[12]

Not only through their observance of the Sabbath have Jews demonstrated the manner in which unique temporal arrangements may function as solidifiers of in-group sentiments. Until this day, all Jewish religious life—and, in modern Israel, all national life as well—is temporally regulated by a pronouncedly distinct calendar, namely, the traditional Jewish calendar. Jews also still adhere to their own distinct chronological dating framework—the Era of the Creation.

The Jewish calendar has been hailed as the single most important book of the people of Israel. It has been said to have preserved the Jews as a people, to have "united all those who had been scattered around the world and made them one people." It has been claimed to have given Jews, wherever they may be, a warm homey feeling and to have helped them inhale "the smell of unity, the commonality of hopes, the unifying destiny, and the mutual pledge."[13]

The reason for this lies in the fact that, to a large extent, it is their collective memories that have kept the Jews together as a people, and most of these probably would have been lost were it not for their having been commemorated in the Jewish calendar.[14] Particularly significant collective memories of events such as the Exodus and the destruction of the Temple, for example, have been commemorated in particular days—Passover and the Ninth of Av—which exist only within the Jewish calendar. If this calendar were to be abandoned, these collective memories might have been lost forever.

It is this fear that the Jewish people might be led "into a cold and strange world which has no Jewish memory in it" that has motivated Joshua Manoach to condemn the increasing use of the Gregorian calendar and the Christian Era alongside the Jewish calendar and the Era of the Creation in modern Israel.[15] His main worry is that it might result in no less than the complete loss of the Jewish national identity:

> The soul of Israel, its religion and its customs, is anchored in its time. Replacing its national-religious time by the time of others . . . is suicidal for a distinct and independent people.[16]

> Every people has its own time, which ties it to its land and place, and in which its history and holidays are embedded. . . . Every people that has tried to separate itself from its time has disappeared and is no longer remembered among the living.[17]

> We have to decide once and for all—either ours or theirs, a Jewish calendar or a Christian calendar. It is impossible to have a common way between these two times.[18]

The use of the term "Christian calendar" is no mere accident. In fact, Manoach actually condemns Israelis for "Christianizing" their time.[19] Along those lines, he also claims that the modern Hebrew temporal formulations "before the count" (for "B.C.") and "the civil date" (for the date according to the Gregorian calendar) ought to be changed to "before the Christians' count" and "the Christian date," respectively.[20] He obviously defies the universalistic claims of the Gregorian calendar and the Christian Era and tries to expose their "real" particularistic nature as nothing but Christian institutions.

Not that Manoach advocates an international, universalistic calendar. In no way does he even try to suggest that the rest of the world ought to consider adopting the Jewish calendar instead of the Gregorian calendar. He simply echoes a trend which used to be popular and which—as we shall see later in this chapter—is gradually dying with the expansion of an international time-reckoning and dating system throughout the entire world. It is an age-old quest to defy standardization and preserve particularistic sentiments by means of maintaining distinct temporal arrangements.

That quest has been manifested on numerous occasions throughout history. Consider, for example, the centrality of the dispute over determining the date of Easter to the split between the Roman Catholic Church and the Greek Orthodox Church. Consider also the cases of Venice and Pisa, which, for two centuries following the Gregorian reform of the calendar, which established 1 January as the standard official beginning of the calendar year, still clung to their traditional practices of beginning the year on 1 March and 25 March, respectively.[21]

Of major interest for the present discussion are the various sectarian calendars that evolved alongside the traditional Jewish calendar—those of the Northern Kingdom (around 900 B.C.), the Samaritans (around 700 B.C.), the Sadducees and the Boethusians (around 200 B.C.), and the Karaites (during the eighth century A.D.).[22] The struggle around those calendars played a prominent part within the broader political struggle of the above sects against the ruling Jewish establishment. With respect to the conflict between the Sadducees and the Pharisees, the two major rival Jewish parties around 200 B.C., for example, it has even been argued by Louis Finkelstein that

> Of all the sectarian controversies raging in the Second Commonwealth, that concerning the dates of the *Omer* and Shabuot inevitably became the most bitter and the most prominent. . . . None of the other controversies involved such profound public and private considerations.[23]

Particularly significant for our discussion is the fact that, all in all, the differences between each of these sectarian calendars and the generally accepted Jewish calendar were relatively minor. After all, the major characteristic of the Boethusian calendar was the fact that it insisted that the Omer—a particular offering brought to the Temple during Passover and on whose counting the date of Shavuoth is based—be offered on the first Sunday after Passover, rather than on the morrow of the first day after that holiday. Similarly, one of the main characteristics of the Karaite calendar is the fact that it insists that Passover and the Feast of Tabernacles be observed for only seven, rather than eight, days.

And yet, despite the fact that the differences between these sectarian calendars and the generally accepted Jewish calendar were so minute, they nevertheless did exist. Furthermore, they were solely responsible for creating situations whereby days that were regarded as most sacred by the Jewish establishment were considered to be profane by particular sects. Thus, even though these calendrical differences may seem to be rather insignificant on the surface, they were nevertheless highly significant from a symbolic standpoint.

If we purposely disregard the theological rationales for establishing and preserving such minor calendrical differences, their latent social function becomes quite apparent. They reflect a particularly strong need on the part of a social group to dissociate itself from another group, usually the one from which it has sprung. As Finkelstein suggested with regard to the Sadducean calendar,

> the problem of the date of the *Omer* and of Shabuot served as continuous reminders of the sectarian cleavage in Jewry, and of the opposition of the Temple priesthood in general, to the whole Prophetic-Pharisaic tradition.[24]

Another sect which—as we have already seen earlier with respect to the Sabbath—also utilized calendrical means as a part of its general attempts to dissociate itself from Judaism was the early Christians. The Quartodeciman controversy, which revolved around the determination of the date of Easter, ought to be seen within the context of the general attempts made by the Church to emancipate itself from the grip of the Jewish calendar.[25]

In its early days, the Church was split over the determination of the date of Easter. While many churches celebrated it on Sunday, some of the Eastern churches still insisted on celebrating Easter on the fourteenth day of the lunar month, that is, with Passover, the Jewish holiday with which it is so intimately associated. Finally, at the meeting of the First Council of Nicaea in A.D. 325, the practice of celebrating Easter with Passover was defined as an act of heresy. The first ecumenical council of the Church ruled that Easter be celebrated on the Sunday following the full moon which coincides with, or falls next after, the vernal equinox.

It is quite obvious that the main motive underlying the ruling of the Council of Nicaea was making sure that Easter and Passover would never coincide. As James Barnett pointed out, "It appears that the Easter celebration was so fixed to avoid its falling on the same date as the Jewish Passover."[26] From a symbolic standpoint, the fact that Easter would always fall on Sunday, the Lord's Day, was only secondary to the fact that it would never coincide with Passover, even if the latter happens to fall on Sunday. The ruling that Easter ought to be celebrated on the Sunday *following* the full moon— which precluded the possibility of ever celebrating it on a full moon —ought to be viewed within the context of the fact that Passover is always celebrated on a full moon. There is virtually no other reason for the Church's insistence that Easter be celebrated only a few days after the full moon. The only purpose of that ruling was to temporally segregate the two major Jewish and Christian holidays—and, with them, the entire Jewish and ecclesiastical calendars—from one another.

It is ironical that, by trying to totally dissociate itself from Judaism, the Church only immortalized its awareness—albeit negative— of the Jewish calendar! It is a classic example of how, by trying to negate something, we only make it more salient. In order to avoid any coincidence of Easter and Passover whatsoever, the Church inevitably had to become forever aware of the Jewish holiday. (Incidentally, the two holidays would not have coincided more than once every nineteen years anyway.) Rather than remain entirely solar, like the Julian calendar on which it is essentially based, the ecclesiastical calendar has had to incorporate some awareness of the lunar cycle (and especially with regard to its most important holiday), an ironic reminder of some fundamental Jewish influence. Until this day, while Jews keep celebrating Passover Eve on a regular basis on the fourteenth day of the lunar month Nisan, Easter remains a "movable" feast vis-à-vis the calendar year. The Church is forced to move it from one date to another every year, so that it will never coincide with its original ancestor.

The inevitable result of all this has been an embarrassing dependence of the ecclesiastical calendar on the calendar from which it was originally meant to be dissociated. A far more successful attempt on the part of a sect to utterly dissociate its holidays from the Jewish holidays was carried out by the sect known to us from the Dead Sea Scrolls and generally referred to as the Qumran Community, or the Dead Sea Sect. This fundamentalist monastic community, which flourished in the Judaean Desert between 100 B.C. and A.D. 70, managed to defy the Jewish calendar in a way that resembles the manner in which the French and Bolshevik revolutions managed to defy the ecclesiastical week, namely, by adhering to a distinct calendar which was based on an annual cycle of an entirely different length.

The calendar to which this sect adhered is mentioned in two pseudoepigraphic works which have been found in the Qumran caves—*The Book of Jubilees* and *The Book of Enoch*:

> And all the days of the commandment will be two and fifty weeks of days, and these will make the entire year complete. . . . And command thou the children of Israel that they observe the years according to this reckoning—three hundred and sixty-four days, and these will constitute a complete year.[27]

> And the sun and the stars bring in all the years exactly, so that they do not advance or delay their position by a single day unto eternity; but complete the years with perfect justice in 364 days.[28]

This calendar was quite distinct from the one adhered to by the Jewish community at large around that time. It was based on a 364-day annual cycle that was divided into fifty-two weeks, as well as into four 91-day seasons, each of which was thirteen weeks long and consisted of three 30-day months plus an additional memorial day.[29]

Both *The Book of Jubilees* and *The Book of Enoch* were written —possibly by traditionalist Sadducees—sometime during the second century B.C., at the height of the rivalry between the Sadducees and the Pharisees. It is not clear whether the solar calendar they depict was actually the traditional Jewish calendar which Moses supposedly introduced, as the author of *The Book of Jubilees* seems to imply. It is well established, however, that its traditionalist adherents clearly reacted against the common tendency during that period—prevalent among Pharisees and Helenized circles alike—to move away from a purely solar calendar toward the Greek lunisolar calendar.[30] According to George F. Moore,

> The motive for [the solar calendrical system] was probably not the mere charm of symmetry, but the desire to create *a distinctively Jewish division of time fundamentally unlike those of other peoples, and particularly that of the Greeks.*[31]

It was probably the Pharisees and Helenized Jews that the author of *The Book of Jubilees* had in mind when he condemned as sinful heretics those who "disturbed the feasts" and "walked according to the feasts of Gentiles," "dislodged the years from their order," and "confounded feasts and holy days with abominable and unclean days" and vice versa.[32]

The Dead Sea Sect definitely regarded such passages as moral imperatives. The rule of that order—*The Manual of Discipline*—is interspersed with references to the obligation of members of the sect to adhere to the "true" temporal location of the "holy seasons." It is quite typical that, already in the opening chapter of the manual, the following condition for entering the community is put forward: "They must not deviate by a single step from carrying out the orders of God at the times appointed for them; they must neither advance the statutory times nor postpone the prescribed seasons."[33]

Probably the major consequence of the adherence of the members of the sect to this solar calendar was that they came to observe the Jewish holidays and festivals on days other than those observed by the Jewish community at large, who went by the lunisolar calendar through which the priesthood—by that time increasingly Pharisaic—regulated the liturgical services in the Temple at Jerusalem.[34] This implied that the members of the Qumran community and the rest of the Jews regarded different days as holy. Furthermore, it meant that the former did not participate with the latter in the public worship services at the Temple.[35] As Yigael Yadin has pointed out,

> They could thus obviously not follow the calendar in use in Jerusalem, which is a lunar calendar. As a result their festivals occurred on different days. They could therefore not partake in the holy service in the Temple, where the official calendar was observed. They could not for the same reason sacrifice offerings.[36]

At a time when the holiday services at the Temple in Jerusalem were definitely the most significant collective events at the societal level, this must have been both a manifestation and a cause of separatistic sentiments. According to A. Dupont-Sommer,

> The followers of the Covenant, being guided by a special calendar, must have celebrated the Sabbaths and festivals at different dates from those of the rest of Jewry. They were consequently completely isolated from the latter in all the practices of liturgical life. Throughout the length of the year, this was a serious circumstance, emphasizing in the most visible and concrete fashion the separatist nature of the sect, and particularly its complete divergence from the Pharisaic party.[37]

And, indeed, a number of scholars have noted the social segregative function of this sectarian calendar:

> Of all the ritual peculiarities visible in the [Dead Sea] Scrolls, the one that sets the Qumran sect most effectively apart from Rabbinic Judaism is thought to be its calendar.[38]

> The use of a divergent calendar and of different systems of reckoning time would have the advantage of enabling the Covenanters to keep themselves in some sense separate from their fellow Jews.[39]

We can now better appreciate the significant role calendars may play in promoting separatism. The case of the Qumran sect is highly suggestive of the tremendous power of the calendar as a social segregator. By creating a new annual rhythm of liturgical activity, the Qumran calendar definitely helped to temporally segregate the holidays of the Dead Sea Sect from those of the rest of the Jews. As such, it was clearly one of the major factors responsible for the actual social segregation of the sect from the Jewish society at large.

According to Jacob Licht, "The sect's adoption of the 364-day calendar was the single most decisive factor of its separation, for *practical symbiosis of two groups using different calendars is impossible.*"[40]

A similar social experiment which was based on the very same principle—and which, 1,350 years after it took place, can certainly be said to have had a tremendous success—was carried out in A.D. 632 by the prophet Mohammed. Like the Qumran sect, he managed to utterly dissociate the Islamic religious holidays he introduced from the pagan Arab festivals from which many of them actually derived, by establishing an entirely new annual cycle. He abolished the intercalary month Nasi—which he regarded as a man-made artifact representing a sinful deviation from the divine order of things—and, thus, replaced the lunisolar calendar that had prevailed in Arabia with an entirely lunar calendar.[41]

It is quite possible that Mohammed's calendrical reform ought to be seen within the context of the rise of the significance of the moon in Islam.[42] However, even if the prophet did actually intend to promote the cult of the moon, his reform has nevertheless had a most fascinating latent function as well. One of the implications of his having replaced the traditional Arab 365-day year with a new Mohammedan 354-day annual cycle was that, already a few generations later, it would have been most difficult to still associate the new Islamic religious festivals with the local pagan Arab holidays from which they had originally derived! As G. E. von Grunebaum pointed out, "This rotation [of the new Muslim months within the traditional solar year] removes the Muslim festivals completely from whatever connection with natural phenomena their pagan origins may have had."[43] Like any other date within the Mohammedan calendar, these festivals very rapidly lost any seasonal character they might have originally had. Being anchored in a purely lunar annual cycle, they can "appear" practically anywhere within the solar or lunisolar calendar year.

Thus, by establishing a new annual rhythm of religious activity, it was much easier for Mohammed to temporally segregate the Islamic holidays from non-Islamic ones. That must have facilitated the actual social segregation of Moslems from non-Moslems, as had been the case with the Qumran sect seven hundred years earlier.

Calendars as Symbols

The above discussion centered around the segregative function of calendars, the way in which they help to establish intergroup boundaries by reflecting, as well as promoting, in-group sentiments. However, it also served to highlight the way in which various social groups attach meanings to their calendars. I shall now focus on these symbolic functions of the calendar.

The tremendous symbolic significance of the calendar is quite evident from the fact that substantial calendrical reforms have always been associated with great social—political as well as cultural—reforms. Consider, for example, the calendrical reforms that accompanied the reform of the Athenian constitution by Cleisthenes in 508 B.C. or the crystallization of the Roman Empire by Julius Caesar in 46 B.C., not to mention the meeting of the first ecumenical council of the Church at Nicaea in A.D. 325 or the Stalinist reforms of the 1920s and the 1930s in the Soviet Union, which I have discussed earlier. Consider also the new calendars that were devised by great religious reformers such as Mohammed, whom I have already discussed, and Moses, as a part of their general reforms. The tremendous cultural and political significance of the adoption of the Gregorian calendar by different countries—which will be analyzed later in this chapter—is also indicative of the symbolic aspect of calendrical reforms.

Deciphering the symbolism underlying temporal arrangements is by no means an easy task.[44] It could be much easier, however, if those who designed those arrangements were to convey to us in an explicit manner what the latter are supposed to symbolically represent. Fortunately, there is one such case that is available to us—the case of the French Republican (or Revolutionary) calendar.

On 20 December 1792, the supreme political body governing Revolutionary France—the National Convention—issued a decree authorizing the Committee of Public Instruction to consider a reform of the existing calendar. The committee produced an extremely detailed proposal, and on 24 November 1793, the National Convention put the Republican calendar into effect. This calendar was in official use in France—as well as in its colonies, "sister republics," and annexed territories—from 1793 until 1 January 1806, when it was abolished by Napoleon.[45]

The French Republican calendrical reform is undoubtedly the most radical attempt in modern history to have challenged the calendrical system that prevails in the world to this day. It is hard to overemphasize the extent to which the reformers obliterated the existing system of units of time as well as the existing time-reckoning and dating frameworks, since almost none of the constituents of those was spared. The scope of the Republican calendrical reform was almost total, since its architects strived to bring about a total symbolic transformation of the existing calendrical system. To understand this, we must appreciate the sociohistorical context within which the reform took place. The Revolutionary calendar was born in an age committed to the idea of total regeneration, an age which advocated the total obliteration of the existing order in the name of progress and modernity. Launching the calendrical reform was primarily a symbolic act which was supposed to mark the total discontinuity between past and present. (This accounts for the fact that it also involved, as we shall soon see, the beginning of a new chronological era—the Republican Era.) It is the symbolism associated with the Revolutionary calendar that also accounts for the fact that it was readopted by the Paris Commune in 1871.[46]

That Maximilien Robespierre himself participated in some of the debates regarding the reform is quite indicative of how seriously the reformers took their task.[47] They were particularly sensitive to the symbolic overtones of their acts. In the decree in which they announced the introduction of the new calendar, they were particularly explicit about "the motives that have determined the decree,"[48] which—as they themselves admitted—were, to a large extent, purely symbolic. Whereas the existing calendar was associated, in their minds, with nothing less than vice, arrogance, stupidity, treason, lies, servitude, cruelty, fanaticism, slavery, and persecution, the new calendar was intended to be associated with "the spirit of our revolution."[49]

It is, therefore, within the sociohistorical context of the French Revolution that the symbolic functions of the Republican calendar ought to be examined. And, indeed, four themes which embody much of the spirit of the French Revolution—secularism, rationalism, naturalism, and nationalism—underlie most of the symbolism associated with the French Republican calendar. Therefore, rather than attempt to provide a total analysis of that calendar, I shall now try to examine the various ways in which its architects managed to design it so that it would symbolically represent each of those four themes of the French Revolution.

Secularism. Ever since antiquity, timekeeping had always been associated with the religious sphere of life. Consequently, it had almost always been the clergy that controlled the calendar. Not surprisingly, at least since Julius Caesar, almost all major calendrical reforms had been introduced and sanctioned by religious authorities such as the first ecumenical council of the Church at Nicaea, the Jewish *nasi* Hillel II, the prophet Mohammed, and Pope Gregory XIII. In this respect, the Revolutionary calendrical reform was to constitute a most significant historical precedent and breakthrough.

As we shall see later in this chapter, the calendar that had been in use in pre-Revolutionary France was symbolically associated quite strongly with the Catholic Church. The powerful symbolic links between the Gregorian calendar and highly significant Catholic institutions like the Saints' Days, the Sunday Letter, and the Golden Number did not escape the reformers' attention.[50] Nor were they oblivious to the fact that the practice of beginning the year on 1 January had been introduced to France by no other than Charles IX, the same king who had also approved the notorious massacre of the Protestant Huguenots on Saint Bartholomew's Day.[51] In short, as far as the reformers were concerned, the calendar that had been in use in France was inherently associated with "Catholic superstition" and with the priesthood.[52]

The secular symbolism implied in the new calendar did not escape the pre-Revolutionary French authorities. When Sylvain Maréchal, one of the originators of the reform, proposed, as early as 1788, to dispose of the Church's Saints' Days as well as to abolish Sunday along with the seven-day week, the Bourbon government ordered his influential *Almanach des Honnêtes Gens* to be torn up and burnt as "impious, sacrilegious, blasphemous, and tending to destroy religion."[53] It is also within this context that the condemnation of the

Revolutionary calendar by John Quincy Adams as "irreligious" ought to be understood.[54]

The tremendous de-Christianizing effects of any reform of the Gregorian calendar were obviously clear to the reformers themselves as well. The major thrust of the French Republican calendrical reform was definitely against religion in general and Christianity in particular, and it is quite typical, for example, that Maréchal opened his *Almanach des Républicains* with the following guideline: "The calendar of the French Republic . . . must not resemble in any respect the official annuals of the apostolic and Roman Church."[55] The new calendar was to function primarily as a de-Christianizer, and the abolition of the traditional temporal reference framework was deliberately meant to strip the Church once and for all of one of its major mechanisms of exercising social control and regulating social life in France. In order to accomplish that, the Revolutionary calendar had to be a *civil* calendar, divested of any ecclesiastical associations. (The Fascists' attempts to secularize the Italian calendar by deliberately introducing many nonreligious holidays into it ought to be seen in the same light.)[56]

The first constituents of the traditional calendar to be left out of the new calendar were those daily and weekly reminders of the Catholic Church—the Saints' Days, the seven-day week, and Sunday. It is hard to overemphasize the tremendous significance of having done away with those sacred elements of the Christian tradition. Furthermore, as shown earlier, the replacement of Sunday by *Décadi,* an official rest day to occur every ten days, also contributed to the disruption of actual church-attending practices, based as they were on the seven-day week. (However, it also entailed a considerable reduction of the total number of rest days. That the new sociotemporal order involved working for nine—rather than six—days straight before having a day of rest certainly did not help to increase its popularity among the French people.)

Another symbolic act of de-Christianization was the establishment of a new annual cycle based on a nonreligious, civil New Year's Day. There are no natural divisions along the temporal continuum, and even though the annual cycle originated in a natural phenomenon (the revolution of the earth around the sun), the decision as to where to fix the cutoff point that marks its "begin-ning" is a purely arbitrary one, based entirely upon social con-vention. One of the major characteristics of any calendar is that it interrupts the continuous flow of time by introducing some regularly recurrent "critical dates."[57] The events that constitute these temporal reference points usually have a particular symbolic significance.

The French Republican calendrical reformers made a most sig-nificant symbolic statement when they replaced 1 January with 22 September as New Year's Day. As we shall see later, there were particular ideological reasons for insisting that the new calendar year would begin on 22 September. For the present discussion, how-ever, the most important thing is that the events with which that date was symbolically associated were not religiously significant. That is why that act had such a profound symbolic significance, as far as secularization was concerned. It is important to remember that, as the date on which the Sunday Letter and the Golden Number were changed and the Feast of Circumcision was celebrated, 1 January had traditionally been symbolically associated with the Catholic Church. It was probably not practical convenience alone, but sym-bolic considerations as well, that led Napoleon to restore the Gre-gorian calendar beginning 1 January 1806, a totally meaningless date within the Revolutionary calendar, yet so symbolically sig-nificant within the traditional calendrical system.

It was for quite similar reasons that the reformers also estab-lished a new chronological dating framework, replacing the tradi-tional Christian Era by the Republican Era, which was to begin retroactively on 22 September 1792. It was time that separated the old order from the new one, and beginning the new age with a "new time" was clearly meant to symbolize the total discontinuity between past and present. Since the flow of history is continuous, the se-lection of those historical events which constitute the "beginnings" of chronological eras—like the selection of those temporal refer-ence points that mark the "beginnings" of annual cycles—is purely arbitrary. This selection process has a tremendous symbolic signifi-cance, since those historical events are almost always imbued with profound collective meaning. Furthermore, the act of counting the passage of historical time from a certain event definitely serves to increase the social awareness of the collective significance of that event. Consider, for example, the sort of "captivity era" introduced in 1979 by some American television networks, which involved counting the number of days from the takeover of the American embassy in Teheran.

As Pitirim Sorokin and Robert Merton noted about any chronological dating framework, "In all cases the point of departure is social or imbued with profound social implications; it is always an event which is regarded as one of peculiar social significance."[58] Note, for example, the tremendous symbolic significance of the foundation of Rome for the ancient Romans, the destruction of the Second Temple for the Jews, the flight of Mohammed from Mecca (the *Hegira*) for the Moslems, the march on Rome for the Fascists, and so on. All these events were charged with profound symbolic connotations, which is why they became the cornerstones of chronological dating frameworks. To appreciate the symbolic significance of chronological eras, note also that, when Dionysius Exiguus first introduced the use of the Christian Era, he made the explicit recommendation that the then-popular Era of Diocletian be abolished, so as not to "perpetuate the name of the Great Persecutor."[59]

Like the date 1 January, the Christian Era clearly did not belong in the new Revolutionary time-reckoning and dating system, because it was symbolically associated with Christianity. The act of substituting the date of the foundation of the French Republic for that of the supposed birth of Christ as the "point of departure" for the new era clearly symbolized the de-Christianization of the French calendrical system. It implied in the most vivid manner that France had entered a new, secular age, wherein the birth of the Republic was to be regarded as far more significant—both historically and symbolically—than the birth of Christianity.

As it turned out, the emphasis on secularization most probably undermined much of the potential success of the French Republican calendrical reform, and certainly ought to be regarded as one of the major factors that were responsible for its eventual failure. The reformers must have underestimated the depth to which religious sentiments were still rooted among the French people, many of whom probably found it quite impossible to depart so abruptly from a sacred symbolic order such as the traditional calendrical system. The fact that the restoration of the Gregorian calendar by

Napoleon was actually an integral part of his general reconciliation with the pope clearly suggests that the eventual failure of the Revolutionary calendrical reform ought to be seen within the context of the overall failure of the French Revolution to de-Christianize France.

Rationalism. As a product of the French Enlightenment, the French Revolution was also supposed to inaugurate an Age of Reason in France. The calendrical reformers were, thus, well aware of the centrality of reason to their reform, claiming that it was "necessary to substitute the reality of reason for the visions of ignorance."[60] Their new calendar was clearly meant to represent the true spirit of the French Revolution by helping to fight ignorance and superstition and to promote precision, promptitude, simplicity, facility, clarity, and enlightenment.[61]

The Revolutionary calendar was meant to be an unprecedented project—a calendar that adhered to the principle of reason alone. It was only natural, therefore, that the chief architect of the Revolutionary calendrical reform, Charles-Gilbert Romme, was a former professor of physics and navigation, whose consultants included respectable scientific authorities such as the famous mathematicians Monge and Lagrange, the astronomers Lalande and Pingré, the chemist Fourcroy, and other distinguished members of the Academy of Sciences. Nor was it by any means a mere coincidence that Monge and Lagrange were also members of the committee that had introduced—only a year before—a major reform of the system of measures and weights. In fact, the French Revolutionary calendrical reform ought to be viewed as an extension of the metric reform. Accordingly, in order to increase the legitimacy of their new time-reckoning and dating system, the reformers also introduced a new system of units of time, based on the decimal principle, that was clearly meant to make their calendar appear more rational and scientific.

With the decimal system as its cornerstone, the new system of units of time looked quite unlike its predecessor. While the Gregorian calendar year consisted of seven thirty-one-day months, four thirty-day months, and one twenty-eight-day—or twenty-nine-day, on leap years—month, the Revolutionary calendar year consisted of twelve uniform thirty-day months. (As in the ancient Egyptian calendar, the five complementary days were grouped together at the end of the year, and a sixth intercalary day was added on leap years.) Each new thirty-day month was divided into three ten-day weekly cycles called *décades*.[62] Furthermore, each day was divided into ten hours, each new hour into 100 "decimal minutes," and each of those into 100 "decimal seconds." All units of time shorter than the month were, thus, interrelated in decimal terms!

In part, all this was done for purely symbolic reasons. The architects of the Revolutionary calendrical reform were quite well aware of the symbolic significance of their act. Given the religious connotations of the number "7" within the Judeo-Christian tradition, they condemned it as "superstitious."[63] The decimal principle, on the other hand, was clearly associated with science and rationality, since it is among the cornerstones of Western mathematics.

However, the reformers must have realized that the act of adopting the very basis of the existing counting system in order to systematize the relations among the various units of time involved not only symbolic implications, but some practical convenience as well, since it definitely promoted facility and simplicity.[64] This was true particularly with regard to the acts of establishing uniform thirty-day months and replacing the seven-day week with the ten-day *décade*. Not only did the Revolutionary calendrical reformers save the users of the new calendar the trouble of having to memorize—as we do— the number of days in each one of the various months of the year, but they accomplished the unprecedented feat of establishing a concordance of the weekly and monthly cycles.

Within our own calendrical system, the week and the month are two distinct temporal reference frameworks that are totally independent of one another, since the cycles from which they derive are based on incompatible rhythms and, therefore, run independently of one another. Our calendar year consists of a number of *complete* months, so that the beginning of the year—1 January—coincides with that of a month. (Interestingly enough, this has not always been the case. Toward the end of the Middle Ages, for example, people used to reckon the years from the Feast of the Annunciation on 25 March.)[65] Fortunately, this is also true of the relations between the month, the day, the hour, the minute, and the second. The only "intruder" in this highly ordered system is the weekly cycle.[66] Weeks do not have to be "completed" in order for a new month or a new year to begin.

As we have seen earlier, a concordance of the weekly and annual cycles had already been accomplished in the past. By adhering to a 364-day calendar, which consisted of fifty-two complete weeks, the Dead Sea Sect managed to associate all its annual holidays with particular days of the week on a regular basis. To appreciate what a remarkable accomplishment that was, note that the *day of the week* and the *date* are two distinct ways of dating events, which are totally independent of one another.[67] Thus, we usually need a calendar in order to determine on what date Labor Day, Thanksgiving Day, or Election Day fall, or on what day of the week Christmas falls, in any given year.

Whereas the Dead Sea Sect had managed to synchronize the weekly and annual cycles, the French Republican calendrical reformers accomplished a no-less-remarkable parallel feat—a concordance of the weekly and monthly cycles. That was made possible by establishing a fixed and simple (1 : 3) mathematical relation between the new thirty-day months and ten-day *décades,* and fixing the beginning of each new month on *Primidi,* the first day of the new week.

Temporal formulations in terms of the date could thus be easily converted to others in terms of the day of the week by simple reference to the last figure of the former. The eighteenth day of the calendar month, for example, would always fall on *Octidi,* the eighth day of the week. The reverse, too, could be achieved by simple reference to the name of the day of the week, because—as we shall soon see—it also reflected its place within the week. As the fifth day of the week, *Quintidi,* for example, would always fall on the fifth, fifteenth, or twenty-fifth day of the month.[68] The tremendous contribution of this simple—yet so sophisticated—arrangement in facilitating the everyday cognitive process of having to deal with two traditionally incompatible levels of temporal reference can hardly be overemphasized.

The name *"Quintidi"* would be immediately associated with the numbers five, fifteen, and twenty-five, because the names of the Revolutionary days of the week reflected their place within the weekly cycle. *Primidi, Duodi, Tridi, Quartidi, Quintidi, Sextidi,*

Septidi, Octidi, Nonidi, and *Décadi* literally meant "first day," "second day," "third day," and so on.

The act of naming the days of the week according to their place within it was highly significant. Like the act of introducing new units of time such as the *décade,* the "decimal minute," and the "decimal second," it was part of a deliberate effort to substitute a pronouncedly quantitative conception of time, as became an Age of Reason, for a qualitative orientation which was associated with the traditional, religious, and "irrational." The relations among the units of time became even more conspicuously quantitative with the introduction of uniform months and the simplification of the mathematical relations between the new monthly and weekly cycles. The new units of time were clearly meant to be regarded as certain "quantities" of duration, which were systematically interrelated in mathematical terms, namely, as multiples of one another. With the abolition of the Church's Saints' Days, Sunday, and the religious holidays of Christianity, the days of the week and of the year lost much of their idiosyncratic, unique character. As mathematically equivalent entities, they became far more interchangeable with one another.

Naturalism. Presenting the new calendar as a particularly rational project certainly helped to make it appear as anything but a merely arbitrary convention. However, in order to make sure that it would be regarded as inevitable, it was also symbolically associated with Nature. Rather than draw its authority from "priestly prestige," the Revolutionary calendar was to be inseparable from "the truth of Nature."[69] It was supposed to symbolize the centrality of natural phenomena to the life of the new society, thus expressing the belief of the French Enlightenment in the essential need for man to be in harmony with Nature.

It is within this context that we ought to understand the new nomenclature of time that was introduced along with the Revolutionary calendar. It is in the nomenclature of time that the symbolism of calendrical systems can be most purely seen, and any analysis of the Revolutionary calendar which would ignore the nomenclatural innovations that were introduced along with it would not provide us with an adequate basis for grasping the full symbolic significance of the French Republican calendrical reform.

It is hardly surprising that the Revolutionary nomenclature of time was the work of a poet, Fabre d'Églantine, since poets are particularly sensitive to the symbolic dimension of words and names. Names are typically charged with meaning,[70] and the French Republican calendrical reformers were well aware of that. As they themselves complained, the names of the months of the Gregorian calendar reminded one of the "oppressive tyrants" of antiquity (such as Julius Caesar and Augustus).[71] By the same token, however, they could also manipulate the symbolism associated with names for their own purposes. Since names invoke images—thus affecting both imagination and memory—there was no reason why the collective memory of an entire society could not be controlled and manipulated through the use of particular names.[72] It was this particular educational function of names that guided Fabre d'Églantine in designing the new nomenclature of time for the people of France. For him, failing to use the symbolism associated with names for the purpose of promoting the ideals of the French Revolution would have been an inexcusable waste of a unique opportunity to manipulate the "collective unconscious" of the French society.

Fabre d'Églantine's purpose was quite explicit—"to consecrate the agricultural system through the calendar," to make sure that the French people would be constantly reminded of nature and rural economy.[73] In order to accomplish that, the days of the year—which had been named until then after the Church's saints—were renamed after phenomena such as trees, plants, fruits, seeds, roots, flowers, farming implements, and domestic animals instead.[74] In addition, the months were renamed after seasonal phenomena that would inevitably remind one of Nature. The new months were named *Vendémiaire* (vintage), *Brumaire* (mist), *Frimaire* (frost), *Nivôse* (snow), *Pluviôse* (rain), *Ventôse* (wind), *Germinal* (seeds), *Floréal* (flowers), *Prairial* (meadows), *Messidor* (harvest), *Thermidor* (heat), and *Fructidor* (fruits).[75] (A similar attempt to replace the traditional names of the months with pagan archaisms associated with seasonal aspects of nature was made, a century and a half later, by the Nazis.)[76]

The names of the new months were deliberately designed so as to remind their user of Nature in a way that even transcended their mere referential function. Being particularly sensitive to the role of names as reminders, Fabre d'Églantine went so far as to invoke

images "by the mere pronunciation of the name of the month."[77]
He managed to achieve that by means of a simple morphological
device, namely, applying suffixes ("aire," "ôse," "al," and "dor")
in a differential manner, roughly corresponding to seasonal variations. As a result of this, both the rhythm and the tone of the
months' names suggested that they were grouped in four distinct
three-month blocks, each associated with a particular season. Thus,
by both semantic and morphological means, the new nomenclature
helped to establish a seasonally based differentiation among the
various months, symbolically representing the unbreakable bond
between the calendrical system of French society and the cycles
of Nature.

A symbolic association of the new social order with Nature was
also attempted through the use of the co-occurrence of the founding
of the French Republic and the autumnal equinox. That such a
unique social event happened to take place on a day which is so
significant in Nature was probably a mere coincidence. Nevertheless, the reformers used this coincidence in order to legitimize their
choice of 22 September as the pivot of the new calendar, on the
basis of establishing a *harmony between the social and the natural.*
The symbolic implications of the multiple significance of 22 September certainly did not escape the attention of the architects of the
Revolutionary calendrical reform. In fact, they could not have been
clearer about their deliberate intention to "maintain the coincidence
of the civil year with the celestial movements."[78] When proposing
to synchronize the annual social cycle with a cycle deriving from the
rhythmicity of Nature, the Committee of Public Instruction stated
quite explicitly:

> The equality of the days and nights was marked in the heavens
> at the same moment that civil and moral equality was proclaimed
> by the representatives of the French people as the sacred
> foundation of their new government.[79]

(Note that, on 22 September, the sun also enters *Libra*, the sign
which is symbolically associated with equality, one of the principal
themes of the French Revolution, which was also symbolically
represented by the introduction of *uniform* months.)

Ironically, while the reformers made considerable efforts to present the new calendar as "natural," they could not rely on its being taken as inevitable, and had to resort to a campaign of promoting its adoption through socializing agents such as parents and teachers.[80] In exposing the alterability and only relative validity of the traditional calendar—so as to account for its disposability—they could not help but expose the conventionality and artificiality of any other calendar, including the new one, at the same time. It was quite hard not to realize, for example, that if the annual cycle beginning on 1 January did not derive from the heavens and was a mere artifact resting upon entirely arbitrary social conventions, so would be any annual cycle, including the one beginning on 22 September. Simply because its users had witnessed its birth and knew that things used to be different in the past, the new calendar could never be viewed as absolutely valid, natural, and inevitable.

Furthermore, given the fact that the traditional calendar had been taken for granted as absolutely valid for many generations, it must have appeared to the French people as far more "natural" than the Revolutionary calendar, despite the considerable naturalistic symbolism built into the latter! As becomes quite clear from the strong resistance toward the introduction of the Gregorian calendar to Britain in 1752 and to Greece and the Greek Orthodox Church in 1924,[81] man has a general tendency to cling to traditional practices of time reckoning and dating. The failure of the French Republican calendrical reform suggests that, even in a totalitarian society such as post-Revolutionary France, it was quite difficult to completely and abruptly abolish a temporal order which, despite its arbitrary and conventional basis, was nevertheless deeply rooted in the general culture, and whose absolute validity had most probably been taken for granted for centuries. (That has since been demonstrated again by Stalin's aforementioned failure to introduce the five-day and six-day weeks to the Soviet Union.)

Nationalism. The Revolutionary calendar was clearly meant to be a French calendar. As a symbolic system, therefore, it was supposed to be symbolically associated with nationalism. Thus, for example, it was in order to "express the joy and the spirit of the French people" that the five annual intercalary days were collectively named *"sansculottides,"* after the French Revolutionary *"sans-culottes."*[82] Similarly, it was "in memory of the [French] Revolution" that the four-year cycle associated with the introduction of leap years was named *"Franciade."*[83] (Among the original suggestions for the names of the new months were also names such as *"La Bastille," "La République,"* and *"La Montagne,"* all of which were symbolically associated with the French Revolution.)[84]

For quite similar reasons, the day on which the French Republic was founded—22 September 1792—was chosen to be the pivot of the new annual cycle as well as the "point of departure" for the new Republican Era. The symbolism was quite obvious to the reformers: "Time is opening a new history book, and in its new movement, majestic and simple as equality, it will engrave with a new and pure chisel the annals of regenerated France."[85] In order to appreciate the particular significance of the year 1792 as a national symbol, note that, even though it was not until 1793 that the reformers decided to establish the new era, it was nevertheless important to them that it would begin retroactively in 1792.

Toward A Universal Calendar

Symbolically speaking, the act of introducing a unique national calendar is functionally analogous to acts such as introducing a national anthem, flag, costume, or dish. And yet, while the co-existence of multiple flags or costumes does not generate any inconvenience or confusion which might hinder international communication, a multiplicity of calendars certainly does.

There was simply no way in which the Revolutionary time-reckoning and dating framework could be synchronized with the conventional one, so that any temporal formulation within the former was totally meaningless to users of the latter around the world. (To this day, historians must resort to the use of concordance lists in order to convert Revolutionary dates so as to locate them within the conventional chronological dating framework.)[86] The days of the *décade,* for example, could not correspond to those of the seven-day week, since these two social cycles—albeit being functionally equivalent—were nevertheless based on two totally incompatible rhythms. As for the Revolutionary and Gregorian calendar months —they were based on very similar rhythms, and yet their beginnings never coincided, since all Revolutionary months began sometime around the twentieth day of Gregorian months. As a result of this staggered pattern, dates within the two types of calendar months never corresponded to one another. Finally, the numerical designation of the Republican year was also totally meaningless to anyone who used the Christian Era.

In an age when international communication already required some temporal coordination on a suprasocietal level, the pronouncedly nationalistic spirit of the Revolutionary calendar proved to be detrimental to its chances of survival, and much of the strong resistance toward it—in other countries as well as in France itself —must also be understood within this context. (Even the official *Moniteur* had no choice but to insert the Gregorian date in brackets after the Republican date!)[87] As Laplace, who chaired the committee which recommended to Napoleon that the calendar be abolished, stated: "The expectation that any other nation would adopt the French innovation was a chimera."[88] The horror of Bentabole, the only representative to the National Convention who had originally opposed the nationalistic fervor of the Revolutionary calendar, was rapidly becoming a reality. Rather than "unite all the peoples through fraternity," this calendar was contributing only to their segregation from one another.[89]

Challenging the Gregorian calendar and the Christian Era when they were already adopted by most of the Western world certainly spelled doom for the Revolutionary calendar, because it entailed the international isolation of France. *The history of the last few centuries is a history of a constant movement toward standardizing temporal reference.* The failure of the most radical attempt in modern history to challenge the existing calendrical system and introduce nationalism at the expense of universalism in the domain of temporal reference is most indicative of the pervasiveness of this historical trend.

The expansion of the boundaries of the social world has involved a parallel expansion of the boundaries of the validity of the use of the *standard temporal reference framework* that prevails in it. The centralization of the calendar which usually accompanies the growth of the polity from the local level to the societal level is a typical case in point.[90] In modern times, the validity of the use of a single standard temporal reference framework has even reached the global level. Given the almost universal use and validity of (*a*) the Christian Era and (*b*) the Gregorian calendar, it is quite possible to identify a standard temporal reference framework that is used today almost all over the world, allowing for an almost universally valid standardization of time reckoning and dating.

The Christian—or Incarnation—Era was introduced in A.D. 532 by Dionysius Exiguus, a Roman abbot who was designing new tables for computing the date of Easter.[91] The Church sanctioned those new Easter Tables and, through their employment, the practice of numbering the years from the supposed birth of Jesus Christ gradually spread all over the Christian world. Incarnation datings— first formulated as *"anno ab incarnatione,"* then as *"anno Domini,"* and eventually as "A.D."—appeared in England as early as the seventh century and became increasingly popular following the publication of the Venerable Bede's influential *De ratione temporum* in 725. During the tenth and eleventh centuries, they also gained popularity in Italy, in France, and in papal documents. In 1180, Catalonia replaced the Spanish Era by the Incarnation Era, and was followed by Aragon in 1350, Castile in 1383, and Portugal in 1422. During the fifteenth century the Christian Era was also adopted by the Greek world, and—with the European colonization of America, Africa, Asia, and Oceania—it gradually came to be not merely a Christian era, but, rather, the prevalent chronological dating framework almost all over the world. Having replaced numerous local and national eras, it is the first era ever to have attained almost universal validity. A temporal formulation such as "in 1946," for example, has precisely the same meaning today in Uruguay, Alaska, Greece, Sweden, Japan, and Nigeria!

Of related significance was the standardization of the beginning of the annual cycle. Interestingly enough, the calendar year did not always begin on 1 January for all users of the Christian Era.[92] Toward the end of the Middle Ages, in Europe alone there were at least six different days from which the reckoning of any particular year could begin. Throughout most of the continent, a year would begin on 25 March following Christmas. However, it would begin on 25 March *before* the Nativity in Pisa (so that 1380 in Florence and 1381 in Pisa would begin on the same day); on 1 March in Venice; on 1 January in Spain and Portugal; on 1 September throughout the Byzantine Empire; and on Easter in the Low Countries, the Rhineland, and the French Chancery. Confusion at the supralocal level was obviously tremendous, since the very same date would have entirely different meanings in different towns and regions. Pope Gregory XIII's ruling from 1582 that the reckoning of the years should begin only from 1 January ought to be appreciated within this context.

A most significant chapter in the history of the standardization of temporal reference, which is highly representative of the typically modern trend of shifting from particularism toward universalism,[93] has been the evolution of the Gregorian calendar as one of the cornerstones of the modern international temporal reference framework. The Gregorian reform of the Julian calendar took place in 1582, that is, at the height of the Reformation period in Europe, when the split between Catholics and non-Catholics within Christianity was most accentuated. It is hardly surprising, therefore, that, as a project that was sponsored and sanctioned by—and even named after—a pope, the Gregorian calendar was regarded by the non-Catholic world right from the outset as an exclusively Catholic institution. Typically enough, it was first used as the prevalent standard temporal reference framework only within the boundaries of the Catholic world. It was adopted right away (in 1582) by Spain, Portugal, France, Flanders, Holland, Lorraine, most of Italy, and most of the German Roman Catholic states.[94] During the following five years it was also adopted by Bavaria, Bohemia, Hungary, Moravia, Poland, Silesia, most of Austria, and cities such as Cologne, Mainz, and Liège. The general trend was quite obvious: for the first 118 years that followed the reform, the Gregorian calendar was an exclusively Catholic calendar.

However, the necessity of standardizing temporal reference on an international level became more and more obvious during the seventeenth and eighteenth centuries, and eventually the Gregorian calendar had to transcend the boundaries of the relatively small Catholic world. Beginning in 1700—the first time a century year was not observed by some countries as a leap year, in accordance with the Gregorian reform of the Julian calendar—the Gregorian calendar was finally adopted by most of non-Catholic Europe:

Norway, Denmark, all the German and Dutch Protestant states, and Protestant Swiss cantons such as Basel, Zurich, Bern, and Geneva. Britain gave in and adopted the "new style" of time reckoning and dating in 1752, and Sweden and Finland followed in 1753.

The Gregorian calendar could not be regarded any longer as an exclusively Catholic institution, yet it nevertheless still was, until the end of the nineteenth century, a Christian calendar only, and its use was restricted—without exception—to Europe and to the European colonies in America, Africa, Asia, and Oceania. And yet, the push toward standardizing temporal reference at the global level was gradually gaining momentum.

In 1873 and 1875 Japan and Egypt became the first non-Christian countries to adopt the Gregorian calendar. Both were then at the very early stages of a radical process of modernization and Westernization, the former following the Meiji restoration in 1868, and the latter during the reign of the khedive Ismail. That set a most significant precedent; from then on, adopting the "European" calendar has been regarded as an actual facilitator of international communication as well as a symbol of modernization and Westernization.

By the time of World War I, adopting the Gregorian calendar seemed to have become almost an obligatory ritual that *had* to accompany every revolution or proclamation of independence. Thus, Albania (1912), Estonia (1917), and Yugoslavia (1919), for example, all adopted the Gregorian calendar right after having proclaimed their independence. China adopted it right after the outbreak of the Chinese Revolution (1912), and Lenin introduced it to the Soviet Union "for the purpose of being in harmony with all the civilized countries of the world" less than three months after the Bolshevik Revolution (in January 1918).[95] Adopting the Gregorian calendar in 1926 was also among the first major steps taken by Atatürk as part of his general effort to modernize and Westernize Turkey.

In order to gain its universal stature and validity, the Gregorian calendar clearly had to be stripped of any particularistic associations it might have originally had. And, indeed, at this stage, it cannot be regarded any longer as a Christian institution; rather, it has become one of the major symbols of Western civilization at large. Today, almost four hundred years after its inception, the Gregorian calendar is almost generally accepted throughout the world. It is the first calendar ever to have attained almost universal recognition and validity as the standard framework to be used for all time-reckoning and dating purposes. As P. W. Wilson noted,

> it is international, inter-religious, inter-occupational and inter-racial. Every day its use and its value are spreading further and further afield. To all intents, this calendar is, or is becoming, universal.[96]

I began this chapter by demonstrating how calendars can promote separatist sentiments. The history of the Gregorian calendar, however, seems to indicate quite clearly what the prevalent trend of the last few centuries has been—a shift from particularism toward universalism, to the point of standardizing time reckoning and dating even at the global level and establishing no less than an international temporal reference framework.

Four

Sacred Time and Profane Time

One of the most significant contributions of applying the sociological perspective to the study of temporality has been the delineation of a pronouncedly nonquantitative, *qualitative conception of time*.[1] The discussion of the symbolic function of calendrical systems in the previous chapter must have revealed one of the main characteristics of the calendar, namely, the fact that, as Clifford Geertz put it, it "cuts time up into bounded units not in order to count and total them but to describe and characterize them, to formulate their differential social, intellectual, and religious significance."[2] Despite the growing prevalence of the quantitative conception of temporality in the modern West, which I have discussed in the second chapter, people clearly do not relate to time only as a physico-mathematical entity. They also view it from a qualitative perspective, as an entity which is imbued with meaning.

The meaning of social acts and situations is largely dependent on their temporal context. The very same social act might have several entirely different meanings at different time periods. The simple act of eating, for example, has an entirely different meaning on a fast day than on any other day. Likewise, the act of having sexual intercourse has two entirely different meanings when it takes place on a first date and on a twentieth date. Nor are we likely to confuse the meanings of drinking alcohol at the age of forty and at the age of fourteen, or of arriving at an official ceremony on time and half an hour late.

All this clearly suggests that the meaning of social acts and situations is, to a large extent, temporally situated. In other words, time seems to constitute one of the major parameters of the context on which the meaning of social acts and situations depends. In the present chapter, I shall try to shed some light on the way in which time functions as a significant context for anchoring the meaning of social acts and situations within one particular domain—religion.

It is the contention of many sociologists of religion, especially since Durkheim, that the essence of the phenomenon of religion lies in the categorical distinction between the sacred domain and the profane domain and their total separation from one another. According to Durkheim,

> the real characteristic of religious phenomena is that they always suppose a bipartite division of the whole universe, known and knowable, into two classes which embrace all that exists, but which radically exclude each other.[3]

For Durkheim, no way of classifying the universe is more fundamental to human cognition than the one between these two categories—the *sacred* and the *profane:*

> In all the history of human thought there exists no other example of two categories of things so profoundly differentiated or so radically opposed to one another. The traditional opposition of good and bad is nothing beside this . . . the sacred and the profane have always and everywhere been conceived by the human mind as two distinct classes, as two worlds between which there is nothing in common.[4]

In order to maintain this mutually exclusive conceptual distinction—and, thus, to prevent any moral confusion—between the sacred and the profane spheres of life, any contamination of the former by the latter must be avoided at all costs. To achieve such an absolute distinction in the human mind, a *total separation* of these two domains in actuality is essential. They must be located in two distinctly different parts of the universe:

> Since the idea of the sacred is always and everywhere separated from the idea of the profane in the thought of men, and since we picture a sort of logical chasm between the two, the mind irresistibly refuses to allow the two corresponding things to be confounded, or even to be merely put in contact with each other;

for such a promiscuity, or even too direct a contiguity, would contradict too violently the dissociation of these ideas in the mind. The sacred thing is *par excellence* that which the profane should not touch, and cannot touch with impunity.[5]

In order to accomplish such a total separation between the sacred domain and the profane domain, man has learned how to employ various dimensions of the world for the purpose of encoding the fundamental mutually exclusive conceptual distinction between the categories of the sacred and the profane.[6] Time is definitely one such dimension, and its role within a domain such as religion, which demands segregation, is, therefore, essential.

I have already noted the potential segregative function of temporality when discussing the schedule. Time can certainly function as a most effective principle of differentiation. Since any particular event can take place only at one point in time, temporality is a dimension of the world that definitely allows us to make sharp and clear-cut distinctions with a minimum of ambiguity. The principle of *temporal segregation* is, therefore, among the fundamentals of social life.

That time functions as an ordering principle by helping to keep things apart is quite evident from considering one of man's most sophisticated social institutions—the taking of turns. Simultaneity must be deliberately avoided at times, and the regulation of non-simultaneous access through the institutionalization of turntaking is essential to social organization at all levels. It is turntaking that helps to prevent chaos by allowing us to engage in intelligible conversations with others as well as to play games such as baseball, chess, and bowling. It is also turntaking that underlies the institution of the queue, thus allowing us to gain access to goods and services in an orderly manner.[7] Finally, it is the notion of the turn that also underlies the entire rotation system, whether it is applied in the social organization of nurses' weekend duties in hospitals,[8] children's participation in housework chores, or the occupation of various political slots in democratic systems.

It is also the principle of temporal segregation that underlies the arrangement that food deliveries and office cleaning usually take place at night, in order to assure that food markets and offices will be open and active during the day.[9] This principle is also at the base of the way in which lawyers manage to see such large numbers of clients on an individual basis, radio programs are scheduled, track meets are organized, and airport traffic is regulated by control towers. Finally, temporal segregation is also central to one of the basic requirements of social organization—some "insulation from observability."[10] The deliberate effort to avoid simultaneity is vital, for example, to the operation of moonlighters—not to mention double agents—and is at the very basis of most illicit love affairs.

Given the fact that time constitutes such an effective principle of differentiation, it is quite understandable that temporal segregation would be indispensable to the social organization of religious life. Given that no event can take place at two different time periods at the same time, any particular act or event would necessarily be located *either* within a sacred time period *or* within a profane time period, yet never in both! Thus, in allowing man to establish in a clear-cut manner and with minimum ambiguity whether something "belongs" within one sphere of life or another, time has come to play a central role in facilitating the dichotomization of the universe into sacred and profane domains which are mutually exclusive. Through the dimension of time, the mutual exclusiveness of the sacred and the profane spheres of life is both manifested and sustained.

Durkheim himself, in his analysis of the social organization of religious life, provided us with the pioneer discussion of the role of temporal segregation as a principle of social organization. Arguing that "the religious life and the profane life cannot coexist in the same unit of time," he brought into focus the fundamental bipartite division of time into two distinct parts that are mutually exclusive—the one being devoted to everyday profane activity and the other being consecrated to the cult:

> It is necessary to assign determined days or periods to the [religious life], from which all profane occupations are excluded. ... There is no religion, and, consequently, no society which has not known and practised this division of time into two distinct parts, alternating with one another.[11]

As we shall soon see, particularly significant for our present discussion has been Durkheim's claim that this bipartite division of time into sacred time and profane time is at the very basis of the institutions of the holiday and the rest day.[12]

The Sanctification of the Sabbath

That only sacred time periods constitute the normatively prescribed loci of certain events and types of activity entails a view of time quite similar to the way we view space, namely, as a part of the ecological niche within which human activity is contained.[13] In fact, Durkheim himself demonstrated that, in segregating the sacred world from the profane world, time is functionally analogous to space.[14] However, in order to shed light on the unique segregative role of time in religious life, I have decided to bring into focus one particular religion which not only represents the traditional primacy of the dichotomization of the universe into sacred and profane domains, but also definitely regards time as far more significant than space in facilitating this process. I am referring here to Judaism, which has been characterized as a "religion of time aiming at the sanctification of time," whose "main themes of faith lie in the realm of time."[15]

It is quite probable that time has been particularly significant for the Jews because, throughout most of their history, they have had no place of their own. Having spent most of their history in exile, away from their holy places—the land of Israel in general, and Jerusalem in particular—they have developed and cultivated a unique dependency on time as a sanctifiable dimension of the universe. For a people who have moved so much and so frequently in space, creating some "provinces of sacredness in time," which could be observed and celebrated *anywhere*, has been quite a necessity.

Thus, while many religions have sanctified both time and space, the notion of sanctity in Judaism has been attached to the former far more than to the latter, so that the sacred quality of time does not vary across space as much as the sacred quality of space varies across time. It is not uncommon, in Judaism, that a sacred space would maintain its sacredness only within the boundaries of certain time periods. (The synagogue table, for example, has a ritual value as a locus of holy items on Sabbaths and holidays, yet it loses that value on regular weekdays, when it serves as a repository for various profane items.)[16] Sacred time periods, on the other hand, maintain their sacred quality everywhere. There is virtually no place on earth where Jews are exempt from observing their holy days.

It is within this context that the rise of the Sabbath ought to be seen. While there is considerable evidence in the Old Testament that it had already been observed prior to the destruction of the First Temple in 586 B.C.,[17] it is particularly during the period of the Exile, which followed it, that the Sabbath became such a central institutional pillar of Jewish life.[18] Establishing a sacred province in time served to fill in the vacuum that had been created by the loss of the traditional sacred province in space. With the decline in the significance of the major annual festivals (Passover, Sukkoth, and Shavuoth), whose celebration had traditionally been linked to the Temple in Jerusalem, observing the Sabbath became almost indispensable to the maintenance of Jewish religious life.[19]

The strict observance of the Sabbath was regarded as one of the fundamental essences of Jewish life already back in antiquity. According to the Torah, the appropriate punishment for those who desecrate the holy day is nothing less than death: "Whosoever doeth any work in the sabbath day, he shall surely be put to death."[20] This may explain why Jews even chose to die rather than desecrate the Sabbath by fighting on it.[21] (According to Josephus, that was one of the factors behind the Romans' success in conquering Jerusalem in 63 B.C.)[22]

The centrality of the Sabbath to Jewish life seems to have so far withstood the onslaught of modernity. Even according to Bialik, the national Jewish poet whose poetry reflects the process of secularization within modern Jewish society, "the Sabbath is indeed the cornerstone of Judaism."[23] It is often claimed today that the Sabbath observance may well become the single most decisive factor in the survival of Judaism, without which it would be quite impossible to preserve the Jewish faith as well as the Jewish people. This may explain why it has become, in recent times, one of the focal concerns among rabbinical circles in the Diaspora as well as in the relatively secularized modern state of Israel. Aḥad Ha'Am, a famous Jewish essayist, once wrote: "It can be said without any exaggeration that, more than Israel have observed the Sabbath, it had preserved *them*."[24]

Why have Jews put so much emphasis on the observance of the

Sabbath, to the point of believing that the destruction of the First Temple had actually resulted from the desecration of this holy day?[25] How did the ancient sages come to the point of claiming that the Sabbath observance outweighs all the other commandments in its significance and that the act of desecrating the Sabbath is equivalent to the act of opposing the entire Torah and desecrating all its precepts?[26] Is it a mere coincidence that, in both versions of the Decalogue, the Fourth Commandment—which deals with the Sabbath observance—is conspicuously far more elaborate than any of the other nine commandments?[27]

In order to answer the above questions and fully understand the unique centrality of the Sabbath to Jewish life, we must examine the Jewish identification of this day with the idea of the *holy* or the sacred. It is important to note that, in the entire Decalogue, the word "holy" (*qadosh*) appears only with regard to the Sabbath! Furthermore, the first time that this word appears in the entire Bible is when God is said to have "blessed the seventh day and hallowed it."[28]

The Sabbath was clearly set apart from all the other Jewish "holy days," and the ancient sages were particularly careful to emphasize the distinction between its sanctity and that of any of the annual festivals. In order to stress this distinction, they likened the difference between any holiday and the Sabbath to the difference between a governor and a king.[29] Thus, even though—as a weekly event—the Sabbath is celebrated fifty-two times more frequently than all the annual festivals, it is definitely regarded as far more sacred than any of them.

That Jews are supposed to distinguish between these two degrees of holiness is also evident from the benediction they traditionally recite at the conclusion of Sabbaths that are immediately followed by holidays: "Blessed be He who maketh a distinction between holy and holy."[30] To appreciate the fact that the sanctity of the Sabbath supersedes that of any annual festival, note that the ceremony of which this benediction is a part—the *havdalah*—always marks the ritual descent from the more sacred to the less sacred, and never vice versa. (Thus, it never takes place at the end of regular weekdays, and it is performed at the conclusion of annual festivals only when they are not immediately followed by the Sabbath. On the other hand, it is performed at the conclusion of every Sabbath, regardless of whether it is immediately followed by a regular week-day or an annual festival.)

At one of the ceremonies which mark the inauguration of the Sabbath—the *kiddush* (which literally means "sanctification")—much emphasis is put on the sanctity of the day: "Blessed art Thou, O Lord, who sanctifiest the Sabbath Day."[31] And yet, it is not only the Sabbath itself that is sanctified during the *kiddush* ceremony; it is also those who observe it, the Jewish people. "Thou hast chosen Israel and Thou hast sanctified us among the peoples in that with love and favor Thou hast given us Thy holy Sabbath as an in-heritance."[32]

That is very much in line with a common traditional Jewish in-terpretation of the origin of the Sabbath: "Moreover also I gave them My sabbaths, to be a sign between Me and them, that they might know that I am the Lord that sanctify them."[33] In other words, Jews have traditionally maintained that, by observing the Sabbath, they themselves are sanctified. Their sense of actual participation in the great spiritual world order and of being imbued with holiness during the Sabbath is even reflected in their popular folk belief that every Sabbath Eve God gives every man an "additional soul" (*neshamah yeterah*), which he takes back from him at the expira-tion of the holy day.[34]

According to Mircea Eliade, religious people believe that, by observing the sacred time periods, they actually become more per-sonally involved with the holy: "In the festival the sacred dimension of life is recovered, the participants experience the sanctity of human existence as a divine creation."[35] That applies particularly to festi-vals that commemorate "beginnings," because the participation in the festival ritual is essentially regarded as an act of imitating the divine powers, the creators:

> The periodic reactualization of the creative acts performed by the divine beings *in illo tempore* constitutes the sacred calendar, a series of festivals.[36]

> Every religious festival, any liturgical time, represents the reactualization of a sacred event that took place in a mythical past, "in the beginning."[37]

For, however complex a religious festival may be, it always
involves a sacred event that took place *ab origine* and that is
ritually made present.[38]

Whereas most festivals involve the periodic celebration of sacred
"beginnings" on an annual basis only, the Sabbath observance entails the reactualization of holy events on a weekly basis. Furthermore, in the case of the Sabbath, the holy event which is supposed
to be periodically reactualized is none other than the Creation
of the World, the Beginning par excellence!

The most conspicuous ritual act of imitating God and reactualiz-
ing the act of the Creation is probably the Sabbath rest, whose intimate association with sanctity is made quite explicitly in the following benediction from the Sabbath Afternoon Service: "Let thy
children perceive and know that this their rest is from thee, and
by their rest may they hallow thy name."[39] According to the Bible,
the temporal pattern of working for six days and then resting on
the seventh is a divine pattern, closely linked to the Creation of the
World: "And on the seventh day God finished His work which He
had made; and He rested on the seventh day from all His work
which He had made."[40] In other words, the Sabbath rest is a ritual
act whose main function is to symbolically reactualize God's rest
following the Creation of the World. Whether the actual Hebrew
name of the Sabbath, *"Shabbath,"* originally derived from the word
"sheva" ("seven"), which refers to the "seventh day," or from
the word *"shavat"* ("ceased"), which refers to God's rest, it is made
quite clear in the Decalogue that God's rest on the seventh day is
the main reason for the entire Sabbath observance.[41]

The Jews' sense of participation in divine activity during the
Sabbath has also been intensified by the sexual symbolism that is
associated with some Sabbath rituals. Fertility symbolism and rites
have traditionally played a central role in origin myths and ceremonies, and their presence in the Jewish festival which reactualizes
the Creation of the World is anything but surprising to the student
of comparative religion.

To this day, upon their return home from the synagogue on
Sabbath Eve, observant Jewish men sing "Eshet Ḥayil" ("woman
of valor"), a song praising the virtuous woman. It is by no means

a mere coincidence that this song is also occasionally chanted at Jewish weddings.[42] As it turns out, it is actually only one of several Jewish rites that take place both at weddings and on Sabbath Eve.[43]

Consider, for example, the performance of a marital act on Sabbath Eve, which the ancient sages regarded as no less than a religious duty (*mitzvah*), to the point of even advising men to eat garlic on Friday, since it is supposed to foster love and increase one's semen.[44] According to the mystical Kabbalists, on Sabbath Eve, Jewish women become the earthly representations of the female aspect of the divine, the *shekhinah*. (The song "Eshet Ḥayil," which actually originated in Kabbalistic circles, initially referred to the *shekhinah*.)[45] Any sexual intercourse between Jewish husbands and wives during that time period is, therefore, symbolically representative of the union between the male and female aspects of the divine. The Kabbalists went as far as to insist that the actual act of copulation be consummated at the precise moment that the male and female aspects of the divine supposedly unite, thus stressing even further the symbolic significance of the Sabbath observance as participation in the holy through imitation of the divine.[46]

Sabbath and Weekdays

As pointed out earlier, time does not necessarily have to be seen as a homogeneous, physico-mathematical entity. In fact, the qualitative conception of temporality puts a particular emphasis on man's sociocultural ability to distinguish between the "qualities" of periods of time that are entirely identical from a mathematical standpoint.[47] We cannot deny, for example, the fact that working on Sunday differs substantially from working the same amount of time on Wednesday or that working on a night shift is categorically distinct from working on a day shift, despite the fact that both shifts may be mathematically equivalent to one another.[48]

This is a result of the fact that culture may assign to different time periods different "qualities" even if those time periods happen to be identical from a quantitative standpoint. Different time periods may have different "qualities" because temporality is not necessarily a homogeneous entity. Whereas the quantitative conception of time stresses its homogeneity, the qualitative view of time emphasizes its *heterogeneity*.

Nowhere is the qualitative conception of time as a heterogeneous dimension more prevalent than within the religious sphere of life. As Eliade has argued,

> For religious man time . . . is neither homogeneous nor continuous. On the one hand there are the intervals of a sacred time, the time of festivals . . . on the other there is profane time, ordinary temporal duration, in which acts without religious meaning have their setting.[49]

Durkheim even went so far as to claim that the category of time in general had actually derived from the fundamental need of religions to qualitatively differentiate between the sacred and the profane spheres of life:

> it was probably the necessity of this alternation [between the sacred and the profane] which led men to introduce into the continuity and homogeneity of duration certain distinctions and differentiations which it does not naturally have.[50]

It is one of the main contentions of cognitive anthropology that the preliminary condition of classification, which is a typically human cognitive skill that allows man to approach nature in an indirect manner, is *discontinuity*.[51] It is essentially through interrupting the continuity of nature, by transforming an undifferentiated continuum into discrete classes and categories, that we manage to transform nature into culture. This is quite evident with regard to temporality: as cultural beings, we have cultivated a special cognitive ability to carve out of the continuum of time segments that are handled discretely, as if they were quantum units.[52]

This implies that, within the qualitative conception of temporality, the flow of time is regarded as uneven. According to Claude Lévi-Strauss, for example, different historical periods may vary in their "pressure," even though they might be of equal duration.[53] Along the same lines, Barry Schwartz has recently demonstrated how culture divides the past into extraordinary, "charismatic" historical epochs and routine, relatively "empty" ones.[54] Our cognitive ability to introduce culturally based discontinuity into the otherwise even flow of natural time is particularly evident within the domain of religion. As Lloyd Warner pointed out, "the holy days and sacred seasons advance not as cold arithmetical numbers, as they appear on a secular calendar, but in dramatic rhythms of emotional intensity and modes of emotions."[55]

The fundamental discontinuity between normal-routine-profane time and abnormal-extraordinary-sacred time was first noted by Durkheim: "Does this not prove that between the profane being which he was and the religious being which he becomes, there is a break of continuity?"[56] This discontinuity has since been discussed by a number of leading anthropologists. In Eliade's words, sacred time periods "have no part in the temporal duration that precedes and follows them":

> For religious man, on the contrary, profane temporal duration
> can be periodically arrested; for certain rituals have the power to
> interrupt it by periods of a sacred time.[57]

Similarly, according to Edmund Leach, "Social time is made to appear discontinuous by inserting intervals of liminal, sacred non-time into the continuous flow of normal secular time."[58] Leach has proposed a "pendulum view of time," claiming that temporality is essentially a discontinuity of repeated contrasts, a "succession of alternations" between the sacred and the profane, with festivals marking the temporary transition from one opposite to another.[59]

The fundamental difference between sacred time and profane time results from the fact that, from a cultural standpoint, they are essentially considered to "belong" on two entirely different planes —and are even represented by two entirely different modalities— of temporality. Basically, whereas profane time is *historical* and is best represented in a *linear* fashion, sacred time is essentially *ahistorical* and is best represented in a *cyclical* manner. No one has described this fundamental difference between the two modalities of temporality better than Eliade:

> Religious man experiences two kinds of time—profane and
> sacred. The one is an evanescent duration, the other a "succession
> of eternities," periodically recoverable during the festivals that
> made up the sacred calendar. The liturgical time of the calendar
> flows in a closed circle.[60]

sacred time, appears under the paradoxical aspect of a circular time, reversible and recoverable, a sort of eternal mythical present that is periodically reintegrated by means of rites.[61]

sacred time is indefinitely recoverable, indefinitely repeatable.[62]

It is important to note that, according to Eliade, religious people experience time in both linear and cyclical fashion. Along with him, I would like to challenge the traditional view according to which cyclical temporality is characteristic of traditional societies alone while linear temporality is an exclusively modern phenomenon. Rather, I would like to contend that both modalities of temporality can and do exist—albeit in varying proportions—within one and the same society or culture.

To return to the example of Judaism, there is one particular Jewish benediction—the blessing over the Hanukkah candles—in which both the linear and the cyclical modalities of temporality are even juxtaposed to one another. In that benediction, Jews bless God for having performed miracles "in those days at this time" (*"bay-amim ha-hem bazman ha-zeh"*). The benediction implies that Hanukkah can actually be regarded as being located on more than just one plane of temporality. On the one hand, it is symbolically associated with a historical event that happened in the past ("in those days"), that is, within linear, profane time. On the other hand, it is also a nonhistorical annual festival which is periodically ("at this time") celebrated in an "eternal present," that is, within cyclical, sacred time. To further appreciate the fact that the liturgical calendar actually entails two distinct planes and modalities of temporality, note also how Hanukkah may *precede* the festival of Purim, for example, by almost three months within the calendar year, even though the historical event with which it is symbolically associated supposedly took place several centuries *after* the one with which Purim is symbolically associated!

Linear-historical-profane time is essentially cumulative. If this year is the 1,980th year of the Christian Era, next year must be the 1,981st. If last 25 November was the day of my thirty-first birthday, next 25 November will then mark my thirty-second. If the last convention of the American Sociological Association was its seventy-fourth annual meeting, the next one will be its seventy-fifth.

None of this applies to sacred, ahistorical time. It is an "eternal present" which is indefinitely recoverable. As Eliade has pointed out, "It can be said of sacred time that *it is always the same,* that it is 'a succession of eternities.' "[63] Any sacred time period is culturally perceived as being one and the same entity which recurs periodically. For all liturgical purposes, its location within historical time is of no consequence and totally insignificant and irrelevant. This may account for the fact that Jews have traditionally referred to their holiest of days as "*the* Sabbath." Whether it fell in April 1716 or September 1379, it has nevertheless always been regarded as one and the same entity.

Given the centrality of the Sabbath to Judaism, it is quite ironical that Eliade himself regards the development of an exclusively linear conception of time as a typically Jewish innovation.[64] After all, the Sabbath is clearly located on a plane of temporality quite different from that of historical time. (That, incidentally, is also true of the institution that has derived from it—the week. Unlike historical events, which are sequentially arranged in an irreversible order, Wednesday, for example, can be viewed both as preceding the Sabbath by three days and as following it by four days!) In fact, by standing out of profane historical time, the Sabbath breaks the continuity of the latter.[65] By observing the Sabbath, Jews manage to culturally arrest the continuous flow of profane historical time every seven days for a sacred period of twenty-four hours. The observance of the Sabbath exemplifies man's cognitive ability to carve out of the continuum of profane historical time a discrete segment that constitutes a province of sacredness which is clearly ahistorical.

It has been suggested by Leach that our entire cultural notion of time periods is actually derivative of the celebration of festivals.[66] It can be argued, for example, that the particular significance of the year as a social cycle essentially derives from the fact that it is the time interval between two occurrences of any major festival. In a similar manner, the entire Jewish institution of the seven-day week can be seen as derivative of the observance of the Sabbath. As F. H. Colson noted, "To the Jew the week is only the interval between two Sabbaths and apart from this no sanctity attaches to it."[67] The Jewish week is definitely an offspring of the Sabbath, and it is not surprising to find out that, in the ancient Jewish literature—Biblical,

Talmudic, and Midrashic—the week was originally called by the very same name, *"Shabbath."*[68]

Given the fact that the Jewish week revolves entirely around the Sabbath, it is understandable that Saturday—the day on which it was celebrated—became right from the beginning, as Colson put it, "The pivot on which the week turns, the day from which the others are measured."[69] It is interesting to note that even the early Christians, before they substituted Sunday for Saturday as the "Lord's day," regarded Saturday as the center of gravity of the week, and related to Friday and Sunday primarily as to the days which preceded and followed it, respectively.[70]

It is by no means a mere coincidence that the six weekdays were originally named in Hebrew "First in the Sabbath," "Second in the Sabbath," and so on, that is, in accordance with their temporal distance from the preceding Saturday.[71] (In modern Hebrew, these names have been abbreviated to "First Day," "Second Day," and so on.) After all, their social meaning derives entirely from their temporal location vis-à-vis Saturday. Friday, for example, derives its entire cultural significance in Judaism from the fact that it is a day of preparations toward the Sabbath. The major significance of Sunday, on the other hand, is as the day which follows the Sabbath. (A famous Sabbath song which depicts the various days of the week as loci of joy which gradually increases toward the Sabbath must also be understood within this context.)[72]

In fact, all six weekdays are traditionally divided in Judaism into two three-day groups, according to their temporal location vis-à-vis the coming Sabbath or the one which has passed. Sunday, Monday, and Tuesday are regarded as the days after the Sabbath, whereas Wednesday, Thursday, and Friday are viewed as the days before the Sabbath. This classification actually has some fundamental liturgical significance. As we shall soon see, the termination of the Sabbath is ritually marked by a special ceremony which usually takes place on Saturday evening. On unusual occasions, it can be postponed, yet it must be performed before the end of Tuesday, which clearly indicates that Wednesday is already considered to "belong" to the following Sabbath.[73]

The Hebrew names of the weekdays are indicative of the pronouncedly quantitative approach toward them in Judaism. This nomenclature suggests that the only basis for differentiating among the weekdays ought to be their temporal distance from the Sabbath. After all, if it were not for the fact that they are differentially located in time vis-à-vis the Sabbath, they probably would have been regarded as absolutely interchangeable with one another!

This quantitative approach toward the weekdays stands in marked contrast to the qualitative approach toward the Sabbath itself, whose name is associated not only with the number seven, but also with the purely qualitative concept of rest. The Hebrew nomenclature of the days of the week thus also reflects the fact that, while the weekdays may be interchangeable with one another, as a group they are clearly perceived as absolutely distinct from the Sabbath.

The special status of Saturday as culturally distinct from all the other days of the week is also evident from the fact that, in contrast to the masculine form of the names of all the weekdays, the name "Shabbath" is in the feminine form. This nomenclatural application of the categorical contrast between masculinity and femininity serves to emphasize the mutual exclusiveness of the categories of sacred time and profane time. As we shall see later, it is also related to the Jewish personification of the Sabbath as a bride-queen.

In the pagan planetary week, each day of the week was consecrated to a different planet-deity, thus having a unique significance of its own. Sunday and Monday, for example, were consecrated to the sun and the moon, respectively, and were, therefore, both regarded as sacred. Such a typically polytheistic arrangement could never be incorporated into a monotheistic belief system such as Judaism. As Jews recognize only one deity, they have consecrated to it only one of the seven days of the week. This has clearly served to promote the cultural perception of the Sabbath as a day which is markedly distinct from any other day of the week.

Religious systems tend to emphasize the qualitative differences between sacred and profane time periods, even though these periods are often identical from a quantitative standpoint. Christians, for example, would never regard 18 June and 25 December as interchangeable—even though both are mathematically identical twenty-four-hour time periods—since the latter, being the temporal locus of Christmas, is more than a merely regular day. In a similar manner, Jews have always regarded the Sabbath as markedly distinct from, and never interchangeable with, any other day of the week. After all, as Abraham Joshua Heschel noted, it is "not a date but an atmosphere."[74]

Jews have traditionally perceived the Sabbath not only as distinct from the weekdays, but essentially as antithetical to them. Whereas the weekdays, traditionally believed to have been the days on which the world was created, have always been regarded as worldly, the Sabbath has clearly always been seen as absolutely otherworldly. The utter contrast between the world of the weekdays and the world of the Sabbath—two worlds which are absolutely mutually exclusive—is well reflected in some common Yiddish linguistic expressions. The contrast between the concepts of *"shabbesdik"* ("Sabbath-like") and *"vokhendik"* ("weekly"), for example, is quite parallel to the contrast between the concepts of "heavenly" and "earthly." Thus, peddlers and the unschooled, for example, are commonly referred to as *"vokhendikeh mentshen"* ("people of the week").[75] Note also that, in modern Hebrew, highfalutin expressions are often referred to as "words of Sabbath" (*"millim shel Shabbath"*). And yet, there is probably no better evidence of the utter contrast between the world of the weekdays and the world of the Sabbath than the fact that the actual Hebrew word for "weekday" is nothing less than "profane day" (*"yom ḥol"*)!

One of the most effective ways of substantiating the categorical distinction between the Sabbath and the weekdays has always been a differential distribution of one's activities between them. As the ancient Jewish sages maintained, during the Sabbath, "thine affairs are forbidden, the affairs of Heaven are permitted."[76] It is within this context that all the interdictions and injunctions relating to the Sabbath observance ought to be understood.

Various cultures use taboos and interdictions in order to substantiate and solidify fundamental conceptual distinctions, especially within the domain of religion.[77] Along these lines, the numerous injunctions which relate to the Sabbath observance ought to be viewed as some of the most effective mechanisms that help to establish and maintain the categorical distinction between the Sabbath and the weekdays in particular, and between the sacred and the profane domains in general. As Hutton Webster noted, these injunctions reveal the intrinsic relationship between taboos and holiness: "The

word 'holy' in [the Sabbath] injunctions has the place of 'set apart
ritually,' 'separated from common use,' i.e. taboo."[78] That these
interdictions apply only to the Sabbath and never to any of the
weekdays serves to further solidify the categorical distinction between the former and the latter.

The mainstream rabbinical tradition within Judaism has, generally speaking, been rather liberal in implementing the injunctions
which relate to the Sabbath observance. As becomes quite evident
from the Talmudic tractate *Eruvin,* the rabbis made considerable
efforts to liberalize the interpretation of the original Biblical injunctions and, thus, to make the observance of the Sabbath much
more feasible. Take, for example, the following Biblical injunc-
tion: "Let no man get out of his place on the seventh day."[79] While
various fundamentalist sects, which have never accepted the Talmud, have traditionally recommended a literal interpretation of
this Biblical imperative,[80] the rabbis institutionalized the "Sabbath
limit" (*tehum Shabbath*), which allows Jews to move during the
Sabbath as far as two thousand cubits (about half a mile) away
from their town. The institution of *eruv* allows even further flexibility.[81]

And yet, even the relatively liberal rabbinical tradition has been
rather specific about what is to be strictly prohibited during the
holy day. An entire Talmudic tractate as well as large portions of
the Code of Jewish Law were devoted to the injunctions involved
in the Sabbath observance. No less than thirty-nine "main labors"
which are prohibited during the Sabbath were enumerated in the
Talmud, yet even that was not sufficient and, in the Code of Jewish
Law, an entire chapter of ninety-three sections was necessary for
some further elaboration and specification.[82] In their instructions,
the rabbis specified in great detail every taboo act that ought to be
avoided during the Sabbath as well as every taboo object (*mukzeh*)
that ought not to be handled on the holy day. To appreciate the
detail of the specifications, consider, for example, the following
typical injunctions from the Code of Jewish Law:

> Mustard, horseradish, or any kind of relish, in which no vinegar
> was put while it was still daylight, may not be prepared on the
> Sabbath, unless we do it in an irregular manner, that is, we first

pour the vinegar into the dish, and then the mustard or the horseradish into it. We must put enough vinegar into it, so that the mixture be soft. Neither should we mix it with a spoon, but with a finger, or shake the vessel until it is well mixed.[83]

It is forbidden to write or to draw a picture, even with the finger, in liquid spilled on the table, or on the rime of window panes, or anything similar to it, no matter how impermanent such writing is. It is even forbidden to make a mark upon any object with the fingernails. Wax, or the like, found on a book, even if it is only on one letter, must not be removed.[84]

A door that is made out of one board, cannot be used to close a doorway with it, if the doorway is not made for regular entrance and exit, even if it has a hinge but it does not swing on it, for since it is made out of one board, it appears as if we were building and closing up an open space. However, it is allowed to close with it an opening which is used for regular entrance and exit, providing there is a threshold, for then it is obvious that it is a doorway.[85]

Shreds of skin which have become separated from the base of the fingernails, should not be removed either by means of an instrument, or by hand, or with the teeth. A nail, most of which has been torn off and causes pain, may be removed with the hand, but not with an instrument. But if less than half has become separated, it should not be removed even by hand.[86]

Obviously, the level of strictness in observing such injunctions varies considerably from one religious group to another within Judaism, and it is probably only the most Orthodox observant believers that approach the level of compliance demanded even by these relatively liberal rabbinical interpretations of the Biblical injunctions. And yet, I am definitely dealing here not with actual behavior, but, rather, with doctrine. After all, it is through the latter, and not the former, that we can best learn about the conceptual distinctions and categorical imperatives which exist in Judaism.

Despite the aforementioned affinity between the Sabbath and any other known "taboo day," there is one fundamental difference between them. The main characteristic of all the injunctions involved in the Sabbath observance is not their prohibitive nature. Rather, it is the fact that they substantiate and accentuate the distinction between the Sabbath and the weekdays in particular, and the mutual exclusiveness of the categories of the sacred and the profane in general. From a logical standpoint, the very same goal may also be achieved by making enjoyment during sacred time periods an imperative.

And, indeed, there has been a general tendency in Jewish tradition to perceive the Sabbath as a joyful delight.[87] The injunctions involved in the Sabbath observance do not necessarily have to be seen in logically negative terms, that is, as involving refrainment from doing or handling certain things. In fact, the Bible itself seems to approach these injunctions from a logically positive standpoint when it maintains that the actual rationale for observing the Sabbath is essentially the human need to rest:

> Six days shalt thou labour, and do all thy work; but the seventh day is a sabbath unto the Lord thy God, in it thou shalt not do any manner of work, thou, nor thy son, nor thy daughter, nor thy man-servant, nor thy maid-servant, nor thine ox, nor thine ass, nor any of thy cattle, nor thy stranger that is within thy gates; that thy man-servant and thy maid-servant may rest as well as thou.[88]

To go back to our earlier discussion of the meaning of the Sabbath observance as an act of imitating divine activity, it is interesting to note that, according to the Jewish tradition, since God rested on the seventh day, it can be said that rest, tranquillity, quiet, and peace were actually created on the Sabbath.[89]

Enjoying oneself during the Sabbath is essentially a moral obligation in Judaism. According to the Code of Jewish Law, on this day "it is meritorious to partake of everything that provides one with pleasure."[90] Thus, for example, Jews are required by their religious codes to particularly enjoy the Sabbath meals. In honor of the holy day, they must use for those meals the better room in the house, "set the table properly," put a clean tablecloth on it, and eat delicacies so as to increase their pleasure.[91] Along the same lines, in order not to spoil the delight of the Sabbath, Jews have traditionally refrained from fasting on it.[92] (This provides further evidence of the primacy of the Sabbath over the annual holidays. The temporal location of the Sabbath can affect that of an annual fast day, but it cannot be affected by it. Whereas annual fast days which fall on

Saturday, with the single exception of the Day of Atonement, have to be "moved" to Sunday on account of the Sabbath, the Sabbath itself is never "moved.")[93] For the same reason, Jews are also required to refrain from displaying any outward signs of mourning during the Sabbath. Furthermore, they are forbidden to desecrate and profane this sacred province of time even by thoughts. Thus, in order to fully enjoy the Sabbath delight, they must rid themselves of all tensions and anxiety and deliberately avoid thinking about matters which might cause worry, such as work and business.[94] (The rules regarding what one may think or feel at certain time periods are quite suggestive of a phenomenon I have discussed at length in the second chapter, namely, the inevitable relation between schedules and calendars and social control.)

Interestingly enough, in order to emphasize the unique holiness of the Sabbath, Jews have felt the need to stress, by means of contrast, the profanity of the weekdays. Thus, since the Sabbath has traditionally been characterized as an anxiety-free day of delight, the weekdays have usually been viewed as lacking any spirituality and as being full of tension and anxiety.[95] This goes along with Durkheim's contention that, upon passing from the profane to the sacred world, religious people believe that they undergo actual metamorphosis.[96] Jews seem to believe that, during the Sabbath, their entire being is transformed from a profane entity into a sacred one. The aforementioned traditional belief that God gives every Jew an "additional soul" on the Sabbath ought to be understood within this context, as are the traditional saying that during the Sabbath every Jew is a king and Heinrich Heine's song that compares the Jew to a dog which is transformed into a human being every Sabbath Eve.[97] According to the ancient Jewish sages, the light upon a Jew's face is different on the Sabbath and on regular weekdays, and one interpretation of the Biblical phrase "I am black but comely" is "I am black all the days of the week and comely on the Sabbath."[98]

According to Eliade,

> It is precisely the reintegration of this original and sacred time that differentiates man's behavior *during* the festival from his behavior *before* or *after* it. For in many cases the same acts are performed during the festival as during nonfestival periods. But religious man believes that he then lives in *another* time.[99]

As I shall now demonstrate, the Jewish people have devoted much thought to distinguishing their behavior and appearance during the Sabbath from their behavior and appearance on the regular weekdays and making sure that the former would not resemble the latter in any way. I shall show how, by deliberately trying to perform even the most mundane activities in a pronouncedly distinct manner during the Sabbath, Jews have managed to substantiate and accentuate the fundamental distinction between sacred and profane time through their own behavior.

For example, during the Sabbath, Jews must walk in a way which differs from their regular way of walking during the rest of the week.[100] (This has to do mostly with pace: the leisurely Sabbath pace is generally regarded as antithetical to the hectic tempo of the rest of the week.)[101] Furthermore, during the Sabbath, they are supposed to wash themselves in a distinct manner, to sit in a particularly dignified way, and even to move things in a special manner which is characteristic of the Sabbath alone.[102] Finally, in order to highlight the contrast between sacred time and profane time, they must even talk during the Sabbath in a manner which would differ from the way they talk on regular days.[103] This accounts for the prohibition of uttering any profane words during the Sabbath,[104] as well as for the evolution of distinct Sabbath greetings, such as *Shabbath Shalom* in Hebrew and *Gut Shabbes* in Yiddish.

A person's outward appearance is also among the most effective ways in which the categorical distinction between sacred time and profane time is ritually marked. As Marshall Sahlins has argued,

> We also substantialize in clothing the basic cultural valuations of time. . . . Each [type of clothes] references the nature of the activities ordered by those times, in the way that weekday apparel is to Sunday "best" as the secular is to the sacred.[105]

It is, thus, quite understandable that an entire chapter of the Sabbath tractate in the Mishnah is devoted to particularly detailed descriptions of how men and women ought to appear in public on the Sabbath.[106]

In order to accentuate the fundamental distinction between sacred time and profane time, Jews have established a cultural differentiation between types of clothing which are associated with each, following the Talmudic imperative, "Thy Sabbath garments should not be like thy weekday garments."[107] This accounts for the evolution of special Sabbath garments such as the Sabbath cap and caftan, as well as for the fact that Jewish women wear special dresses and jewelry during the Sabbath which they do not wear on regular weekdays.[108]

The injunctions concerning the Sabbath clothing have usually been interpreted as requirements that one would display one's best garments and jewelry during the holy day. And yet, as I shall soon demonstrate also with regard to food, *the association of the sacred with delight is only secondary to its separation from the profane.* The primacy of the Jewish categorization of the universe into sacred and profane domains which are mutually exclusive is evident even from the manner in which some Jews, according to Mark Zborowski and Elizabeth Herzog, have traditionally stored their clothes: "Storage space is divided according to weekday and holiday clothes, not according to individual ownership."[109] Jews have traditionally been required to own at least two distinct sets of clothes, so that one can be used exclusively on the Sabbath. Furthermore, according to tradition, if a man does not own two sets of clothes, he should at least let his cloak down more than usual during the Sabbath, for no other reason than making a distinction![110]

The cultural valuation of time in Judaism is also expressed through foodways. As Claude Lévi-Strauss and Mary Douglas have demonstrated, people use food not only for the purpose of eating, but also for the purpose of thinking, that is, for classifying the universe and substantiating and accentuating certain fundamental cognitive—as well as moral—distinctions.[111] In order to highlight the fundamental categorical distinction between sacred time and profane time, not only have Jews been required, as mentioned earlier, to use the better room in the house for the Sabbath meals and to put a clean tablecloth on the table; these meals are also distinguished from regular weekday meals by special table hymns (*zemirot*) that are sung exclusively on them. Most significant, though, is the requirement that the food consumed on the Sabbath be different than that consumed on regular weekdays.[112] The fundamental contrast and opposition between sacred time and profane time is culturally marked by contrasts such as that between the white Sabbath *hallah*

bread and the dark rye bread of regular weekday meals, or the one
between the costly seasoned fish of the Sabbath and the salt herring
of regular weekdays.[113] However, despite the fact that Jews are
traditionally supposed to eat delicacies during the Sabbath, we
ought to remember that—as noted earlier, with regard to the Sabbath clothing—the association of the sacred with pleasure is only
secondary to its distinction and separation from the profane. This
accounts for the traditional ruling that the Sabbath meals be served
either some time earlier or some time later than usual, but never at
the same time that meals are served on regular weekdays,[114] a routine which exists solely for the purpose of marking some conspicuous
change.

Judaism has always been particularly explicit—as well as ritually
articulate—about the necessity to maintain the categorical distinction between the sacred and the profane at all costs. According to
Douglas, the Jewish faith provides an extreme example of a cultural
obsession with distinctions and separations: "Being holy means
being set apart. The Israelites cherish their boundaries and want
nothing better than to keep them strong and high."[115] It is the Jews
who, every year on Passover, emphasize the centrality of the distinction between the categories of the sacred and the profane—as well
as their temporal segregation from one another—by instructing their
young to ask the ritual question, "Why is this night *different* from all
other nights of the year?"

This cultural obsession with separations accounts for all the patterns I have depicted above, patterns of ritual demarcation of the
fundamental distinction between the Sabbath and the regular weekdays as two antithetical categories. Given their basic need to emphasize the mutual exclusiveness of the categories of the sacred and the
profane as well as their temporal segregation from one another,
Jews have always regarded the contamination of sacred time periods
by profane activities as an abomination. This is why they have
traditionally avoided performing the very same activities in the very
same manner on both the Sabbath and regular weekdays. Performing a weekday activity on the Sabbath has always been regarded as
a desecration or profaning of the latter (*hillul Shabbath*)—definitely one of the most abominable sins.[116]

The temporal segregation of the holy day from the "profane days"

is, by far, the most essential feature of the Jewish week. That it is
far more basic and central to Judaism than the actual temporal
location of the holy day within historical time is even evident from
the ancient rabbinical ruling that, if a traveler loses count of the
days of the week, he should still observe the Sabbath every seven
days, even though it may very well be on the wrong day.[117] As
P. W. Wilson pointed out, "The significance of the week lies mainly
in the fact that one day out of seven differs from the other six."[118]

Hence the unique significance of the *havdalah,* a ritual ceremony
which is performed at the expiration of the holy day and—as we
shall see later—without which no Sabbath can ever be terminated.
This particular ceremony, whose name literally means "separation,"
or "distinction," is a classic example of how Jews ritualize the
temporal segregation of the sacred and the profane from one another, and thus also manage to accentuate the categorical distinction between them. In the words of Joseph Herman Hertz, former
chief rabbi of the British Commonwealth, "The deeper meaning of
the ceremony is thus to impress upon us *the reality of moral distinctions* in the universe."[119]

Emphasizing the distinction between the Sabbath and the weekdays serves to clarify and accentuate the categorical distinction between the sacred and the profane in general. It is, therefore, ritually
associated with two other fundamental distinctions, both of them
between categories that are most clearly mutually exclusive opposites: light and darkness, and Israel and the heathen nations. The
customary benediction goes like this:

> Blessed art thou, O Lord our God, King of the universe, who
> makest a distinction between holy and profane, between light
> and darkness, between Israel and the heathen nations, between
> the seventh day and the six working days. Blessed art thou,
> O Lord, who makest a distinction between holy and profane.[120]

(It should be added that, until the end of the first millennium, it was
also customary, in the *havdalah* ceremony, to bless God for distinguishing between three additional mutually exclusive opposites:
the clean and the unclean, the sea and the land, and the upper and
the lower waters.)[121]

Nowhere better than in the "distinction," or "separation," ceremony can the function of time as a segregator of holiness and profanity be seen. As we shall see later, this ceremony also serves to mark the boundary between the provinces of sacred time and profane time, as well as to allow the transition from the former to the latter.

Boundaries—Separation and Transition

Not only must the sacred and the profane be conceptually distinguished from one another; they also ought to be actually separated from one another. If the two are to be viewed as absolutely distinct, mutually exclusive categories, their actual segregation from one another is essential. Any overlap between them might involve the profaning or desecration of the sacred and must, therefore, be strictly avoided. As suggested earlier, time can play a most significant role here. The actual temporal segregation of the sacred and the profane allows one to anchor them in distinctly separate parts of the universe and, thus, to maintain their mutual exclusiveness as conceptual categories. Some clear boundaries between sacred time and profane time are, therefore, essential.

However, religious people must experience *both* sacred time and profane time, since the former would have been meaningless were it not contrasted with the latter. Therefore, while sacred time and profane time ought to be separated from one another, there must also be some way of passing from one to the other. I shall now demonstrate that the same boundaries which serve to separate sacred time from profane time also serve to allow the transition between them.

To go back to the example of the Sabbath—how are the separation of this holy day from the regular weekdays and the transition between them accomplished? How are believers to know when they ought to eat, dress, walk, talk, and think in a "Sabbath-like" manner and when they ought to go back to being their usual, "profane" selves?

Throughout history Jews have been particularly meticulous in their efforts to determine the temporal boundaries of the Sabbath in the most precise manner. Scores of Jewish scholars have engaged—at least since the time of the Talmud—in endless debates regarding the precise determination of the time at which the Sabbath ought to be inaugurated and the time at which it must depart.[122] They have always regarded the determination of the precise boundaries of the Sabbath as a uniquely responsible task, therefore leaving no room for flexibility.

The particular zeal and rigidity with which the problem of determining the Sabbath boundaries has always been approached in Judaism must be understood within the context of the horrible fear on the part of Jews that they might break the Fourth Commandment. Precision is so central to the strict observance of the Sabbath, because any slight error in calculating the boundaries of the holy day might involve some extremely grave consequences. If the Sabbath is ever to be inaugurated too late or terminated too early, one might desecrate it by performing profane activities at time periods which are only erroneously defined as "Friday" or "Sunday."

In order to determine the boundaries of the Sabbath in the most precise manner, Jews have traditionally resorted to Nature, choosing the setting of the sun as the major natural phenomenon with which to associate the inauguration and the termination of the holy day. However, since it is much easier to designate a time *interval* during which those transitions take place than a precise *point* in time at which one day ends and the night of the following one begins, the ancient sages decided to associate the boundaries of the Sabbath with "twilight."[123] Having admitted the enormous difficulties inherent to determining the temporal boundaries of twilight, they nevertheless tried their best to do so, using, as a point of reference, the number of visible stars in the sky or the time it takes one to walk a certain fixed distance after sunset. Their efforts ought not to be regarded as mere academic hairsplitting, given the seriousness of the task of determining the precise boundaries between sacred time and profane time.

Precaution has always been the main theme underlying any effort to determine the Sabbath boundaries. Two types of situations must be avoided at all costs: inaugurating the Sabbath too late and concluding it too early. In order to avoid such situations, the Talmud recommends that the holy day be inaugurated as early as possible and concluded as late as possible, within reasonable limits.[124] Thus, for the sake of precaution, Jews have been required to add to the

Sabbath two short time intervals, usually a little more than three minutes long each. (In order to avoid desecrating the Sabbath, the length of these intervals ought to be adjusted for latitude and season.)[125] These time intervals are to be added as safety measures at the end of Friday between sunset and the beginning of twilight, as well as right before the beginning of Sunday, following the end of the twilight period (which is marked by the appearance of three stars in the sky). Aside from the addition of these time intervals, which is regarded as obligatory, a voluntary addition of still another time interval beyond them has been recommended by some scholars for extra precaution.[126]

What becomes quite apparent is that the Sabbath can legitimately be inaugurated somewhat earlier than is necessary or concluded somewhat later than is necessary, within certain reasonable limits. Notice that, for the sake of precaution, the added time intervals—literally referred to as "addition to the Sabbath" (*"hossafath Shabbath"*)[127]—are essentially regarded as an integral part of the holy day. (As we shall see later, however, the status of the entire liminal period near the boundaries of the Sabbath is rather ambiguous.) They actually involve stretching out the Sabbath at both ends, extending it at the expense of some time taken off both Friday and Sunday. In other words, they involve a deliberate act of "adding from the profane time to the sacred time."[128] This is indicative of an interesting asymmetrical element in the relation between the sacred and the profane: whereas profaning sacred time is generally regarded as an abominable sin, "sanctifying" profane time as a safeguard against it is definitely not!

The temporal boundaries of the Sabbath are determined in accordance with natural phenomena such as the setting of the sun and the appearance of three stars in the sky. However, in order to achieve uniformity and make sure that all Jews would welcome and escort the Sabbath *together,* as a group, some communication system that would allow for large-scale synchronization of activities has always been essential. In their attempts to achieve temporal symmetry on a communal level, Jews have chosen to apply a system based on the same principle which we have encountered earlier in the case of the Benedictine monastery bells—auditory signaling.

The signal which marked the beginning (as well as the conclu-

sion) of the Sabbath two millennia ago was the act of blowing a ram
horn or a trumpet from the top of a high building.[129] This was done
by a Temple priest in Jerusalem and by the community sextons in
all other towns. All in all, six blasts were blown. The first blast
marked the interruption of the work in the fields, allowing field
workers sufficient time to return to town. Those who worked in
town could still work until the second blast was heard, whereby all
shops were to be closed. The third blast was blown just before sunset and was the signal for performing last-minute preparatory activities such as removing the hot food from the stove and storing it for
the Sabbath, removing one's phylacteries, and kindling the Sabbath
lights. Following a short time interval—its duration defined as the
time during which one can roast a small fish or arrange a loaf in the
oven—the last three blasts were blown in rapid succession. First
came a long, sustained blast (*teki'ah*), then a series of short, broken
blasts (*teru'ah*), and finally another long, sustained blast. Whereas
the first three blasts signaled the interruption of all work, the last
three were supposed to symbolically demarcate the separation of the
weekdays from the Sabbath. The actual Sabbath observance was to
begin right after the sixth blast was heard.

Jews' deep fear of desecrating the Sabbath is quite evident from
an interesting Talmudic debate regarding whether the signals were to
be given by a trumpet or a ram horn. The debate revolved around
whether either of the two instruments was forbidden for handling
during the holy day.[130] The rabbis were debating whether the Sabbath could be inaugurated right after the sixth blast, given that the
sexton still had to carry his instrument from the high roof back to
his home! Obviously, no standard additional time period could be
applied, since the distance from the roof to the sexton's house varied
across sextons. This debate should by no means be seen as merely an
exercise in academic hairsplitting; it serves to highlight once again
the tremendous fear Jews have of desecrating their holiest of days.

Signaling the beginning of the Sabbath by trumpet or horn blowing was still popular during the Middle Ages. Indeed, a modern
version of that practice—announcing the moment of transition by a
siren—was still in use even in modern Israel. And yet, auditory
signaling gradually gave way with the spread of the use of clocks
and watches, which allowed for clock-time designation of the mo-

ments of the inauguration and the conclusion of the Sabbath. Thus, today, the precise clock-time designations of the times of the setting of the sun and of the appearance of three stars in the sky, calculated for all Friday and Saturday nights throughout the year, are regularly published by rabbinical authorities in annual almanacs, noted on the official calendar, and announced by synagogue beadles.[131]

Aside from defining the strict boundaries which separate sacred time from profane time, Jews have also institutionalized a series of rites that would allow the transition from one to the other. Various cultures demarcate the boundaries between conceptual categories by ritual activity. These rites are necessary not only for making the distinction between those categories more conspicuous, but also for allowing some possible transition from one to another. As Leach has pointed out,

> the change of status from "unmarried" to "married" is simply a
> switch of categories, but at the level of action the switching
> calls for a ritual, a crossing of social frontiers.[132]

Ritual activity can definitely help man cross the boundaries between sacred time and profane time in both directions. To quote Eliade, "By means of rites religious man can pass without danger from ordinary temporal duration to sacred time."[133] Obviously, such ritual activity also allows him to return from sacred time back to profane time.

Such ritual activity symbolizes transition, the crossing of thresholds, *passage*. Time is, after all, the main dimension along which any social passage takes place.[134] This makes Arnold van Gennep's classic discussion of "rites of passage" most relevant to the present discussion.

Van Gennep himself pointed out that "those rites which accompany and bring about the change of the year, the season, or the month, should also be included in ceremonies of passage."[135] Ironically, however, he later made the following erroneous statement: "Since the week is nothing more than a subdivision of the month, it is not marked by rites of passage except as it may be related to market days (especially in Africa)."[136] I have demonstrated throughout this chapter that the Jewish week is far more than a mere subdivision of the month. We should, therefore, not be surprised to find out that the boundaries of the Sabbath are actually marked by a rich variety of "rites of passage."

In order to accentuate the fundamental categorical distinction between the Sabbath and the weekdays and make sure that the former would never be perceived as merely one of the seven days of the week, Jews have traditionally gone as far as to personify it as a bride, and even as a queen.[137] Within the Jewish tradition, the Sabbath is generally viewed as a personified entity which comes periodically to "visit" the profane world, as if to sanctify it by its sheer presence. This accounts for the traditional ritualization of her "arrivals" and "departures." Thus, for example, the conclusion of this holy day has traditionally been referred to as "the exit of the Sabbath" (*"motzaeh Shabbath"*), and at least at some point in history the opposite term, "the arrival of the Sabbath" (*"movaeh Shabbath"*), was also used to refer to its inauguration.[138] The "arrival" of the holy entity was even ritualized in the most vivid fashion by the sixteenth-century Kabbalists of Safed, who used to go out to the fields on Friday afternoons to welcome the Bride-Queen Sabbath by reciting special prayers and hymns in her honor.[139] Their hymn "Lekha Dodi," which opens with the words "Come, my friend, to meet the Bride; Let us receive the face of Sabbath," is still one of the most popular Sabbath hymns, and the entire rite of "welcoming the Sabbath" (*"kabbalath Shabbath"*) has survived in many Jewish communities—albeit in a modified form—to this day. It is complemented by the opposite rite of "escorting the Queen" (*"melaveh malkah"*), which is performed at the conclusion of the Sabbath. The very names of these two rites are indicative of the perceived nature of the two events they serve to ritually mark: the "entrance" and the "exit" of the holy "visitor."

As might be suggested by the fact that the Sabbath was traditionally ushered in by six blasts rather than just one, the transition from profane time to sacred time and back again is not an abrupt one. The Sabbath is supposed to "arrive" and to "depart" in a rather gradual manner. Thus, it is not only the precise points in time which designate the actual boundaries of the sacred time period that are ritually marked, but also the entire temporal areas around them.

According to van Gennep, transition rites are usually preceded by "pre-liminal" *separation rites*.[140] Prior to the transition from the profane world to the sacred world, some ritual activity which helps to separate the two worlds from one another ought to take place. In the same way that Jews must perform the rite of burning all the leaven—which is taboo on Passover—before that holiday can begin, they must also finish their preparations for the Sabbath before ushering it in. Thus, much of what takes place in Jewish homes on Friday—as well as on parts of Thursday—ought to be seen as preparations toward the transition from profane time to sacred time. These include ritual activities such as cleaning one's house, putting a clean tablecloth on the table and fresh coverings on one's bed, arranging one's furniture, sharpening one's knives, trimming one's fingernails, immersing one's body and face in hot water, and wearing fresh garments that have not been worn during the week.[141] All of the above are *purification rites* which must be performed in honor of the "arriving visitor" and are supposed to facilitate the separation between the realms of sacred time and profane time and the transition from the latter to the former.

It is interesting to note that, while all of these activities are essentially preparations for the sacred, they nevertheless ought to be concluded before the Sabbath "arrives"; that is, they ought to be concluded within profane time. This, along with the fact that, after all, on their Sunday meals, Jews usually eat leftovers from the Sabbath meals, seems to indicate that they do not mind at all that some of the holiness of sacred time would also be imbued on the area of profane time which lies near the boundaries separating the two realms. As I have already pointed out when discussing the safety measures pertaining to the "addition to the Sabbath," the overlap between these two realms is clearly one-sided. While Judaism does not mind at all adding some sanctity to profane time, it abhors any "invasion" of the Sabbath by the regular weekdays. Thus, Jews may very well spend much of Thursday and most of Friday making preparations for the Sabbath, yet they would strongly refrain from "contaminating" the latter by even thinking about weekday-related matters on it.

While the boundaries of the Sabbath may seem to stretch across some time interval, there are nevertheless two precisely designated points in time which mark the exact moments when the holy visitor "enters" and "exits." There is a single point in time, designated in Jewish almanacs and calendars in the most precise manner, which is supposed to separate the Sabbath from the preceding week.[142] For at least two thousand years, this point has been ritually marked by a single rite: the kindling of the Sabbath lights.[143] As Zborowski and Herzog put it, "Once the candles have been lighted, Sabbath is within the home."[144]

The Sabbath is believed to "enter" Jewish homes at the precise moment that the benediction over the kindling of the lights is completed, yet this involves a serious conflict with another traditional custom. It is customary, in Judaism, to recite the benediction over precepts *before* they are performed. And yet, if the Sabbath is to be ushered in right after the benediction is completed and the latter is to precede the act of kindling the lights, that would inevitably involve desecrating the holy day, since kindling any lights during the Sabbath is strictly prohibited. (It is quite possible that the act of kindling lights was chosen for marking the boundary which separates the Sabbath from the weekdays for the very reason that it is one of the most obvious taboos involved in the observance of the holy day.)

In order to resolve this problem, it was decided that, in this particular case, the traditional sequential relations between precepts and the benedictions over them be reversed and the benediction be recited only *after* the kindling of the lights.[145] This, however, meant that the benediction would be recited over a precept that had already been performed, which, from the traditional Jewish standpoint, is quite an absurdity. In order to resolve this abnormal situation, an interesting compromise was introduced. As if to ignore and deny the fact that the lights have already been kindled, one is supposed to cover one's eyes with one's hands while reciting the benediction![146] (Incidentally, this practice is quite similar to the custom of covering the *hallah* bread—which "belongs" to the Sabbath, yet the preparation of which must be completed during the profane Friday—until the Sabbath "arrives," so as not to "contaminate" it by profane time, as well as not to see it.)

All this presupposes—and is indicative of—the centrality of the act of reciting the benediction over the kindling of the Sabbath lights as the single most important rite which marks the actual inauguration of the holy day. Jews are particularly concerned with the way in which it is sequentially arranged vis-à-vis the actual act of kindling the lights, because it is precisely there that they believe that the Sabbath boundary passes. The difference between kindling the Sabbath lights before the benediction or right after it cannot be overemphasized. It basically involves a decision whether the act of kindling the lights lies within or outside the Sabbath boundaries and, thus, whether or not it actually desecrates the holy day.

The rite of kindling the Sabbath lights is performed at home not by the master of the house, but, rather, by his wife. While this may seem peculiar to anyone who is familiar with the relatively insignificant role of women within traditional Jewish liturgy, it ought to be understood within the context of the entire sexual symbolism of the Sabbath observance, which I have discussed earlier. Basically, around the inauguration of the holy day, every Jewish community is sexually segregated! At the moment the Sabbath is supposed to "arrive," all the men usher it in together at the synagogue, while every woman does it by herself at home. Thus, the Sabbath is actually inaugurated through two distinct and absolutely separate ritual procedures. As the Authorized Daily Prayer Book puts it, "The Sabbath is inaugurated in the Home by the kindling of the Sabbath lights; and in the Synagogue, by special psalms and the Lechoh Dodi hymn prior to the Evening Service."[147]

The evening service (*arvit* or *ma'ariv*) usually begins in the synagogue after the appearance of stars in the sky. On Friday, however, because of the precaution measures mentioned earlier, it begins as early as an hour and a quarter before sunset.[148] The laws of the Sabbath are supposed to apply from the singing of "Lekhah Dodi" and of the ninety-second psalm, "Mizmor Shir Le'yom Ha' Shabbath" ("A psalm, a song for the Sabbath day"), both of which open the service.[149] (Interestingly enough, no attempt is ever made to synchronize the men's act of singing these songs in the synagogue with the women's act of kindling the Sabbath lights at home.) In the middle of the service, the "sanctification" ("*kiddush*") ceremony is performed. This rite is performed once again later, at home, right after the first Sabbath meal begins. (Prior to the evolution of the men's custom of congregating in the synagogue before the meal, this ceremony used to take place only once, right after the kindling of the Sabbath lights.)[150]

I have noted earlier the gradual nature of the transition from profane time to sacred time, which, as we shall soon see, is also characteristic of the transition from sacred time back to profane time. One major implication of this is that, even though the two are generally perceived as mutually exclusive categories, some overlap between them is inevitable. This makes the status of the temporal area around the boundaries between them rather ambiguous, which goes along well with the anthropological claim that ambiguity is one of the most typical characteristics of liminality in general and of transition rites in particular.[151]

The ambiguous status of twilight within Jewish tradition is a perfect case in point. Being a period of transition from day to night, this liminal period is in itself neither day nor night in any clear-cut manner. The twilight periods around the boundaries of the Sabbath can, therefore, never be identified in an absolute manner as either purely sacred (as parts of the Sabbath) or purely profane (as parts of the preceding Friday or the following Sunday). Hence the ruling that, whenever there is an emergency, Jews can break the Sabbath laws during the twilight period which separates Saturday from Sunday, even though that period is officially regarded as part of the Sabbath.[152] Thus, as demonstrated earlier with regard to the distinction between the Sabbath and the annual festivals and holidays, despite the fact that, in theory, sacred time and profane time constitute a dichotomy, various subprovinces of sacred time nevertheless seem to have different degrees of sanctity attached to them.

The ambiguous nature of the liminal temporal areas around the boundaries which separate sacred time from profane time also makes them somewhat fearsome. Hence the many superstitions which have developed around transition rites that mark the passage from profane time to sacred time and vice versa. After all, even the custom of covering one's eyes while reciting the benediction over the kindling of the Sabbath lights may be seen in this light. This may also be one reason for the prayers which are traditionally recited around the "arrival" of the Sabbath (when the lights are kindled) as well as when it is about to "exit" (when three stars appear in the sky), asking God to protect the Jews in general and one's loved ones in particular.[153]

The time around the "departure" of the holy "visitor" is particularly fearsome for Jews. Given their traditional belief that, during the Sabbath, God gives them an "additional soul," the conclusion of the holy day is associated with spiritual impoverishment. Around their anxiety about being stripped of their extra spirituality, a peculiar rite has evolved, namely, the custom of smelling pungent spices and blessing them as part of the *havdalah* ceremony. This rite is performed explicitly in order to soothe one's soul, which is supposed to sadden around the "departure" of the Sabbath.[154] It is interesting to note that no benediction over the spices is ever required when the conclusion of the Sabbath happens to coincide with the beginning of one of the annual festivals, that is, when one still remains within the realm of sacred time.[155]

The fragrant odors of the spices are also believed to help one fight the influence of evil spirits. Apparently, this is also the latent function of ritual practices such as examining one's fingernails by the light of the *havdalah* candles and pouring out some of the wine over which a benediction has been recited during that ceremony.[156] Such practices ought to be seen within the context of the popular Jewish belief that Satan and all evil forces are deprived of their power during the Sabbath, as a consequence of which all the sinful souls and spirits leave hell during the holy day, only to return there at its conclusion.[157] Upon their return to hell, the influence of all evil forces is believed to increase, which makes the time around the expiration of the Sabbath particularly fearsome.

Within this context, it is also not surprising that Jews make many efforts to manipulate the boundaries of the Sabbath and postpone its "departure." Thus, for example, it is not only for the sake of precaution that the service for the conclusion of the holy day begins and ends at a later hour than usual; given the popular belief that the evil spirits and lost souls cannot return to hell until that service is concluded, that practice is also meant to prolong the temporary relief from their evil influence as much as possible. This is also why it was customary among the Kabbalists to protract the singing of the word "*Barkhu*" ("Bless") as long as one's breath would allow. For precisely the same reason, it is still customary among Hassidic circles to postpone the "departure" of the Sabbath by prolonging the *melaveh malkah* ("escorting the Queen") meal and festivities far into the night.[158]

The actual separation of the Sabbath from the following week, however, is ritually marked by the "separation" or "distinction" (*havdalah*) ceremony, which I have discussed earlier. It should come as no surprise that, at the end of this ceremony, the master of the house blesses all his family with the ritual greeting "*shavu'a tov*" ("a good week").[159] Nor is it by any means a coincidence that, during this ceremony, God is blessed for having created "the light of the fire."[160] After all, was it not on Sunday—traditionally believed to have been the first day of the Creation—that God separated the light from the darkness?[161] There is no doubt that it is the *havdalah* ceremony that marks the actual boundary which separates the Sabbath from Sunday and the following week, thus inaugurating the latter two.

I have discussed earlier the benediction that deals exclusively with separations. That benediction is clearly an integral part of the *havdalah* ceremony, since only this ceremony can separate sacred time from profane time and allow a smooth transition from the Sabbath to the weekdays. The tremendous significance and the unique role of the *havdalah* ceremony cannot be overemphasized. Performing it constitutes essentially a fulfillment of the minimal requirement pertaining to the Sabbath observance—the separation of sacred from profane time!

It is interesting to note that if, for some unusual reason, a person must break the Sabbath laws by performing some taboo activity, he or she can do so *only after performing the havdalah ceremony*.[162] In other words, before the Sabbath has been ritually separated from the following week, absolutely no transition from sacred to profane time is possible. This strongly supports my general theory as to the main function of the entire institution of the Sabbath—the absolute separation of the sacred domain from the profane domain.

Five

Private Time and Public Time

In the previous chapter I demonstrated how, by managing to accentuate fundamental categorical distinctions, time can function as a most effective principle of differentiation. The establishment of cultural institutions such as the Sabbath certainly helps people to perceive different periods of time as if they were actually different in their qualities. Furthermore, time seems to enable people to maintain the mutual exclusiveness of the sacred and profane domains. In the present chapter I shall try to demonstrate that, in a very similar fashion, time also serves another major social function, namely, keeping the private and public spheres of life apart.

The Temporal Structure of Social Accessibility

One of the fundamental characteristics of modern society is man's multiple participation in the social world, a phenomenon which was probably best described by Georg Simmel.[1]

According to Simmel, in premodern societies, all of one's social involvements were interdependent. Thus, for example, just from knowing a person's familial affiliation one could fairly accurately guess his or her political and religious affiliations as well. In other words, the traditional pattern of an individual's involvements in social life might be graphically represented as a set of concentric circles, whereby affiliation with any particular social group or network necessarily entailed—as well as was actually "contained" in—affiliations with some other groups or networks.

Given the growing division of labor and the resulting

differentiation of spheres of life in modern society, this has undergone a most fundamental change. A person's familial affiliation does not necessarily tell us anything about his or her religious, political, or—for that matter—occupational affiliations anymore. The modern pattern of an individual's involvements in social life can be graphically represented as a web of overlapping, intersecting circles, whereby most of one's social affiliations are not "contained" in— and are, therefore, at least in part, independent of—one another.

Multiple participation means segmented participation. And, indeed, one of the major implications of the multiple participation of modern individuals in the social world has been their "segmentation" along the lines of their affiliations with various social groups and networks. That these affiliations are, to a large extent, independent of one another necessarily implies that none of them encompasses the modern individual in toto. Whereas membership in concentric social circles entails being totally absorbed by them, each of the various intersecting social circles with which modern individuals are affiliated demands from them only a *partial involvement* in it. In other words, modern social structures are typically characterized by the pattern of *divided commitment*. As Lewis Coser has pointed out,

> Modern non-totalitarian societies typically come to terms with
> such competing demands on individuals through a structural
> arrangement by which these individuals, far from being fully
> immersed in a particular sub-system, are in fact segmentally
> engaged in a variety of social circles, none of which should
> demand exclusive loyalty.[2]

> As a rule, in the urban and industrial world (except for
> totalitarian countries), each person belongs to a variety of groups
> and circles all of which claim allegiance while none makes
> exclusive demands on commitments.[3]

As a result of all this, modern society is typically characterized by a social structural, as well as existential, distinction between the modern person and each of the various social *roles* that he or she assumes. Never being totally identified with any one of these roles, the modern individual is necessarily only partially involved in each of them. That no one social role circumscribes the modern individual in toto is at the basis of the modern bureaucratic distinction between doing and being.

All of this explains the rise of the institution of privacy as one of the fundamental necessities of the modern individual. The distinction between "person" and "role" is quite parallel to the distinction between the private and public spheres of life. That none of the various social roles which modern individuals assume circumscribes them in toto implies various residues of privacy. The competing claims on individuals by the various social circles with which they are affiliated and the often-conflicting demands entailed by the variety of social roles they play make the institutionalization of periodic withdrawal from publicity into privacy absolutely essential to modern social life.[4] In other words, the partiality of each of the individual's various involvements in social life necessarily entails some degree of inaccessibility.

It should be added, though, that privacy or inaccessibility must not be regarded as absolute notions, since they are essentially defined in a relative fashion. After all, the notion of the "private self" is purely analytic, since a person with no social roles or affiliations whatsoever simply does not exist. With the possible exception of extreme situations such as being asleep, meditating, or being locked in a bathroom,[5] one is never inaccessible in an absolute manner, but always vis-à-vis somebody. The state of being inaccessible to one's boss or clients, for example, does not necessarily entail privacy vis-à-vis one's spouse and children as well. In the same manner, neither does the state of privacy vis-à-vis one's students necessarily entail being inaccessible to one's close friends as well.

How is privacy possible? How do we manage to regulate our social accessibility and withdraw periodically into our "private selves"? How do we maintain the partiality of each of our various involvements in social life? After all, it has been demonstrated that, as social actors, we manage quite successfully to partially insulate ourselves from observability as well as to segregate the audiences of our various—not always congruous—performances.[6]

One dimension of the world along which we manage to regulate our social accessibility is space. As various studies of personal space and territoriality have shown, space is a most significant parameter of privacy and inaccessibility. And yet, the private or public quality of any given space very often varies across *time*. Private "back regions," for example, wherein individuals are insulated from being observable by their audience, are defined not only in spatial terms, but in temporal terms as well. As Erving Goffman has pointed out, "There are many regions which function *at one time* and in one sense as a front region and *at another time* and in another sense as a back region."[7]

It is this relatively neglected temporal dimension of social accessibility and privacy that is at the center of the present discussion. I would like to demonstrate how *time functions as one of the major dimensions of social organization along which involvement, commitment, and accessibility are defined and regulated in modern society*. With the increasing functional and structural differentiation within individuals' webs of social affiliations and the growing bureaucratic split between "person" and "role," time has become one of the major organizational principles which facilitate the institutionalization of privacy as well as the "segmentation" of modern individuals along the lines of their various social involvements. By providing some fairly rigid boundaries that segregate the private and public spheres of life from one another and to which the association of person and role is confined, time has become indispensable to the regulation of the social accessibility of modern individuals as well as to the maintenance of the partiality of each of their various social involvements.

In other words, time seems to function as a segmenting principle. Similar to the way in which it helps to keep the sacred domain and the profane domain apart, it also helps to segregate the private and public spheres of life from one another, as well as to separate persons from each of their various social roles.[8]

The indispensability of *scheduling* to the maintenance of privacy has already been pointed out by Goffman:

> By proper scheduling of one's performances, it is possible not only to keep one's audiences separated from each other . . . but also to allow a few moments in between performances so as to extricate oneself psychologically and physically from one personal front, while taking on another.[9]

While manifestly participating in one system of roles, the

individual will have some capacity to hold in abeyance his involvement in other patterns, thus sustaining one or more dormant roles that are enacted roles on other occasions. This capacity supports a life cycle, a calendar cycle, and a daily cycle of role enactments; such scheduling implies some jurisdictional agreements as to where and what the individual is to be when.[10]

The reason that the various social involvements of modern individuals are essentially partial is that they are restricted to certain time periods, whereas during other time periods they do not even exist. Our life is socially organized and temporally structured in such a way that, whereas during some time periods we must be accessible to others, there are other time periods during which we may be legitimately inaccessible to them. This is why time is so central to the definition and regulation of social involvement, commitment, and accessibility.

I would like to propose here that we view time from yet a novel perspective, namely, that of territoriality.[11] That would help us to identify a temporally defined *niche of inaccessibility* which resembles both the "home territory" and "personal space" in that we expect to have far more control over our social accessibility within it than outside of it. In other words, within this "niche," we can be legitimately inaccessible.

We are actually dealing here with a sort of "preserve" that is bounded by some temporally defined "involvement shields,"[12] which, though certainly not as visibly conspicuous as spatial boundaries, are nevertheless socially regarded as no less binding. Claiming control over one's social accessibility within this "preserve" ought to be regarded, therefore, as any other territorial claim. Consequently, any violation of this claim—such as telephoning people around 3:30 A.M.—is as unacceptable as a violation of their personal space such as standing or sitting too close to them. Such a violation is justifiable only on the grounds that it is necessitated by an extreme emergency. That calling people around that hour may constitute a practical joke[13] is based on the assumption that a telephone call made during what is socially accepted as sleeping hours must be an emergency.

The individual's basic right to be inaccessible at certain times is also evident from the way society punishes offenders by taking

control over their social accessibility out of their hands. A typical
case in point is the prison, a social milieu wherein people have
almost no time during which they may be legitimately inaccessible,
where "inmates are *almost continually* in one another's presence or
in sight of authorities."[14] I should add here that time is probably
the most significant dimension of the "total" aspect of "total institutions" in general. Inmates, soldiers, and hospital patients, for
example, are *always* socially accessible, and have no time whatsoever within which they can screen out nonintimates. It is not
surprising, therefore, that, in his original definition of the "total institution," Goffman listed time as the first dimension of the "en-
compassing tendencies" of institutions in general.[15] (L. Coser also
regards time as one of the two main resources of individuals over
which social institutions compete.)[16]

I suggest that we view the relative degree of the individual's
social accessibility at any given time as a proportion between two
hypothetical constructs: *private time* and *public time*. Private time
is essentially "sociofugal," in the sense that—like certain socially
defined spaces—it is deliberately designed to prevent, or at least
discourage, the formation of human contact and to separate people
from one another. Public time, on the other hand, is essentially
"sociopetal," in the sense that, like various other spaces, it is deliberately meant to promote the establishment of human contact
and to draw people together. In other words, private time and public time are the nonspatial analogues of the library and the dancing
floor, respectively.[17]

I should point out, however, that—like "privacy" and "publicity" in general—private time and public time must not be regarded as mutually exclusive categories which together constitute
an exhaustive conceptual dichotomy. Both of them are only hypothetical constructs, and neither of them exists in pure form in
actuality. Therefore, they ought to be regarded as the ideal-typical
polarities of a hypothetical continuum which bears a striking re-
semblance to another continuum that relates to the spatial aspects
of social accessibility, namely, the one lying between "intimate
distance" and "public distance."[18] In other words, rather than view
given time periods as *either* private *or* public, we ought to regard
every moment of an individual's time as some combination of *both*

private and public elements, that is, as being located somewhere along that continuum. That would certainly allow us to compare various degrees of social accessibility. As I pointed out earlier, only rarely can one be said to be absolutely and totally inaccessible. The time during which I read yet can be interrupted by my children is by no means absolutely private. And yet, compared with the time during which we play together, it is certainly far less public than the latter.

We should also remember that the definition of any given time period as relatively private or public is not unidimensional. After all, as pointed out earlier, the notions of accessibility and privacy are inherently relative, since one is always "accessible" or "inaccessible" vis-à-vis somebody. Thus, during my office hours, which are clearly defined as public vis-à-vis my students, I am absolutely inaccessible to my friends. On the other hand, on open-house evenings, when I am absolutely free from any professional commitments, I am nevertheless committed to be absolutely accessible to any friend or acquaintance who bothers to drop by.

The situation, however, is by no means chaotic. With the sole exception of professional commitments, which I shall soon discuss at great length, the degree of social distance between the individual and others seems to be the single most significant factor that accounts for the variability of the temporal boundaries of social accessibility. For example, it is usually considered quite appropriate to call a close friend some time past the temporal boundary beyond which calling a mere acquaintance or a stranger would be regarded as an intrusion. It is usually also my closest circle of intimates who have access to me during time periods that are socially defined as essentially private: holidays, vacations, periods of hospitalization, recuperation, mourning, and so on.

It should be pointed out, however, that, in general, there are actually no explicit rules which provide a clear-cut definition of the temporal boundaries of social accessibility, so that these are very often subject to negotiation. Even though there is usually much consensus around them, the fact that various people may define them differently inevitably introduces some ambiguous situations that sometimes even result in conflicts.

The definitional relativity of private time and public time also stems from the fact that their "location" is not defined in an absolute manner in terms of particular times of the day, days of the week, or parts of the year. Since—as demonstrated in the first chapter—much of social life is temporally structured along regularly recurrent patterns, private time periods and public time periods are usually defined as being "located" within certain phases of particular social cycles. The latter, however, might very well vary.

Nighttime, for example, is regarded by most people in our society as a relatively sociofugal, private time period, whereas daytime is generally regarded as relatively public and sociopetal. (Note, however, that precisely because social interaction is usually far more exclusive at night than during the day, when people do interact at nighttime their interaction is often particularly intimate. It has also been claimed that people are generally much more friendly and helpful to others at nighttime than during the day.[19] Almost paradoxically, precisely because nighttime is generally defined as a sociofugal time period, interpersonal barriers fall there much faster than during the daytime!) That, however, does not apply to night workers, for example. During my fieldwork in the hospital, I once heard a night nurse telling an intern how very surprised and annoyed she was at being called at home by her head nurse at 10:30 A.M. She first referred to that time as "the middle of the day," but then added immediately, "in the middle of the night *for me,* that is," as if to emphasize the relativity of the sociopetal quality of daytime. Furthermore, the definition of the temporal boundaries which separate the more private time periods from the more public ones may also vary across cultures. The social meaning of calling someone at 3:00 P.M., for example, depends to a large extent on whether or not that act takes place within a cultural context in which it is customary to take afternoon naps.

The temporal boundaries of social accessibility also vary across interactional channels, even within one and the same culture. Being socially accessible through the telephone, for example, is quite distinct from being available for a face-to-face contact. Consequently, it is usually not considered inappropriate to call someone on the telephone some time past the temporal boundary beyond which an actual visit would be regarded as an intrusion. It should be pointed out, in this regard, that giving others one's telephone number—especially if it is not listed in the telephone directory—is a most significant act of displaying accessibility to them. Aside from the practical significance of granting them actual access to one, it also serves the function of symbolically incorporating them into a selective and exclusive social circle of intimates.

Note, however, that privacy can be violated not only by an actually ringing telephone, but also by the sheer knowledge that it *might* ring any moment! Hence the practice of enhancing one's inaccessibility by using a receptionist to screen telephone calls or—even more simply—by taking one's telephone off the hook. And yet, even such an act must conform to a certain temporal definition if it is to be socially acceptable! Generally speaking, it is far more legitimate to cut oneself off from the rest of the world during time periods which are regarded as sociofugal anyway. Therefore, we usually find it much more offensive and frustrating to be barred from having access to others during the daytime than at nighttime.

At the other extreme, the deliberate refrainment from ever taking one's telephone off the hook is a symbolic display of a particular social quality—*ever-availability*. This quality involves a particular temporal definition of social commitments, namely, being *always* accessible. As I shall soon demonstrate with regard to the modern bureaucratization of professional commitments, this quality, a most powerful symbol of a rapidly dying traditional social order, is becoming more and more of an anachronism. And yet, within the more traditional spheres of life, it is still strongly cherished. *The extent to which one approximates an ideal-typical state of ever-availability is probably still one of the most important criteria for evaluating how good a parent, child or grandchild, spouse, sibling, relative, or friend one is.*

It is quite obvious that the temporal organization of social accessibility is heavily imbued with symbolic significance which transcends its merely practical value. Consider, for example, *lead time*.[20] On the surface, inviting someone for dinner a long time in advance may appear to be merely a practical device used in order to secure his or her participation. However, lead time also functions as a symbolic display of politeness and respect for the privacy of others, for their basic right to be inaccessible at times. A "short notice," for example, seems to imply that others' availability is taken for granted and, therefore, involves some lack of respect for their claim to some social inaccessibility.

Like the temporal boundaries of social accessibility, only rarely is the length of lead time explicitly defined (as in the highly formalized diplomatic world, for example). Usually, it is regulated by tacit rules of etiquette, varying at regular patterns across relative social status as well as social distance. Thus, as far as social status is concerned, it is well known that distinguished speakers who are invited to deliver guest lectures, for example, usually demand not only a higher fee, but also a longer lead time than do less-known speakers. Note, in this regard, that a "short notice"—as in "I need it right away," for example—may also function as a purely symbolic display of exercising social power over someone. As far as social distance is concerned, note, for example, that while very close friends may be invited to come "in an hour or so," many people might decline an invitation for a first date if they are given "only" two days' notice, even if they are actually free on that particular day. Interestingly enough but for the very same reason, a "short notice" may be deliberately meant to function as a purely symbolic display of intimacy. People may call one another "at the last moment," for example, precisely in order to present themselves as less distant socially and to suggest that they do not regard the relationship as very formal. (Given the socially perceived sociofugality of nighttime, that is also true of some telephone calls that are made deliberately at particularly "late" hours!)

The Bureaucratization of Professional Commitments

There is an obvious conceptual affinity between "private time" and "free time" (or "leisure time"). And yet, in the same way that "privacy" in general ought to be distinguished from "freedom," these two categories must not be confused with one another, since they emphasize two distinct aspects of social life. Whereas the main focus of the work/leisure dichotomy in sociology is the use of time, the present conceptual framework revolves around the temporal aspects of social accessibility. Thus, whereas leisure is traditionally characterized essentially as time which is optionally used, private time is characterized here primarily as time during which one is socially inaccessible, *regardless of how it is used*. To appreciate the fundamental distinction between these two concepts, note that people often engage in public activities during their leisure time, while trying their best to emphasize their inaccessibility when they work. Note also that, whereas leisure is defined in a unidimensional manner—always as time free *from work*—private time is essentially defined in a multidimensional fashion. As shown earlier, there is a variety of social entities vis-à-vis whom individuals may claim privacy, so that, at one and the same time period, one may be absolutely inaccessible to one person and yet totally accessible to another.

And yet, even though I have characterized public time and private time as pronouncedly distinct from work time and leisure time, it is nevertheless in the domain of work that the temporal segregation of the private and public spheres of life from one another can best be appreciated. Probably nowhere is the modern temporal segregation of the "private self" from the "public self" more clearly evident than within this domain.

The premodern social order is characterized by relatively *diffuse* relations between person and role.[21] This implies a perceived identity between individuals and their occupational roles, as if the former *were,* indeed, the latter. Who people are is essentially inseparable from what they do.

Such a social order does not tolerate any significant institutionalized distinction between the private and public spheres of life. And, indeed, privacy is a rather modern phenomenon. The premodern social order is characterized by patterns of undivided commitment, with social institutions making *total* claims on their members. Within such a social context ever-availability is widely cherished and one would not expect to find any well-developed concept of private time.

The traditional conception of the relations between person and occupational role can still be identified in some professions, at least on the ideological level. Being involved in religious service, politics, police work, military service, medicine, or diplomacy, for example, usually entails a vision of individuals who are inseparable from their occupational roles, of "professionals" who are *always* "on the job." Many students also tend to believe that some approximation of ever-availability ought to be among the major criteria for a professional evaluation of university professors.

To appreciate the centrality of the temporal structure of professional commitments to the traditional definition of the relations between person and occupational role, consider, for example, the case of medicine as a profession. It is quite typical, for instance, that the first chapter of the code of ethics of the American Medical Association begins with the words, "A physician should not only be ever ready to obey the calls of the sick . . ."[22] That phrasing clearly implies that physicians regard ever-availability as such a fundamental professional obligation that they even tend to take it for granted. The physician is traditionally depicted as the prototype of the professional who is always "on the job." To appreciate the particular symbolic significance of ever-availability in medicine, note, for example, how family physicians of the "old style" often dramatize their professional commitment by making a point of emphasizing that they will willingly go and visit a patient in need at *any* time of the day and on *any* day of the week. This is probably also the main reason why the modern hospital is always open[23] and why some Health Maintenance Organization clinics list round-the-clock, *continuous* coverage as their single most significant attraction to private patients.

Even in the modern age, medicine is among the very few professions that still adhere, at least ideologically, to the traditional conception of the "professional" as inseparable from his or her occupational role. Physicians are held continuously responsible and accountable for their patients' well-being and are, therefore, expected to activate their professional duties *whenever* they are in demand. At least in theory, they have practically no periods of time which are defined as utterly private and not vulnerable to intrusion. In other words, at least in theory, *they are always accessible!*

Thus, when physicians leave the hospital for the day, they are usually expected to leave instructions as to how they can be reached. Furthermore, it is not unusual that they would actually be called at home for consultation. Finally, with the introduction of a special one-way radio system into many hospitals, modern physicians also carry "beepers" with them, which implies—practically as well as symbolically—that they can be reached *at any time*. The physician who is unexpectedly "beeped" out of a movie theater or a party has become a symbol of total, undivided commitment to one's professional obligations. Like the telephone, the "beeper" intrudes upon one's privacy not only when it actually "beeps," but also indirectly, by the sheer knowledge that it might "beep" any moment. As some physicians whom I interviewed claimed, they do not experience total privacy even when they are in a bathroom by themselves!

The manner in which society defines the professional commitments of physicians is quite evident from the way in which medical coverage in hospitals is temporally structured. One of the most significant structural characteristics of doctors' work schedules, in accordance with which their professional duties are defined from a temporal standpoint, is their relative *temporal flexibility*. Physicians' coverage systems in the hospital are based on time slots which are fairly flexible, as far as their length is concerned, since their end is usually marked by what is socially defined as the actual completion of the physician's daily tasks in the hospital, rather than being dictated by the clock. In other words, *doctors do not have any rigidly fixed leaving times beyond which they may legitimately refuse to see patients.*

Given the fact that the institutionalization of private time is a fairly modern phenomenon, it is not surprising that, in professions which adhere to the traditional definition of the relations between person and occupational role, private time is essentially defined as a residual category. In other words, from a logical standpoint, private time is traditionally defined in a negative fashion, that is, as time during which one is *in*accessible, *not* involved or committed. (Interestingly enough, this typically traditional definition of private time is parallel to the typically modern definition of leisure as time which is not work time.)[24] Modern individuals who choose a career as politicians, detectives, physicians, diplomats, policemen, ministers, reporters, businessmen, or military officers must be aware of the fact that they commit themselves to a very particular life-style, which, as we shall soon see, differs in a most significant way from the life-style of most other people today. Such careers involve a definition of private time as a pronouncedly residual category, namely, as that period of time during which one is free from one's professional commitments.

Admittedly, this is partly true of most other modern professions as well. And yet, it is particularly in careers such as medicine or the military that one's time with one's family, for example, is defined in a residual manner, that is, as the time that one is not required to stay at one's hospital or base! It is not a coincidence that the concept of "resident" evolved in the context of the hospital, where, traditionally, house staff actually resided at the hospital almost continuously. That the institutional temporal order in social milieus such as the hospital is organizationally prior to the personal one[25] is also manifested in the chronological priority accorded the scheduling of public time over private time. It can even be argued that the former is logically prior to the latter, since it is usually the relatively fixed and unalterable starting point in accordance with which most of the latter is organized. Doctors, for example, usually plan their vacations in accordance with the annual rotation schedule of their hospital. Also, like policemen and military personnel, they must refer to their weekly or monthly night-duty schedule before they can make any reservations for shows or plans with friends for particular evenings and weekends. With the sole exception of the category "special requests," the scheduling of their private time never precedes that of their public time.

The traditional conception of professional commitments is still preserved today not only in certain professions, but also in the upper echelons of almost any professional group. In other words, the degree of one's separability from one's occupational role is a function not only of one's occupation, but also of one's social status.

It is quite true that high-ranking officials exercise much tighter control over their social accessibility than do low-ranking personnel. In the same way that the rich, for example, use butlers, they use secretaries and receptionists to screen visitors, telephone calls, and mail, and it is usually quite difficult to get an appointment with them. As Schwartz has noted,

> In organizational life the privacy of the upper rank is insured structurally; it is necessary to proceed through the lieutenant stratum if the top level is to be reached. In contrast, the lower rank, enjoying less control over those who may have access to it, find their privacy more easily invaded.[26]

And yet, almost paradoxically, high social status usually involves a much less clear-cut segregation between the private and public spheres of one's life than does low social status.[27] This results from the fact that the definition of the professional commitments and responsibilities associated with high social status is far more diffuse than the definition of those associated with low social status.

In general, there seems to be a very close relationship between the level of specificity or diffuseness at which professional responsibilities and commitments are defined and the degree of rigidity or flexibility of the definition of their temporal boundaries. Thus, the fairly diffuse definition of the professional commitments and responsibilities of high-ranking officials usually implies a relatively flexible definition of their temporal boundaries. They are almost always held responsible and accountable. In contrast, the far more specific definition of the professional commitments and responsibilities of lower-echelon personnel usually entails a far more rigid definition of their temporal boundaries. In other words, all other things being equal, *flexibly defined temporal boundaries of professional commitments are usually associated with high status, and rigidly defined ones wtth low status.*

This implies that the time of the executive in any bureaucratic organization, for example, has a markedly more public quality to it than the time of hourly paid employees who work in the very same organization. The temporal boundaries of the responsibility of the director of an emergency room for his service, for instance, are rather fluid and quite flexibly defined, compared with those of any orderly who works there. It is precisely because his social status within the emergency room is significantly higher than that of the orderly that it would always be he, rather than the orderly, who will be called at home in the middle of the night in case something goes wrong there.

I shall soon discuss at length the temporal structure of nurses' professional commitments. That these commitments are temporally defined in a far more rigid manner than those of physicians is closely related to the fact that physicians are located much higher than nurses within the social hierarchy of the hospital. However, the patterns which I have just discussed are identifiable even *within* each professional group. Given the fact that continuity of coverage is intrinsically related to indispensability,[28] it is not surprising that head nurses, who are socially defined as far less dispensable than regular nurses—the former are held *personally* responsible for the units of which they are in charge—also present a much closer approximation of the ideal-typical model of the professional who is always "on the job." Thus, they usually arrive at work before most regular day nurses, often leave some time after them, and are generally far more accessible than the latter during their nonhospital time.

It should be noted that, given the markedly distinct temporal profile of the professional commitments associated with high social status, high-ranking officials very often arrive at work "early" and leave "late" for the purely symbolic purpose of displaying their high status! Ever-availability has indeed become a symbolic expression of being professionally committed, which, indirectly, is indicative of high status. Hence the rise of the "beeper" as a modern status symbol, not only in medicine. By carrying a "beeper," one appears to be more important. Woody Allen's friend's habit of calling his answering service every now and then during his nonwork time in order to report his current location (in *Play It Again, Sam*) is another colorful example of the close symbolic relationship between one's ever-availability and one's importance.

And yet, people of high social status and those who choose professional careers such as politics, medicine, or the priesthood are a relatively small minority and do not represent the typical modern work situation. All in all, it seems that ever-availability is a gradually dying phenomenon, the professional who is always "on the job" is increasingly becoming a rare species, and *it is the rigid manner in which professional commitments are temporally defined today that seems to be one of the key characteristics of modern social organization.*

That the relationship between modern individuals and their roles tends to be more specific than diffuse[29] also implies that it is essentially a *temporary* relationship. Consider, for example, the temporal rigidity of the modern definition of authority. Unlike "traditional" or "charismatic" authority, which involves the entire person who has it, modern "legal-rational" authority essentially involves only that part of him or her which is temporarily associated with the "office."[30]

As such, it necessarily involves *fixed temporal boundaries*. Whereas the authority of traditional or charismatic leaders such as Louis XIV, Nicholas II, Mao Tse-Tung, or Kwame Nkrumah, for example, was temporally bounded only by death or a "nonscheduled" political insurgence, the legal-rational authority of leaders such as Harold Wilson or Jimmy Carter has been procedurally bounded in a most rigid fashion by the fixed, "scheduled" end of their *term* in office. In fact, this is one of the most cherished prides of modern Western constitutional democracy.

The very same pattern characterizes the distinction between the authorities of the traditional master and the modern boss. Much insight into the symbolic significance of the growing "privatization" of time might be gained by contrasting, for example, the traditional power relations between masters and servants with the modern power relations between superiors and subordinates. The human dignity of the modern underling is symbolically expressed by the fact that, unlike the traditional servant, he or she is not *only* a subordinate! In the modern West, subordinates are never regarded as inferior by nature to their superiors. The essential partiality of their identification as relatively inferior to them is institutionally assured by the structural fact that their association with their occupational roles is actually temporary. It is temporally bounded in a most rigid manner by the fixed beginning and end of the working day and the workweek, and is periodically suspended. As Alexis de Tocqueville so ably described it,

> they only become so *for a time,* by covenant. Within the terms of this covenant the one is a servant, the other a master; beyond it they are two citizens.[31]

> In democracies the condition of domestic service does not degrade the character of those who enter upon it, because it is freely chosen and adopted *for a time only.*[32]

A most significant ideological change has taken place in the modern West. With the spread of the democratic belief in the universality of human dignity and given the increasing demand for privacy, it has become generally accepted that every person has a basic right to be socially inaccessible at certain times, for practical as well as symbolic reasons. Within the domain of work, the official recognition given to the "privatization" of some parts of individuals' time—that is, to their right to periodically dissociate themselves from their occupational role and be professionally inaccessible at times—is most evident from the institutionalization of "paid time off" as one of the most common forms of employees' fringe benefits. Hence the introduction of paid nonwork time periods such as annual holidays, vacations, sick leaves, jury leaves, voting time, coffee and rest breaks, meal periods, and wash-up time.[33] (Interestingly enough, like the traditional conception of private time in general, these typically modern institutions are essentially defined in a traditional manner as being away from something, that is, as a residual category. That the word "vacation" in itself derives from *"vacuus,"* which is the Latin word for "empty," speaks for itself.)

I am actually talking here about the right of modern individuals to claim control over their social accessibility during their private time as a sort of personal possession. This point was driven home to me one day when a supermarket employee whom I asked— apparently a couple of minutes past the official end of her workday —to weigh some vegetables for me, made the following comment: "I hope you appreciate this. It's *my* time!"

Given the modern conception of time as a commodity, which I have already discussed in the second chapter, it is only natural that one of the most common ways of legitimately denying individuals the right to claim control over their social accessibility during their private time would be to *buy* it from them. (I once heard an employee remarking that she had told her boss that, while he could not own her, he could nevertheless "rent" her.) Working time may be regarded as time which employers buy from their employees.[34] By buying it, they gain the right to transform it from a private time period to a public one. It is within this context that we ought to consider the rise of what is certainly one of the most typical modern capitalist institutions—the *time wage.*[35]

The professional accessibility of modern individuals is institutionally restricted to the temporal boundaries of the part of their time which they have "sold." Beyond those boundaries, they have the right to refuse to be actively associated and identified with their occupational role.

That there is a strong ideological resistance in the modern West to the notion that people can be forced to work *beyond their "regular hours" of work* is quite evident from the etymology of a term which refers to a typically modern phenomenon—*"overtime."* As an American legislator sponsoring a bill which would prohibit employers from firing or even disciplining employees who refuse to work overtime recently asked: "Should individuals' time be ruled by the large corporations that they work for, or should people have the basic right to live their own lives, on their own time?"[36]

Obviously, the more private the individual's time is, the more expensive it is. When employees agree to work overtime, not only must their employers pay them—or give them some "compensatory time" off some other working day—for having "sold" them their right over their time; they must also pay them at a higher rate than usual—"time and a half" or even "double time"—for having "surrendered" to them the more private parts of it![37]

For precisely the same reason, employees also get paid at a considerably higher rate than usual for working evenings or nights. Here again we encounter the qualitative conception of time, which—as demonstrated earlier with regard to the fundamental distinction between the Sabbath and regular weekdays—puts a particular emphasis on man's sociocultural ability to distinguish between the qualities of time periods which are absolutely identical from a mathematical standpoint. From a purely quantitative standpoint, night, evening, and day shifts are usually interchangeable, as are "regular" and "overtime" hours. However, given the general sociofugality of nighttime, the qualitative distinction between them in terms of privacy and publicity is nevertheless officially recognized.

Note also that, when they are asked to work overtime or on a night shift, employees usually expect to be notified enough in advance. This is indicative of their particular sensitivity about having due respect symbolically displayed toward their private time. Generally speaking, it is also largely employees' demand to be able to plan their private time enough in advance that accounts for the particular efforts which managers usually make to design work schedules as early as possible.

In their constant efforts to improve the working conditions of the modern individual, labor unions have always put much emphasis on accomplishments such as the shortening of the workday and the workweek or the increase in the number of annual vacation days. Others have noted the introduction of flexible working hours as a most significant promoter of individualism.[38]

And yet, "flexitime" involves a change only in the degree of rigidity or flexibility of the temporal location of the boundaries between the private and public spheres of life. Far more significant, I believe, is the change in the degree of rigidity or flexibility of these boundaries themselves! If I had to point out the single most significant temporal feature of the modern work situation which symbolically represents the official recognition of the modern individual's right to be professionally inaccessible at times, I would definitely point out the *temporal rigidity of modern work schedules.* I believe it to be one of the key structural characteristics of modern social organization. The temporal rigidfication of work has also been pointed out by Wilbert Moore as one of the most significant characteristics of industrialization:

> The transition from a temporally lax and variable work pattern to a *tightly timed and temporally recompensed work schedule* is one of the major changes in attitude required of the newly recruited worker in underdeveloped areas undergoing economic modernization.[39]

One of the most significant aspects of the "rationalization" of social life in modern Western civilization is the increasing *bureaucratization of professional commitments,* which is clearly manifested through the rigidification of their temporal boundaries. There is an important temporal dimension to the bureaucratic segmentation of the modern individual into a "person" and an incumbent of a particular occupational role. It is clearly seen in the fact that *the partiality of our involvement in our occupational roles and our association with them is very often defined in temporal terms.*

Most occupational commitments today are officially defined in such terms as a number of hours a day or a number of days a week, not to mention, of course, the common bureaucratic distinction between "full-time" and "part-time" employees, a typically modern phenomenon.[40] That so many wage earners today are being paid by units of time such as the hour or the day also reflects, as well as reinforces, the temporal rigidity of their work schedules and the partiality of their professional commitments. Even that part of the year during which we are not actively associated with our occupational roles, namely, the vacation, is nevertheless defined primarily in temporal terms. Thus, we may be free to spend our vacations wherever and with whomever we like, yet we are nevertheless officially restricted as to when we can take them and how long they may last.

The commitments and the responsibilities which are involved in most modern occupational roles are officially restricted to those public time periods to which the participation of their incumbents is institutionally confined. As becomes a pronouncedly bureaucratic age, the time of modern individuals is rigidly segmented into parts during which they are officially supposed and expected to be professionally accessible, and others during which they are not. As L. Coser has pointed out,

> Thus, in modern society, for example, the amount of time that an individual legitimately owes to his employer is normatively and even legally established; this makes it possible for him to have time for his family or other non-occupational associations.[41]

The association of modern individuals with their occupational roles is essentially partial, since it is institutionally confined to a rigidly defined period of time. This explains why many job descriptions today are extremely rigid in explicitly specifying the temporal boundaries of the professional commitments entailed in the job. The rigidity of these boundaries derives from the fact that they are usually *fixed* in time, being officially circumscribed by the calendar and the clock (for example, "a five-day, nine-to-five job with a three-week annual vacation").

The professional commitments of modern individuals are usually not expected to transcend the temporal boundaries which are supposed to separate them as "persons" from their occupational roles. With relatively few exceptions, most of which I have discussed earlier, we are not always "on the job" and, outside the temporal boundaries of certain public periods, we may be quite legitimately professionally inaccessible.

I propose that these time periods be called *"duty periods,"*[42] since their boundaries are actually the boundaries between the states of being "on duty" and "off duty." I regard the popular bureaucratic distinction between being "on" and "off" duty—a typical characteristic of a civilization which emphasizes so much the bureaucratic distinction between "person" and "role"—primarily as a temporal distinction (actually, as a particular instance of the distinction between public time and private time which pertains to the domain of work). And, indeed, from a social organizational standpoint, the temporal definition of the boundaries of most modern professional commitments is definitely prior to—and far more binding than—say, their spatial definition. The professional commitments of modern individuals are defined primarily by the temporal boundaries of some "duty periods." Outside those boundaries, we are usually considered to be off duty, even if we are physically present at our working place. Even when taken at one's working place, "breaks" such as the office coffee break and lunch break are classic examples of some institutionalized forms of temporary suspension of individuals' association with their occupational roles. I shall soon discuss some other occasions whereby persons who are "at work" from a spatial point of view may nevertheless legitimately decline any professional responsibilities on the grounds that they are already off, or not yet on, duty.

The bureaucratization of professional commitments is most characteristic of work situations such as those of bank tellers, assembly-line workers, or secretaries. And yet, it is by no means restricted to them. Consider, for example, the bureaucratization of a traditionally "charismatic" profession like teaching. The institutionalization of conference days which are deliberately scheduled to take place at the expense of teaching time is a typically modern arrangement designed to protect teachers' private time. Along the same lines, consider also the phenomenon of university professors who are not expected to assume any teaching-related responsibilities—even when they are actually on campus—while on official "leaves."

In fact, the bureaucratization of professional commitments has already penetrated even the most sacred domains of life. Let us explore, for example, the temporal structure of modern professional commitments within a domain such as health care, where acute problems of life and death are a daily matter. Within such a domain one would expect to find at least some approximation of a total identity between an occupational role and its incumbent. If professional commitments are bureaucratized in such a domain, it would probably be most difficult to find any realm of social life where they are not.

I have discussed earlier the medical profession as a classic case of an institutionalized attempt to approximate ever-availability and a total identity between an occupational role and its incumbent. And yet, even in the case of the medical profession we can already detect some bureaucratization of professional commitments in the recognition—even though so far only semiofficial—of some notion of the individual's right to periodically withdraw into professional inaccessibility.

To begin with, an increasing number of therapeutic relationships today are restricted to outpatient care, whether in clinics or emergency rooms. Within that context, the doctor-patient relationship is relatively *discontinuous,* in striking contrast to inpatient hospital care. Most outpatient clinics operate on a five-day, nine-to-five basis, as a result of which many physicians' duty periods are durationally rigid, being bounded by leaving times which are fixed at particular times of the day.

Consider also the typically modern phenomenon of medical group practice. It was invented by private physicians deliberately so that they could ensure the privacy of their time off from the clinic, while still being able to comply with the moral imperative of providing continuous coverage.[43] Sharing their responsibility for any particular patient with other physicians—or even with other health professionals, as in the case of the Health Maintenance Organization—allows physicians to provide continuous medical coverage of patients without sacrificing their claim for some professional inaccessibility.

With the decline of private practice—and of personal responsibility in general[44]—in medicine, it is not surprising that the physician who makes house calls in the middle of the night is increasingly becoming a rare species. The admiration which some young residents, interns, and medical students express for senior staff physicians who do come to the hospital on weekends or holidays when they are needed for consultation only indicates that the physician's ever-availability should by no means be taken for granted today. This also applies to nighttime, as Murray Melbin has pointed out: "Night nurses decide not to wake up the doctor on duty because he gets annoyed at being disturbed for minor problems."[45]

Such caution is also displayed by other physicians. Whenever house officers encounter problems or difficulties in the middle of the night and feel the urge to call their attending physicians at home for consultation, they always make sure first that this is justifiable as an emergency and usually offer some apology for having intruded during nonhospital time. Moreover, interns usually think twice before waking up in the middle of the night the resident who is on call at the hospital, even though he or she is officially supposed to be accessible all night! Their caution is definitely reinforced by residents' joking comments such as, "If there is any emergency, don't hesitate *not* to wake me up," which, though made as jokes, certainly cannot be understood only as such. Finally, note that physicians themselves also admit—even though unofficially—that the practice of turning one's "beeper" off under some circumstances is not that uncommon among them.

And yet—ideologically, at least—the medical profession still adheres to the traditional conception of the professional as inseparable from his or her occupational role, and many people still expect physicians to be always "on the job." The bureaucratization of professional commitments within the domain of health care is certainly far more evident in the case of the nursing profession.

The comparison between the medical profession and the nursing profession in terms of the temporal structure of the commitments they involve is striking. Since both professionals operate within the very same organizational settings and activate their commitments and responsibilities vis-à-vis the very same patients, it is quite clear that any fundamental differences between them in terms of the temporal structure of their professional accessibility can be attributed solely to differences between their respective definitions as "professionals."

In the same way that the degree of temporal rigidity or flexibility in defining professional commitments can help us to distinguish among various status rankings within a stratification system, it can also be most helpful to us in identifying and differentiating various occupational roles as well as professional ethics. The relative rigidity or flexibility of the definition of the temporal boundaries of professional commitments and responsibilities may point to fundamental differences in ethical codes among various professions. As I shall soon show, it may also point to the coexistence of several different professional ethics within one and the same organization.

The contrast between the degree of rigidity or flexibility of the temporal boundaries of nurses' and physicians' professional commitments supports Durkheim's claim that, in modern, highly differentiated society, the occupational group constitutes a most significant locus of morality.[46] As I shall now demonstrate, while ever-availability is definitely among the major moral imperatives which characterize the medical profession, the nursing profession does not even pretend to regard it as a binding ethical principle.

When contrasted temporally with the role of physician, the role of nurse is impressive sociologically not only because of the considerably shorter workday and workweek involved, but also because of the relatively rigid definition of the temporal boundaries of professional commitment and accessibility. One of the most significant structural characteristics of the organization of nursing coverage in the hospital, for example, is the temporal rigidity of nurses' duty periods. This rigidity pertains both to the length of these duty periods and to their temporal location within the daily cycle. It is built into the nurses' coverage system through the institutionalization of *fixed arrival and leaving times* which constitute the official boundaries of their professional commitments as nurses. Generally speaking, unlike physicians, nurses stop working not upon having completed their daily work assignments, but, rather, when the clock indicates the end of their shift. Their "report," which is a highly ritualized ceremony that dramatizes the acts of getting into and out of the occupational role of nurse and of assuming and relinquishing professional responsibilities, is institutionally scheduled for fixed times of the day and is usually not postponed by more than a few minutes, even when a service is particularly busy.

The particular rigidity of the temporal boundaries of nurses' professional commitments derives from the fact that they are circumscribed by the clock. Ending one's work in accordance with the clock obviously entails more temporal rigidity than doing it according to the completion of tasks. Moreover, it is also far more artificial. In order to appreciate the artificial basis of the temporal rigidity of nurses' coverage systems, note that not only are the boundaries of their shifts fixed in time, but they are usually also designated in conventionally rounded off temporal formulations. Thus, nurses shifts usually begin and end on the hour rather than at times such as 4:14 or 8:37. This also implies that their length is designated in rounded-off terms of complete hours rather than, say, in time periods of seven hours and forty-two minutes.

Unlike physicians, nurses are paid by the hour, since their professional obligations are officially defined in terms of number of working hours per week. Their time is officially segmented into rigidly defined periods during which they are supposed to be accessible in their capacity as nurses and others during which they may be professionally inaccessible. They are expected to be actively associated with their occupational role only within the temporal boundaries of their duty periods. Outside those boundaries, they are officially relieved from having to assume any professional responsibilities.

The social world of the nurse is generally characterized by a most rigid temporal segregation of privacy and publicity, that is, by a sharp division into private and public time periods. Nurses' time outside the hospital has a far more private quality to it than that of physicians. Unlike physicians, nurses do not carry "beepers" with them, they are not expected to leave instructions as to where and how they can be reached on evenings and weekends, and it is most unusual for them to be called at home for consultation. In short, they are well assured that, once they leave the hospital grounds, the privacy of their off-duty time will be respected.

Whenever nurses are asked by their head nurse or nursing supervisor to work overtime, it is officially understood that they have the right to refuse. If they do agree to it, they get paid at a considerably higher rate than usual, as if to be adequately compensated for having relinquished their claim over some of their private time. (Since nighttime is generally recognized as having a far more private quality than daytime, nurses also get paid at a higher hourly rate than usual for working on the evening and night shifts.)

Furthermore, they expect to be approached about working overtime or on the evening or night shift as far in advance as possible. Not only is it quite impractical not to allow a nurse enough lead time regarding working overtime—for otherwise she might make in the meantime some other plans for that particular evening; it is also considered rather impolite, since nurses are particularly sensitive about having due respect paid their claims to their private time. Thus, even though there are no official rules which specify explicitly how long in advance nurses should call in when sick, most of them seem to agree about a certain temporal threshold beyond which calling in sick is regarded as inappropriately late, since it does not allow those of them who are asked to work overtime enough lead time. Nurses usually get annoyed at any nurse who violates or disregards this informal rule of courtesy, since such behavior actually shows a lack of respect for the private time of the fellow nurses who have to cover for their ailing colleague. Such a symbolic display of respect is expected even by nurses who are on call at home. Despite the fact that they do get paid—even though at a relatively low hourly rate—for just staying at home (in case they might actually be called in), they nevertheless expect to be given some advance notice when they are called in, if only for symbolic reasons. (The situation of being at home on call is a very good example of a most delicate combination of actual privacy and potential publicity. As such, it is indicative of the fact that private time and public time do not constitute a mutually exclusive dichotomy and are, indeed, only the ideal-typical polarities of a hypothetical continuum.)

Interestingly enough, on the very rare occasions when physicians do refuse to see patients beyond a certain hour, they are harshly criticized not only by their colleagues, but by nurses as well! Nurses' own professional ethics, however, allow them to legitimately abstain from assuming any professional responsibilities beyond the official temporal boundaries of their duty periods. If a nurse has not received a report yet or if she has already finished giving hers, she is officially considered to be off duty, even if she is physically present at her own service. Nurses often arrive at their service some time before their shift begins (so as not to be late), being well assured that no one expects them to start working right away. It may happen, too, that a nurse will be sitting at her station some time past the end of her shift, yet remind anyone who asks her to do something that she is already off duty. (I should add, though, that this rigidity does not apply to head nurses and that such instances are far more common in emergency rooms, where the patient turnover is considerably more rapid and staff-patient relationships, therefore, are far less continuous and personal, than in inpatient units.) The nurses' report is a sort of closing ceremony, and the period which immediately follows it—as well as the period which immediately precedes it, as far as arriving nurses are concerned—has the same ambiguous quality which, as shown in the previous chapter, seems to be so characteristic of the liminal periods around the temporal boundaries which separate the sacred from the profane domain. Thus, nurses may be legitimately required to stay in the hospital even after their shift has ended and their report has been delivered, but only for the purpose of completing tasks which are supposed to have been completed during the duty period and which, therefore, sort of "belong" to it. Nurses might be required, for example, to stay in the hospital some time past having completed their report in order to finish writing up progress notes on each of their patients, a task they must perform before leaving for the day. (Unless a shift is unusually quiet, it is almost impossible to finish writing up all one's progress notes—which, obviously, must be as updated as possible—before report time. Since reports may be quite long, it is not unusual that a nurse would leave the hospital only about an hour, or even an hour and a half, past the official end of her shift.) On such occasions, however, they are clearly not expected to fulfill and assume any other nursing duties and responsibilities.

That nurses often arrive at work some fifteen or twenty minutes ahead of time only to sit at their station without even glancing at a bed or a chart—because they are not on duty yet—clearly demonstrates that even pure concern and motivation can be bureaucratized. That these are artificially regulated in such a rigid fashion by the clock implies that they cannot be fully accounted for on a psychological level alone.[47] The bureaucratization of professional commitments is particularly impressive in the case of a profession like nursing, since it implies its having already penetrated one of the most sacred domains of our life, namely, health care. If commitments, concern, and motivation can be bureaucratized in a domain where literally vital problems are a daily matter, is there any domain of social life where they cannot be?

Given the symbolism which is still associated with ever-avail-ability, it is hardly surprising that many modern "professionals" regard such typically bureaucratic behavioral patterns as quite contemptible. Many physicians, for example, regard being paid by the hour as professionally demeaning and look down on "nonprofessionals" or "paraprofessionals," who very often refuse to work beyond their "regular hours." From a Marxist viewpoint, a situation in which a secretary leaves her desk promptly at 5:00 P.M., even if she is in the middle of doing some work, is a classic manifestation of the alienation of modern labor, for whom "doing" is distinctly dissociated from "being."

And yet, it is precisely this aspect of bureaucratization that protects the modern individual from being entirely "swallowed" by what L. Coser has called "greedy institutions."[48] It is precisely the rigidity of the temporal boundaries of our professional commitments that allows us to claim some privacy. It is precisely the low-status technician, orderly, secretary, or aide whose private time is institutionally protected far more than that of any physician. In short, the very same institutions that are directly responsible, as I have demonstrated throughout this book, for much of the rigidification of our life—namely, the schedule and the calendar—can also be seen as being among the foremost liberators of the modern individual!

Notes

Introduction

1. Eviatar Zerubavel, *Patterns of Time in Hospital Life* (Chicago and London: University of Chicago Press, 1979).

2. Ibid., p. xvii.

3. Eviatar Zerubavel, "The French Republican Calendar: A Case Study in the Sociology of Time," *American Sociological Review* 42 (1977): 868–77; Eviatar Zerubavel, "Private Time and Public Time: The Temporal Structure of Social Accessibility and Professional Commitments," *Social Forces* 58 (1979): 38–58; Eviatar Zerubavel, "The Benedictine Ethic and the Modern Spirit of Scheduling: On Schedules and Social Life," *Sociological Inquiry* 50 (1980): 157–69.

4. Max Weber, *The Methodology of the Social Sciences* (New York: Free Press, 1949), pp. 55–61, 67–68, 90.

5. Max Weber, *The Protestant Ethic and the Spirit of Capitalism* (New York: Charles Scribner's Sons, 1958); Georg Simmel, *The Philosophy of Money* (London: Routledge & Kegan Paul, 1978).

6. Lewis Coser, *Greedy Institutions* (New York: Free Press, 1974).

Chapter One

1. Eviatar Zerubavel, "Timetables and Scheduling: On the Social Organization of Time," *Sociological Inquiry* 46 (1976): 88–90. See also David Kantor and William Lehr, *Inside the Family* (San Francisco: Jossey-Bass, 1975), pp. 82–86; Robert H. Lauer, "Temporality and Social Change: The Case of 19th Century China and Japan," *Sociological Quarterly* 14 (1973): 452.

2. Lewis Mumford, *Technics and Civilization* (New York: Harbinger, 1963), p. 269. On the indispensability of regularity to a machine-based industrial economy, see also F. W. Dillistone, *Traditional Symbols and the Contemporary World* (London: Epworth, 1973), p. 109.

3. Peter L. Berger and Thomas Luckmann, *The Social Construction of Reality* (Garden City: Anchor, 1967), pp. 27–28.

4. Julius A. Roth, *Timetables* (Indianapolis: Bobbs-Merrill, 1963).

5. On the temporal structure of meals in general, see Mary Douglas, "Deciphering a Meal," in *Implicit Meanings* (London: Routledge & Kegan Paul, 1975), pp. 255–57.

6. Barry Schwartz, "Waiting, Exchange, and Power: The Distribution of Time in Social Systems," *American Journal of Sociology* 79 (1974): 841–71; "Queues, Priorities, and Social Process," *Social Psychology* 41 (1978): 3–12.

7. Harriet A. Zuckerman, "Patterns of Name Ordering among Authors of Scientific Papers: A Study of Social Symbolism and Its Ambiguity," *American Journal of Sociology* 74 (1968): 276–91.

8. Irenäus Eibl-Eibesfeldt, *Ethology* (New York: Holt, Rinehart & Winston, 1970), pp. 184–90.

9. Harold T. Christensen and George R. Carpenter, "Timing Patterns in the Development of Sexual Intimacy: An Attitudinal Report on Three Modern Western Societies," *Marriage and Family Living* 24 (1962): 30–35.

10. Stanford M. Lyman and Marvin B. Scott, "On the Time Track," in *A Sociology of the Absurd* (New York: Appleton-Century-Crofts, 1970), pp. 195–96; Roth, *Timetables*, p. 81.

11. Ray L. Birdwhistell, "Sequence and Tempo," in *Kinesics and Context* (Philadelphia: University of Pennsylvania Press, 1970), p. 159.

12. Ibid.

13. Alvin Toffler, *Future Shock* (New York: Bantam, 1971), p. 43.

14. Avery Sharron, "Time and Space in Oral and Print Communication Systems: A Note on Musical Improvisation," presented at the Conference on Time and Temporal Structures, Urbana-Champaign, March 1980.

15. Lyman and Scott, "On the Time Track," p. 198.

16. C. Neil Bull, "Chronology: The Field of Social Time," *Journal of Leisure Research* 10 (1978): 294.

17. Murray Wax, "Ancient Judaism and the Protestant Ethic," *American Journal of Sociology* 65 (1960): 452.

18. E. E. Evans-Pritchard, "Nuer Time-Reckoning," *Africa* 12 (1939): 201.

19. Wilbert E. Moore, *Man, Time, and Society* (New York: John Wiley, 1963), p. 25.

20. Radhakamal Mukerjee, "Time, Technics, and Society," *Sociology and Social Research* 27 (1943): 261.

21. Roth, *Timetables*.

22. Wax, "Ancient Judaism," p. 452.

23. John Horton, "Time and Cool People," *Trans-action* 4, no. 5 (1967): 5–12.

24. Bull, "Chronology," pp. 290–93; Emile Durkheim, *The Elementary Forms of the Religious Life* (New York: Free Press, 1965), pp. 23, 32n, 245–51, 391, 488; Amos Hawley, *Human Ecology* (New York: Ronald, 1950), pp. 288–316; Henri Hubert and Marcel Mauss, "Etude Sommaire de la Représentation du Temps dans la Religion et la Magie," *Mélanges d'Histoire des Religions* (Paris: Librairies Félix Alcan et Guillaumin Réunies, 1909), pp. 189–229; Jiri Kolaja, *Social System and Time and Space* (Pittsburgh: Duquesne University Press, 1969); Marcel Mauss, *Seasonal Variations of the Eskimo* (London: Routledge & Kegan Paul, 1979), pp. 79–80; Murray Melbin, "City Rhythms," in *The Study of Time III,* ed. Julius T. Fraser et al. (New York: Springer-Verlag, 1978), pp. 444–65; William Michelson, "Some Like It Hot: Social Participation and Environmental Use as Functions of the Season," *American Journal of Sociology* 76 (1971): 1072–83; John R. Seeley et al., *Crestwood Heights* (New York: Science Editions, 1963), pp. 63–85; Pitirim A. Sorokin, *Social and Cultural Dynamics,* vol. 4 (New York: Bedminster, 1941); Eviatar Zerubavel, *Patterns of Time in Hospital Life* (Chicago and London: University of Chicago Press, 1979).

25. Emile Durkheim, *The Division of Labor in Society* (New York: Free Press, 1964), pp. 257ff.; *Suicide* (New York: Free Press, 1966), pp. 198–202.

26. For some earlier sociological attempts to apply the musical concept of "tempo" to the analysis of rates of recurrence of periodic social activity, see Gladys Engel-Frisch, "Some Neglected Temporal Aspects of Human Ecology," *Social Forces* 22 (1943): 43–47; Hawley, *Human Ecology,* pp. 288–316; William R. Rosengren and Spencer DeVault, "The Sociology of Time and Space in an Obstetrical Hospital," in *The Hospital in Modern Society,* ed. Eliot Freidson (New York: Free Press, 1963), pp. 266–92; Sorokin, *Social and Cultural Dynamics,* vol. 4; Zerubavel, "Timetables and Scheduling," p. 90.

27. Sorokin, *Social and Cultural Dynamics,* vol. 4, pp. 542–51; *Sociocultural Causality, Space, Time* (Durham: Duke University Press, 1943), pp. 190–97.

28. Zerubavel, *Patterns of Time in Hospital Life,* pp. 28–30.

29. Mukerjee, "Time, Technics, and Society," p. 259.

30. Mumford, *Technics and Civilization,* pp. 197–98; Georg Simmel, *The Philosophy of Money* (London: Routledge & Kegan Paul, 1978), pp. 485–91.

31. Kevin Lynch, *What Time Is This Place?* (Cambridge: MIT Press, 1972), p. 119. See also George B. Dantzig and Thomas L. Saaty, *Compact City* (San Francisco: W. H. Freeman, 1973), pp. 194–96.

32. Mumford, *Technics and Civilization,* p. 271.

33. Bruno Bettelheim, *The Informed Heart* (London: Paladin, 1970), p. 131.

34. Dorothy Nelkin, "Unpredictability and Life Style in a Migrant Labor Camp," *Social Problems* 17 (1970): 472–87.

35. Toffler, *Future Shock,* pp. 42–43.

36. On "socially expected durations," see also Robert K. Merton, *Social Theory and Social Structure* (New York: Free Press, 1968), pp. 365–66; *Sociological Ambivalence and Other Essays* (New York: Free Press, 1976), pp. 24–25, 164–65.

37. Elijah Anderson, *A Place on the Corner* (Chicago and London: University of Chicago Press, 1978), p. 63.

38. Zerubavel, *Patterns of Time in Hospital Life.*

39. Ibid., pp. 82, 110–22.

40. Dalton Trumbo, *Johnny Got His Gun* (New York: Bantam, 1970), pp. 126–43.

41. Quoted in Lawrence Wright, *Clockwork Man* (London: Elek, 1968), p. 147.

42. F. H. Colson, *The Week* (Cambridge: Cambridge University Press, 1926), p. 64.

43. *Tractate Shabbath* 69b. Unless otherwise specified, all Tractate references apply to sections of *The Babylonian Talmud* (London: Soncino, 1938).

44. *Tractate Megillah* 13a.

45. Sholem Asch (also spelled Ash), *Kiddush Ha-Shem* (Philadelphia: Jewish Publication Society of America, 1926), pp. 12–19.

46. Daniel Defoe, *The Life and Strange Surprising Adventures of Robinson Crusoe of York, Mariner* (London: Oxford University Press, 1972), p. 64.

47. Mark Zborowski and Elizabeth Herzog, *Life Is with People* (New York: Schocken, 1962), p. 61.

48. Colson, *Week,* pp. 62–63.

49. Hans Christian Andersen, *Andersen's Fairy Tales* (New York: Grosset & Dunlop, 1978), p. 293.

50. For a classic discussion of this, see Kurt Koffka, *Principles of Gestalt Psychology* (New York: Harcourt & Brace, 1935), pp. 177–210.

51. Maurice Merleau-Ponty, *Phenomenology of Perception* (New York: Humanities Press, 1962).

52. Harold Garfinkel, *Studies in Ethnomethodology* (Englewood Cliffs: Prentice-Hall, 1967).

53. Ibid., pp. 79–94; R. Abelson et al., *Theories of Cognitive Consistency* (Chicago: Rand McNally, 1968); Peter McHugh, *Defining the Situation* (Indianapolis: Bobbs-Merrill, 1968).

54. Benjamin Lee Whorf, "Science and Linguistics," in *Language, Thought, and Reality,* ed. John B. Carroll (Cambridge: MIT Press, 1956), p. 209.

55. Gregory Bateson, "Toward a Theory of Schizophrenia," in *Steps*

to *An Ecology of Mind* (New York: Ballantine, 1972), pp. 201–27. Durkheim, *The Rules of Sociological Method* (New York: Free Press, 1964); *Suicide* (New York: Free Press, 1966). Sigmund Freud, *The Psychopathology of Everyday Life* (New York: W. W. Norton, 1960). Garfinkel, *Studies in Ethnomethodology.*

56. Erving Goffman, "Normal Appearances," in *Relations in Public* (New York: Harper Colophon, 1972), pp. 300–301.

57. Trumbo, *Johnny Got His Gun*, p. 155 (italics added).

58. Goffman, "Normal Appearances," p. 241.

59. Hadley Cantril, *The Invasion from Mars* (New York: Harper Torchbooks, 1966), pp. 91–95.

60. Chaim Nachman Bialik, "The Short Friday," in *A Treasury of Jewish Humor*, ed. Nathan Ausubel (Garden City: Doubleday, 1956), pp. 59–73.

61. Ibid., p. 70.

62. Zborowski and Herzog, *Life Is with People*, p. 363.

63. Bialik, "Short Friday," p. 70.

64. Ibid., p. 71.

65. Ibid., p. 72.

Chapter Two

1. Emile Durkheim, *The Elementary Forms of the Religious Life* (New York: Free Press, 1965), p. 23.

2. Reinhard Bendix, *Max Weber* (Garden City: Anchor, 1962), pp. 315–18; R. W. Southern, *The Making of the Middle Ages* (New Haven: Yale University Press, 1953), pp. 154–69; Max Weber, *The Protestant Ethic and the Spirit of Capitalism* (New York: Charles Scribner's Sons, 1958).

3. Harold A. Innis, *The Bias of Communication* (Toronto: University of Toronto Press, 1951), p. 72.

4. Lewis Mumford, *Technics and Civilization* (New York: Harbinger, 1963), pp. 13–14.

5. Bendix, *Max Weber*, p. 318.

6. Lawrence Wright, *Clockwork Man* (London: Elek, 1968), p. 153.

7. Dom David Knowles, *The Monastic Order in England* (Cambridge: Cambridge University Press, 1949), p. 4.

8. *The Rule of Saint Benedict*, trans. Justin McCann (London: Sheed & Ward, 1970), ch. 15.

9. Ibid., chs. 8, 10, 41.

10. Knowles, *The Monastic Order*, pp. 456, 466; Wright, *Clockwork Man*, p. 41.

11. *Rule*, ch. 13. See also ch. 18.

12. Ibid., chs. 11, 41; Wright, *Clockwork Man*, p. 41.

13. *Rule*, chs. 18, 35, 38.

14. Ibid., ch. 48.
15. Ibid., ch. 8.
16. Ibid., ch. 41.
17. Ibid., chs. 8, 10, 16.
18. Mumford, *Technics and Civilization*, p. 16.
19. *Rule*, ch. 47.
20. Ibid., ch. 43.
21. Ibid.
22. Ibid., chs. 47, 50.
23. Ibid., ch. 43.
24. Ibid., ch. 10.
25. Ibid., ch. 11.
26. Ibid., ch. 13.
27. Ibid., ch. 18.
28. F. H. Colson, *The Week* (Cambridge: Cambridge University Press, 1926), pp. 43–49; Hutton Webster, *Rest Days* (New York: Macmillan, 1916), pp. 217–18.
29. Alfred M. Schroll, *Benedictine Monasticism as Reflected in the Warnefrid-Hildemar Commentaries on the Rule* (New York: Columbia University Press, 1941), p. 108; G. J. Whitrow, *The Nature of Time* (New York: Holt, Rinehart & Winston, 1972), p. 69.
30. *Rule*, chs. 8, 10, 41.
31. Mumford, *Technics and Civilization*, p. 14 .
32. John Beckmann, *A History of Inventions, Discoveries, and Origins*, vol. 1 (London: Henry G. Bohn, 1846), p. 349; Sebastian de Grazia, *Of Time, Work, and Leisure* (Garden City: Anchor, 1964), p. 40; H. Alan Lloyd, "Timekeepers—an Historical Sketch," in *The Voices of Time*, ed. Julius Thomas Fraser (New York: Braziller, 1966), pp. 389–91; Marshall McLuhan, *Understanding Media* (New York: Signet, 1964), p. 135; Mumford, *Technics and Civilization*, p. 13; J. D. North, "Monasticism and the First Mechanical Clocks," in *The Study of Time II*, ed. Julius Thomas Fraser and N. Lawrence (New York: Springer-Verlag, 1975), pp. 382–83; Wright, *Clockwork Man*, pp. 56–58.
33. *Rule*, chs. 9, 11, 12, 13, 18.
34. Ibid., ch. 11.
35. Henri Hubert and Marcel Mauss, "Etude Sommaire de la Représentation du Temps dans la Religion et la Magie," in *Mélanges d'Histoire des Religions* (Paris: Libraries Félix Alcan et Guillaumin Réunies, 1909), pp. 189–229; Pitirim Sorokin, *Social and Cultural Dynamics*, vol. 4 (New York: Bedminster, 1941), pp. 542–51; Sorokin, *Sociocultural Causality, Space, Time* (Durham: Duke University Press, 1943); Pitirim Sorokin and Robert K. Merton, "Social Time: A Methodological and Functional Analysis," *American Journal of Sociology* 42 (1937): 615–29; Eviatar Zerubavel, *Patterns of Time in Hospital Life* (Chicago and London: University of Chicago Press, 1979).

36. *Rule,* chs. 47, 48, 50.

37. Georg Lukács, *History and Class Consciousness* (Cambridge: MIT Press, 1971), pp. 83ff.; Karl Marx, *Capital,* vol. 1 (New York: International Publishers, 1967), pp. 71–83.

38. Peter L. Berger and Thomas Luckmann, *The Social Construction of Reality* (Garden City: Anchor, 1967), p. 89. See also pp. 134–45.

39. Peter S. Beagle, *The Last Unicorn* (New York: Ballantine, 1968), p. 199.

40. Emile Durkheim, *The Rules of Sociological Method* (New York: Free Press, 1964), p. 3.

41. W. Lloyd Warner, *The Family of God* (New Haven: Yale University Press, 1961), pp. 367–70.

42. After writing this, I learned that the Israeli government had recently introduced an interval of a few days between those two days!

43. Wright, *Clockwork Man,* p. 213 (italics added).

44. Mumford, *Technics and Civilization,* pp. 269–70.

45. Durkheim, *Rules of Sociological Method,* p. 6.

46. Barry Schwartz, "Notes on the Sociology of Sleep," *Sociological Quarterly* 11 (1970): 485–99.

47. Quoted in Wright, *Clockwork Man,* p. 29.

48. Joost Meerloo, "The Time Sense in Psychiatry," in *The Voices of Time,* ed. Julius Thomas Fraser (New York: Braziller, 1966), p. 249; Wright, *Clockwork Man,* p. 213.

49. George Woodcock, "The Tyranny of the Clock," *Politics* 1 (1944): 265–66.

50. Emile Durkheim, *Suicide* (New York: Free Press, 1966), pp. 246–54.

51. Erving Goffman, "On the Characteristics of Total Institutions," in *Asylums* (Garden City: Anchor Books, 1961), pp. 3–124.

52. Talcott Parsons, *The Social System* (New York: Free Press, 1951), p. 302 (italics added).

53. *Rule,* p. 4 (italics added).

54. Ibid., ch. 18.

55. Ibid., ch. 22 (italics added).

56. Ibid., ch. 48.

57. Ibid., ch. 8.

58. Ricardo J. Quinones, *The Renaissance Discovery of Time* (Cambridge: Harvard University Press, 1972), p. 10 (italics added).

59. John R. Hall, *The Ways Out* (Boston: Routledge & Kegan Paul, 1978), pp. 40–42.

60. Richard Baxter, *A Christian Directory* (London: Robert White, 1673), p. 281.

61. Ibid., pp. 288–92.

62. Quoted in Weber, *The Protestant Ethic and the Spirit of Capitalism,* p. 48.

63. Ibid., p. 50.

64. For a general historical survey of the relations between time and industry, see E. P. Thompson, "Time, Work-Discipline, and Industrial Capitalism," *Past and Present* 38 (1967): 56–97.

65. George Soule, *What Automation Does to Human Beings* (London: Sidgwick & Jackson, 1956), pp. 86–101.

66. De Grazia, *Of Time, Work, and Leisure.*

67. Staffan Linder, *The Harried Leisure Class* (New York: Columbia University Press, 1970), pp. 77–109.

68. Ibid., p. 85.

69. Ibid., p. 79.

70. Walter Kerr, *The Decline of Pleasure* (New York: Simon & Schuster, 1962), pp. 136–37.

71. Linder, *Harried Leisure Class,* p. 90 (italics added).

72. Lukács, *History and Class Consciousness,* p. 90.

73. For the prevalence of this notion within the world of newsmen, see Philip Schlesinger, "Newsmen and Their Time-Machine," *British Journal of Sociology* 28 (1977): 341–42.

74. Benjamin Lee Whorf, "The Relation of Habitual Thought and Behavior to Language," in *Language, Thought, and Reality,* ed. John B. Carroll (Cambridge: MIT Press, 1956), p. 140; see also Victor Gioscia, "On Social Time," in *The Future of Time,* ed. Henry Yaker et al. (Garden City: Anchor Books, 1972), p. 82.

75. Stan Bernstein, "Getting It Done: Notes on Student Fritters," *Urban Life and Culture* 1 (1972): 275–92; C. Neil Bull, "Chronology: The Field of Social Time," *Journal of Leisure Research* 10 (1978): 294.

76. C. Northcote Parkinson, *In-Laws and Outlaws* (Cambridge, Mass.: Riverside, 1962), p. 71.

77. McLuhan, *Understanding Media,* p. 135.

78. Ibid. See also Maurice Halbwachs, *The Collective Memory* (New York: Harper Colophon, 1980), p. 100.

79. Irving Hallowell, "Temporal Orientation in Western Civilization and in a Pre-Literate Society," *American Anthropologist* 39 (1937): 669.

80. Wright, *Clockwork Man,* pp. 160–67.

81. Hall, *Ways Out,* pp. 54–55.

82. Zerubavel, *Patterns of Time in Hospital Life,* pp. 60–61.

83. McLuhan, *Understanding Media,* p. 142.

84. Daniel J. Boorstin, *The Americans—the Democratic Experience* (New York: Random House, 1973), p. 362; Wright, *Clockwork Man,* p. 206.

85. Alfred Schutz, "Making Music Together: A Study in Social Relationship," in *Collected Papers,* vol. 2, ed. Arvid Brodersen (The Hague: Martinus Nijhoff, 1976), pp. 159–78.

86. Avery Sharron, "The Time Signature: An Alternative Concept of

Togetherness," presented at the Conference on Time and Temporal Structures, Urbana-Champaign, March 1980.

87. Durkheim, *The Division of Labor in Society* (New York: Free Press, 1964).

88. *Rule*, ch. 24.

89. George B. Dantzig and Thomas L. Saaty, *Compact City* (San Francisco: W. H. Freeman, 1973), p. 29.

90. Yevgeny Zamyatin, *We* (New York: Bantam, 1972), p. 12.

91. Mumford, *Technics and Civilization*, p. 269.

92. Wright, *Clockwork Man*, p. 216.

93. Goffman, "On the Characteristics of Total Institutions."

94. Zerubavel, *Patterns of Time in Hospital Life*, pp. 82–83. See also the characterization of the social relations among "night people" in Murray Melbin, "Night as Frontier," *American Sociological Review* 43 (1978): 3–22.

95. Zerubavel, *Patterns of Time in Hospital Life*, pp. 60–83.

96. Durkheim, *Division of Labor in Society*.

97. Wilbert E. Moore, *Man, Time, and Society* (New York: John Wiley, 1963), pp. 121–22; Zerubavel, *Patterns of Time in Hospital Life*, pp. 60–61.

98. Georg Simmel, "The Metropolis and Mental Life," in *The Sociology of Georg Simmel*, ed. Kurt H. Wolff (New York: Free Press, 1950), pp. 412–13.

99. Zerubavel, *Patterns of Time in Hospital Life*, pp. 60–83.

100. Georg Simmel, "The Web of Group Affiliations," in *Conflict and the Web of Group Affiliations* (New York: Free Press, 1964), pp. 127–95.

101. Zerubavel, *Patterns of Time in Hospital Life*, pp. 60–83.

Chapter Three

1. Max Weber, *Ancient Judaism* (New York: Free Press, 1952), p. 354.

2. *Midrash Rabbah Exodus* (London: Soncino, 1951), 25.11.

3. *Ezekiel* 20.12. See also Samuel M. Segal, *The Sabbath Book* (New York: Thomas Yoseloff, 1957), pp. 179–80.

4. *The Book of Jubilees* 2.19, in *The Apocrypha and Pseudoepigrapha of the Old Testament*, ed. R. H. Charles, vol. 2 (Oxford: Oxford University Press, 1913).

5. Abraham Joshua Heschel, *The Sabbath* (New York: Farrar, Straus & Giroux, 1951), pp. 51–55.

6. Abraham P. Bloch, *The Biblical and Historical Background of Jewish Customs and Ceremonies* (New York: Ktav Publishing House, 1980), pp. 108–9.

7. *Nehemiah* 13.15–22.

8. Weber, *Ancient Judaism*, pp. 150, 354.

9. Hutton Webster, *Rest Days* (New York: Macmillan, 1916), pp. 267–71.

10. Abraham E. Millgram, *Sabbath* (Philadelphia: Jewish Publication Society, 1944), p. 365; Germano Pàttaro, "The Christian Conception of Time," in *Cultures and Time,* ed. Louis Gardet et al. (Paris: UNESCO Press, 1976), p. 183.

11. Sherrard B. Burnaby, *Elements of the Jewish and Mohammedan Calendars* (London: George Bell, 1901), p. 387.

12. Leonard Hubbard, *Soviet Labour and Industry* (London: Macmillan, 1924), pp. 47, 59, 98; Wilbert E. Moore, *Man, Time, and Society* (New York: John Wiley, 1963), p. 122; Bhola D. Panth, *Consider the Calendar* (New York: Teachers College of Columbia University, 1944), pp. 79–81.

13. Joshua Manoach, "The People of Israel—the People of Time," in *Calendar for 6000 Years* (in Hebrew), ed. A. A. Akavia (Jerusalem: Mossad Harav Kook, 1976), pp. xi, xiv, xx–xxi.

14. Ibid., pp. xiv, xvii–xviii, xx.

15. Ibid,, p. xvi.

16. Ibid., p xxii. See also pp. xiv, xix.

17. Ibid., p. xx. See also pp. vii–viii.

18. Ibid., p. xix.

19. Ibid.

20. Ibid., pp. xvi–xvii.

21. L. E. Boyle, "Medieval Chronology: The West in the Middle Ages," *New Catholic Encyclopaedia,* vol. 3 (New York: McGraw-Hill, 1967), p. 675; Reginald L. Poole, "The Beginning of the Year in the Middle Ages," *Proceedings of the British Academy* 10 (1921–23): 118, 124.

22. "Boethusians," *Encyclopaedia Judaica,* vol. 4 (Jerusalem: Keter, 1972), p. 1169; G. R. Driver, *The Judaean Scrolls* (Oxford: Basil Blackwell, 1965), pp. 230, 321; Louis Finkelstein, *The Pharisees,* vol. 2 (Philadelphia: Jewish Publication Society of America, 1962), pp. 641–54; Joseph Heller and Leon Nemoy, "Karaites," *Encyclopaedia Judaica,* vol. 10 (Jerusalem: Keter, 1972), p. 779; Julian Obermann, "Calendaric Elements in the Dead Sea Scrolls," *Journal of Biblical Literature* 75 (1956): 292–93; Ellis Rivkin, *A Hidden Revolution* (Nashville: Abingdon, 1978), pp. 263–67; "Sectarian Calendars," *Encyclopaedia Judaica,* vol. 5 (Jerusalem: Keter, 1972), pp. 50–51.

23. Finkelstein, *Pharisees,* pp. 648–49. See also J. Van Goudoever, *Biblical Calendars* (Leiden: E. J. Brill, 1961), pp. 15–29.

24. Finkelstein, *Pharisees,* p. 650.

25. P. W. Wilson, *The Romance of the Calendar* (New York: Norton, 1937), p. 198; Lawrence Wright, *Clockwork Man* (London: Elek, 1968), p. 37.

26. James H. Barnett, "The Easter Festival: A Study in Cultural Change," *American Sociological Review* 14 (1949): 63.

27. *Book of Jubilees* 6.30–32.

28. *Book of Enoch* 74.12, in *Apocrypha and Pseudoepigrapha of the Old Testament.* See also ibid., 82.6.

29. Millar Burrows, *The Dead Sea Scrolls* (New York: Viking, 1955), pp. 238–42; Driver, *Judaean Scrolls,* pp. 316–30; Charles T. Fritsch, *The Qumran Community* (New York: Macmillan, 1956), p. 70; Van Goudoever, *Biblical Calendars,* pp. 62–70; Lucetta Mowry, *The Dead Sea Scrolls and the Early Church* (Chicago and London: University of Chicago Press, 1962), pp. 207–10; J. van der Ploeg, *The Excavations at Qumran* (London: Longman, Green & Co., 1958), pp. 126–30; Chaim Rabin, *Qumran Studies* (London: Oxford University Press, 1957), pp. 77–81; Kurt Schubert, *The Dead Sea Community* (Westport, Ct.: Greenwood Press, 1959), pp. 57–58; Edmund Sutcliffe, *The Monks of Qumran* (Westminster: Newman Press, 1960), pp. 112–13; Geza Vermes, *The Dead Sea Scrolls* (Cleveland: Collins & World, 1978), pp. 175–78; Solomon Zeitlin, "The Book of Jubilees: Its Character and Its Significance," *Jewish Quarterly Review,* n.s. 30 (1939): 25–28.

30. Driver, *Judaean Scrolls,* pp. 318–19; Zeitlin, "Book of Jubilees," p. 14.

31. George Foot Moore, *Judaism in the First Centuries of the Christian Era,* vol. 1 (Cambridge: Harvard University Press, 1958), p. 194 (italics added).

32. *Book of Jubilees* 6.32–38.

33. *The Manual of Discipline* 1.14, in *The Dead Sea Scriptures,* ed. Theodor H. Gaster (Garden City: Doubleday Anchor, 1956), pp. 39–40.

34. Rivkin, *Hidden Revolution,* pp. 266–67; Schubert, *Dead Sea Community,* pp. 57–58; Sutcliffe, *Monks of Qumran,* p. 112.

35. Driver, *Judaean Scrolls,* pp. 84, 330; Yigael Yadin, *The Scroll of the War of the Sons of Light against the Sons of Darkness* (London: Oxford University Press, 1962), p. 206.

36. Yigael Yadin, *The Message of the Scrolls* (New York: Simon & Schuster, 1957), p. 174.

37. A. Dupont-Sommer, *The Jewish Sect of Qumran and the Essenes* (London: Vallentine, Mitchell & Co., 1954), pp. 107–8.

38. Rabin, *Qumran Studies,* p. 77.

39. Driver, *Judaean Scrolls,* p. 330. See also van der Ploeg, *Excavations at Qumran,* p. 129.

40. Jacob Licht, "The 364-Day Solar Calendar," *Encyclopaedia Judaica,* vol. 5 (Jerusalem: Keter, 1972), p. 52 (italics added).

41. Burnaby, *Elements of the Jewish and Mohammedan Calendars,* pp. 367–71.

42. Louis Gardet, "Moslem Views of Time and History," in *Cultures and Time* (Paris: UNESCO Press, 1976), p. 202.

43. G. E. von Grunebaum, *Muhammadan Festivals* (New York: Henry Schuman, 1951), p. 53.

44. W. Lloyd Warner's analysis of the Church's calendar as a symbolic system serves as a notable example of an attempt to do so. See his *Family of God* (New Haven: Yale University Press, 1961), pp. 345–73.

45. For a complete protocol of the report of the Committee of Public Instruction, see *Procès-Verbaux du Comité d'Instruction Publique de la Convention Nationale,* ed. J. Guillaume, vol. 2 (Paris: Imprimerie National, 1894), pp. 437–51, 579–91, 693–713, 872–93. For some historical accounts of the Revolutionary calendar, see George B. Andrews, "Making the Revolutionary Calendar," *American Historical Review* 36 (1931): 515–32; Jacques Godechot, *Les Institutions de la France sous la Révolution et l'Empire* (Paris: Presses Universitaires de France, 1951), pp. 363–66; Aug. Herrmann, *Concordance des Calendriers Grégorien et Républicain* (Strasbourg: Heitz, 1938).

46. Edward S. Mason, *The Paris Commune* (New York: Macmillan, 1930), p. 241; Wilson, *Romance of the Calendar,* p. 155.

47. *Procès-Verbaux,* pp. 696, 706.

48. Ibid., pp. 875–82.

49. Ibid., pp. 441, 445, 876.

50. Ibid., pp. 448, 703.

51. Ibid., p. 877.

52. Ibid., pp. 696, 698.

53. Andrews, "Making the Revolutionary Calendar," p. 516.

54. Joseph Lovering, "A Note on the Republican Calendar," *Proceedings of the American Academy of Arts and Sciences* 8 (1872): 350.

55. Andrews, "Making the Revolutionary Calendar," p. 525.

56. Herbert W. Schneider, *Making the Fascist State* (New York: Oxford University Press, 1928), p. 226.

57. Henri Hubert and Marcel Mauss, "Étude Sommaire de la Représentation du Temps dans la Religion et la Magie," *Mélanges d'Histoire des Religions* (Paris: Librairies Félix Alcan et Guillaumin Réunies, 1909), pp. 197–208.

58. Pitirim Sorokin and Robert K. Merton, "Social Time: A Methodological and Functional Analysis," *American Journal of Sociology* 42 (1937): 623; see also pp. 618–19; Pitirim Sorokin, *Sociocultural Causality, Space, Time* (Durham: Duke University Press, 1943), p. 174.

59. John Adam Robson, "Christian Chronology," *Encyclopaedia Britannica,* vol. 5 (Chicago: Encyclopaedia Britannica, 1972), p. 728.

60. *Procès-Verbaux,* p. 697.

61. Ibid., pp. 440, 444–45, 696, 876, 882.

62. The French were not the first ones, however, to have institution-

alized a 10-day weekly cycle. For other historical precedents, see Webster, *Rest Days,* pp. 188–92.

63. *Procès-Verbaux,* pp. 444, 881.

64. Ibid., p. 444.

65. Poole, "Beginning of the Year."

66. F. H. Colson, *The Week* (Cambridge: Cambridge University Press, 1926), p. 2.

67. Eviatar Zerubavel, *Patterns of Time in Hospital Life* (Chicago and London: University of Chicago Press, 1979), p. 103.

68. *Procès-Verbaux,* p. 702.

69. Ibid., pp. 448, 697.

70. Ernst Cassirer, *Language and Myth* (New York: Dover, 1953), pp. 44–62; Claude Lévi-Strauss, *The Savage Mind* (Chicago: University of Chicago Press, 1966), pp. 172–216.

71. *Procès-Verbaux,* p. 445.

72. Ibid., pp. 697–99.

73. Ibid., pp. 698–99, 703–4.

74. Ibid., pp. 707–13.

75. Ibid., pp. 700–701.

76. Richard Grunberger, *The 12-Year Reich* (New York: Holt, Rinehart & Winston, 1971), p. 446.

77. *Procès-Verbaux,* p. 701.

78. Ibid., p. 874.

79. Ibid., pp. 442, 877.

80. Ibid., pp. 449–50, 584, 875.

81. Van der Ploeg, *The Excavations at Qumran,* p. 129; Wilson, *Romance of the Calendar,* pp. 150–51, 156; Wright, *Clockwork Man,* p. 100.

82. *Procès-Verbaux,* p. 704.

83. Ibid., pp. 583, 880.

84. Ibid., pp. 446–47, 580.

85. Ibid., p. 877.

86. See, for example, Herrmann, *Concordance des Calendriers.*

87. Andrews, "Making the Revolutionary Calendar," pp. 528, 531n.

88. Lovering, "Note on the Republican Calendar," p. 349.

89. *Procès-Verbaux,* p. 585.

90. See, for example, Cyrus H. Gordon, *The Ancient Near East* (New York: Norton, 1965), p. 186n.

91. F. F. Arbuthnot, *The Mysteries of Chronology* (London: William Heinemann, 1900); Boyle, "Medieval Chronology," p. 675; Oscar Cullmann, *Christ and Time* (Philadelphia: Westminster, 1964), p. 18; Julius T. Fraser, *Of Time, Passion, and Knowledge* (New York: Braziller, 1975), p. 53; Panth, *Consider the Calendar,* p. 70; Poole, "The Beginning of the Year," p. 120; Robson, "Christian Chronology," p. 728; G. J. Whitrow, *The Nature of Time* (New York: Holt, Rinehart

& Winston, 1972), p. 17; Wilson, *Romance of the Calendar*, pp. 135, 332; Wright, *Clockwork Man*, p. 42.

92. Boyle, "Medieval Chronology," p. 675; Panth, *Consider the Calendar*, pp. 66, 70; Poole, "Beginning of the Year"; Wilson, *Romance of the Calendar*, p. 296.

93. Talcott Parsons, *The Social System* (New York: Free Press, 1951).

94. A. A. Akavia, *Calendar for 6000 Years* (Jerusalem: Mossad Harav Kook, 1976), pp. 608–10; Colin Alistair Ronan, "Western Calendar," *Encyclopaedia Britannica*, vol. 4 (Chicago: Encyclopaedia Britannica, 1972), p. 619; Wilson, *Romance of the Calendar*, pp. 149–56, 333–35.

95. Panth, *Consider the Calendar*, p. 79.

96. Wilson, *Romance of the Calendar*, pp. 29–30.

Chapter Four

1. See, for example, Henri Hubert and Marcel Mauss, "Etude Sommaire de la Représentation du Temps dans la Religion et la Magie," in *Mélanges d'Histoire des Religions* (Paris: Librairies Félix Alcan et Guillaumin Réunies, 1909); Georg Lukács, *History and Class Consciousness* (Cambridge: MIT Press, 1971), pp. 89–90; Karl Mannheim, *Essays on the Sociology of Knowledge* (London: Routledge & Kegan Paul, 1952), pp. 281–83; Barry Schwartz, *Queuing and Waiting* (Chicago and London: University of Chicago Press, 1975); Eviatar Zerubavel, *Patterns of Time in Hospital Life* (Chicago and London: University of Chicago Press, 1979), pp. 113–17.

2. Clifford Geertz, "Person, Time, and Conduct in Bali," in *The Interpretation of Cultures* (New York: Basic Books, 1973), p. 391.

3. Emile Durkheim, *The Elementary Forms of the Religious Life* (New York: Free Press, 1965), p. 56.

4. Ibid, pp. 53–54.

5. Ibid., p. 55.

6. On the use of food and space for that purpose, see, for example, Mary Douglas, *Purity and Danger* (New York: Praeger, 1966), pp. 41–57; Mircea Eliade, *The Sacred and the Profane* (New York: Harcourt, Brace & World, 1959), pp. 20–65.

7. Schwartz, *Queuing and Waiting*.

8. Zerubavel, *Patterns of Time in Hospital Life*, p. 119.

9. Wilbert E. Moore, *Man, Time, and Society* (New York: John Wiley, 1963), p. 119.

10. Rose Laub Coser, "Insulation from Observability and Types of Social Conformity," *American Sociological Review* 26 (1961): 28–39; Robert K. Merton, *Social Theory and Social Structure* (New York: Free Press, 1968), pp. 428–30.

11. Durkheim, *Elementary Forms of the Religious Life,* p. 347.

12. Ibid., pp. 345–47.

13. Murray Melbin, "Night as Frontier," *American Sociological Review* 43 (1978): 5.

14. Durkheim, *Elementary Forms of the Religious Life,* pp. 346–47.

15. Abraham Joshua Heschel, *The Sabbath* (New York: Farrar, Straus & Giroux, 1951), p. 8.

16. Samuel C. Heilman, *Synagogue Life* (Chicago and London: University of Chicago Press, 1976), p. 34.

17. *Amos* 8.5; *Hosea* 2.13; *Isaiah* 1.13; *II Kings* 4.23.

18. Max Weber, *Ancient Judaism* (New York: Free Press, 1952), pp. 150, 354.

19. Abraham E. Millgram, *Sabbath* (Philadelphia: Jewish Publication Society, 1944), p. 344.

20. *Exodus* 31.15. See also ibid., 35.2; *Numbers* 15.32–36.

21. *I Maccabees* 2.32–38.

22. Josephus, *Complete Works* (Grand Rapids: Kregel, 1960), *The Antiquities of the Jews* xiv, iv, 2–3.

23. Millgram, *Sabbath,* p. 254.

24. Aḥad Ha-Am, *Kol Kitvey Aḥad Ha-Am* (Jerusalem: Jewish Publishing House, 1947), p. 286. Note that, in Hebrew, there is one word for both "observe" and "preserve."

25. *Jeremiah* 17.27; *Tractate Shabbath* 119b. Unless otherwise specified, all Tractate references apply to sections of *The Babylonian Talmud* (London: Soncino, 1938).

26. *The Jerusalem Talmud: Tractate Nedarim* 3.9; Maimonides, *The Book of Seasons* (New Haven: Yale University Press, 1961), *Sabbath* 30.15; *Midrash Rabbah: Exodus* (London: Soncino, 1951), 25.12; *Tractate Ḥullin* 5a; *The Zohar* (London: Soncino, 1933), *Beshalaḥ* 47b.

27. *Deuteronomy* 5.12–15; *Exodus* 20.8–11.

28. *Genesis* 2.3; Heschel, *Sabbath,* p. 9.

29. *Tractate Pesaḥim* 103a–104a.

30. *The Code of Jewish Law,* ed. Solomon Ganzfried (New York: Hebrew Publishing Company, 1961), 96.5; Maimonides, *Book of Seasons, Sabbath* 29.22.

31. Millgram, *Sabbath,* p. 35.

32. Ibid.

33. *Ezekiel* 20.12.

34. *Tractate Beẓah* 16a; *Tractate Ta'anit* 27b.

35. Eliade, *Sacred and the Profane,* p. 89.

36. Ibid., p. 85.

37. Ibid., pp. 68–69. On the commemoration of "beginnings" as events that belong within the domain of sacred time, see also Barry Schwartz, "The Iconography of Origins," presented at the annual meeting of the Pacific Sociological Association, Anaheim, April 1979.

38. Eliade, *Sacred and the Profane*, p. 88.

39. *The Authorized Daily Prayer Book*, ed. Joseph H. Hertz (New York: Bloch Publishing Co., 1960), p. 579.

40. *Genesis* 2.2.

41. *Exodus* 20.8–11.

42. "Eshet Hayil," *Encyclopaedia Judaica*, vol. 6 (Jerusalem: Keter, 1972), p. 887.

43. Raphael Patai, *The Hebrew Goddess* (New York: Avon, 1978), pp. 245, 248.

44. Maimonides, *The Book of Seasons, Sabbath* 30.14; Joshua Trachtenberg, *Jewish Magic and Superstition* (New York: Atheneum, 1970), p. 186; *Tractate Baba Kamma* 82a; *Tractate Kethuboth* 62b.

45. Patai, *Hebrew Goddess*, p. 249.

46. Ibid., pp. 251–54.

47. Hubert and Mauss, "Etude Sommaire," pp. 207–8.

48. Zerubavel, *Patterns of Time in Hospital Life*, pp. 113–17.

49. Eliade, *Sacred and the Profane*, p. 68.

50. Durkheim, *Elementary Forms of the Religious Life*, p. 347.

51. Claude Lévi-Strauss, *The Savage Mind* (Chicago: University of Chicago Press, 1966), p. 199.

52. Zerubavel, *Patterns of Time in Hospital Life*, pp. 2–3.

53. Lévi-Strauss, *Savage Mind*, pp. 258–61.

54. Schwartz, "Iconography of Origins."

55. W. Lloyd Warner, *The Family of God* (New Haven: Yale University Press, 1961), p. 347.

56. Durkheim, *Elementary Forms of the Religious Life*, p. 54.

57. Eliade, *Sacred and the Profane*, pp. 71–72.

58. Edmund R. Leach, *Culture and Communication* (Cambridge: Cambridge University Press, 1976), p. 83.

59. Edmund R. Leach, "Two Essays concerning the Symbolic Representation of Time," *Rethinking Anthropology* (London: Athlone, 1961), pp. 133–34.

60. Eliade, *Sacred and the Profane*, p. 104.

61. Ibid., p. 70.

62. Ibid., p. 69. See also ibid., pp. 72, 90; Warner, *Family of God*, pp. 345–73.

63. Eliade, *Sacred and the Profane*, p. 88 (italics added).

64. Ibid., pp. 110–11.

65. For an attempt to graphically represent this peculiar relationship between sacred time and profane time as two entirely distinct planes of temporality, see Leach, "Two Essays," p. 134.

66. Ibid., pp. 132–36.

67. F. H. Colson, *The Week* (Cambridge: Cambridge University Press, 1926), p. 107.

68. *Leviticus* 23.15–16; *Midrash Rabbah: Genesis* 11.5; *Tractate Ta'anit* 29b.

69. Colson, *Week*, p. 29.

70. Ibid., pp. 27–29.

71. *Tractate Ta'anit* 27b, 29b.

72. Millgram, *Sabbath*, p. 49.

73. *Code of Jewish Law* 96.15; Maimonides, *Book of Seasons, Sabbath* 29.3; *Tractate Pesahim* 106a; Mark Zborowski and Elizabeth Herzog, *Life Is with People* (New York: Schocken, 1962), p. 37.

74. Heschel, *Sabbath*, p. 21.

75. Zborowski and Herzog, *Life Is with People*, pp. 59–60, 142, 363.

76. *Tractate Shabbath* 113a.

77. Douglas, *Purity and Danger;* Durkheim, *Elementary Forms of the Religious Life*, pp. 337–65.

78. Hutton Webster, *Rest Days* (New York: Macmillan, 1916), p. 242n.

79. *Exodus* 16.29. See also ibid., 23.12, 34.21, 35.2–3; *Jeremiah* 17.22–27; *Nehemiah* 13.15–22.

80. Hayyim Schauss, *The Jewish Festivals* (New York: Schocken, 1962), p. 11.

81. *Tractate Eruvin.*

82. *Code of Jewish Law* 80; *Mishnayot: Tractate Shabbath* (New York: Judaica Press, 1963), 7.2.

83. *Code of Jewish Law* 80.7.

84. Ibid., 80.62.

85. Ibid., 80.70.

86. Ibid., 80.55.

87. Isaiah 58.13.

88. *Deuteronomy* 5.13–14 (italics added). See also *Exodus* 23.12.

89. Louis Ginzberg, *The Legends of the Jews,* vol. 5 (Philadelphia: Jewish Publication Society of America, 1953), p. 111; *Midrash Rabbah: Genesis* 10.9.

90. *Code of Jewish Law* 77.22.

91. Ibid., 72.7, 77.22; Maimonides, *Book of Seasons, Sabbath* 30.5; *The Midrash on Psalms* (New Haven: Yale University Press, 1959), 92.3; *Tractate Shabbath* 119a–119b; Zborowski and Herzog, *Life Is with People*, pp. 46, 59.

92. Maimonides, *Book of Seasons, Sabbath* 30.12; *Tractate Ta'anit* 27b.

93. *Tractate Megillah* 5a.

94. *Code of Jewish Law* 90.6; Maimonides, *Book of Seasons, Sabbath* 24.1; Zborowski and Herzog, *Life Is with People,* pp. 47–48, 57.

95. Heschel, *Sabbath*, p. 65.

96. Durkheim, *Elementary Forms of the Religious Life,* p. 54.

97. Millgram, *Sabbath,* pp. 295–96; Zborowski and Herzog, *Life Is with People,* p. 38.

98. *Midrash Rabbah: Genesis* 11.2; *Midrash Rabbah: Song of Songs* I.5, 2.

99. Eliade, *Sacred and the Profane,* p. 85.

100. Maimonides, *Book of Seasons, Sabbath* 24.4; *Tractate Shabbath* 113a.

101. Zborowski and Herzog, *Life Is with People,* pp. 50, 56, 64.

102. *Code of Jewish Law* 86; Maimonides, *Book of Seasons, Sabbath* 24.12–13, 30.2.

103. Maimonides, *Book of Seasons, Sabbath* 24.4; *Tractate Shabbath* 113b.

104. *The Zohar, Beshalah* 47b.

105. Marshall David Sahlins, *Culture and Practical Reason* (Chicago and London: University of Chicago Press, 1976), p. 182.

106. *Mishnayot: Tractate Sabbath* 6.

107. *Tractate Shabbath* 113a. See also *Code of Jewish Law* 72.16; Maimonides, *Book of Seasons, Sabbath* 30.3; *Midrash on Psalms* 92.3.

108. Zborowski and Herzog, *Life Is with People,* pp. 41–42.

109. Ibid., p. 363.

110. Israel Abrahams, *Jewish Life in the Middle Ages* (New York: Atheneum, 1975), pp. 288–89; Maimonides, *Book of Seasons, Sabbath* 30.3; Samuel M. Segal, *The Sabbath Book* (New York: Thomas Yoseloff, 1957), p. 115; *Tractate Shabbath* 113a.

111. Douglas, *Purity and Danger,* pp. 41–57; Mary Douglas, *Implicit Meanings* (London: Routledge & Kegan Paul, 1975), pp. 249–75; Claude Lévi-Strauss, *The Raw and the Cooked* (New York: Harper Torchbooks, 1970).

112. Maimonides, *Book of Seasons, Sabbath* 30.8.

113. Zborowski and Herzog, *Life Is with People,* p. 60.

114. Maimonides, *Book of Seasons, Sabbath* 30.8; *Tractate Shabbath* 119a.

115. Douglas, *Implicit Meanings,* p. 304.

116. *Exodus* 31.14; *Ezekiel* 20.13–24; *Isaiah* 56.2–6; *Nehemiah* 13.17–18.

117. *Tractate Shabbath* 69b.

118. P. W. Wilson, *The Romance of the Calendar* (New York: Norton, 1937), p. 274.

119. *Authorized Daily Prayer Book,* p. 744.

120. Ibid., p. 749; Millgram, *Sabbath,* p. 91.

121. Jacob Mann, "Genizah Fragments of the Palestinian Order of Service," *Hebrew Union College Annual* 2 (1925): 318.

122. See, for example, the bibliography in Edgar Frank, *Shabbath—the Time of Its Beginning and Termination* (New York: Philipp Feldheim, 1964).

123. *Tractate Shabbath* 34b–35.

124. *Tractate Berakoth* 52.

125. Frank, *Sabbath—the Time of Its Beginning and Termination,* pp. 11, 22, 42.

126. Ibid., p. 52.

127. Ibid., pp. 25, 29.

128. *Tractate Yoma* 81b.

129. Abrahams, *Jewish Life in the Middle Ages,* p. 56; Josephus, *Complete Works, War of the Jews,* iv, ix, 12; Maimonides, *Book of Seasons, Sabbath* 5.18–20; Schauss, *Jewish Festivals,* pp. 13–14; *Tractate Shabbath* 35b, 114b.

130. *Tractate Shabbath* 35b.

131. Abraham P. Bloch, *The Biblical and Historical Background of Jewish Customs and Ceremonies* (New York: Ktav Publishing House, 1980), p. 121; Zborowski and Herzog, *Life Is with People,* p. 42.

132. Leach, *Culture and Communication,* p. 34.

133. Eliade, *Sacred and the Profane,* p. 68.

134. Barney G. Glaser and Anselm L. Strauss, *Status Passage* (Chicago and New York: Aldine and Atherton, 1971).

135. Arnold van Gennep, *The Rites of Passage* (Chicago: University of Chicago Press, 1960), p. 178.

136. Ibid., p. 181.

137. *Tractate Shabbath* 119a.

138. Heschel, *Sabbath,* p. 113; *Mishnayot: Tractate Berakoth* 2.5. See also *Tractate Shabbath* 118b–119a.

139. Patai, *Hebrew Goddess,* pp. 243–48.

140. Van Gennep, *Rites of Passage.*

141. *Code of Jewish Law* 72.7; Maimonides, *Book of Seasons, Sabbath* 30.2; Segal, *Sabbath Book,* pp. 13–16.

142. Frank, *Sabbath—the Time of Its Beginning and Termination,* p. 32.

143. Schauss, *Jewish Festivals,* p. 33.

144. Zborowski and Herzog, *Life Is with People,* p. 43.

145. *Code of Jewish Law* 75.4.

146. *Authorized Daily Prayer Book,* pp. 343–44.

147. Ibid., p. 342.

148. *Code of Jewish Law* 76.1; Segal, *Sabbath Book,* p. 26.

149. *Code of Jewish Law* 75.1; *Authorized Daily Prayer Book,* p. 342; Segal, *Sabbath Book,* p. 28.

150. Millgram, *Sabbath,* p. 346.

151. Victor W. Turner, *The Ritual Process* (London: Penguin, 1974), pp. 80–118; Douglas, *Purity and Danger,* pp. 37–40.

152. Maimonides, *Book of Seasons, Sabbath* 24.10.

153. *Authorized Daily Prayer Book,* p. 344; Millgram, *Sabbath,* p. 13; Schauss, *Jewish Festivals,* p. 26.

154. Maimonides, *Book of Seasons, Sabbath* 29.29; Trachtenberg, *Jewish Magic and Superstition*, p. 67; *Tractate Pesahim* 102b.

155. Segal, *Sabbath Book*, p. 136.

156. Trachtenberg, *Jewish Magic and Superstition*, pp. 167, 308.

157. Ginzberg, *Legends of the Jews*, vol. 4, p. 201, vol. 6., p. 22; Segal, *Sabbath Book*, p. 185; Trachtenberg, *Jewish Magic and Superstition*, pp. 66–67.

158. *Authorized Daily Prayer Book*, p. 725; *Code of Jewish Law* 96.2; Patai, *Hebrew Goddess*, pp. 319–21; Harry Rabinowicz, "Melavveh Malkah," *Encyclopaedia Judaica* (Jerusalem: Keter, 1972), vol. 11, p. 1277; Segal, *Sabbath Book*, p. 127; Trachtenberg, *Jewish Magic and Superstition*, p. 66.

159. Zborowski and Herzog, *Life Is with People*, p. 58.

160. *Authorized Daily Prayer Book*, p. 747.

161. *Genesis* 1.4.

162. *Code of Jewish Law* 96.5; Segal, *Sabbath Book*, p. 132.

Chapter Five

1. Georg Simmel, "The Web of Group Affiliations," *Conflict and the Web of Group Affiliations* (New York: Free Press, 1964), pp. 127–95.

2. Lewis A. Coser, *Greedy Institutions* (New York: Free Press, 1974), p. 3.

3. Ibid.

4. Erving Goffman, *The Presentation of Self in Everyday Life* (Garden City: Anchor Books, 1959), pp. 106–40; Erving Goffman, *Behavior in Public Places* (New York: Free Press, 1963), pp. 39–40; Robert K. Merton, *Social Theory and Social Structure* (New York: Free Press, 1968), pp. 428–30; Barry Schwartz, "The Social Psychology of Privacy," *American Journal of Sociology* 73 (1968): 741–42.

5. For a sociological analysis of sleep as the most important institutionalized form of periodic remission, see Barry Schwartz, "Notes on the Sociology of Sleep," *Sociological Quarterly* 11 (1970): 485–99. On the use of the locked bathroom, see, for example, Philip Roth, *Portnoy's Complaint* (New York: Bantam, 1970), pp. 18–23.

6. Rose Laub Coser, "Insulation from Observability and Types of Social Conformity," *American Sociological Review* 26 (1961): 28–39; Goffman, *Presentation of Self in Everyday Life*, p. 49; Merton, *Social Theory and Social Structure*, pp. 428–30.

7. Goffman, *Presentation of Self in Everyday Life*, p. 126 (italics added).

8. For another way in which time functions as a segmenting principle in social life, see Erving Goffman, *Frame Analysis* (New York: Harper Colophon, 1974), pp. 251–69.

9. Goffman, *Presentation of Self in Everyday Life*, p. 138.

10. Erving Goffman, "Role Distance," in *Encounters* (Indianapolis: Bobbs-Merrill, 1961), pp. 90–91. See also Gerald D. Suttles, "Friendship as a Social Institution," in *Social Relationships,* ed. George J. McCall et al. (Chicago: Aldine, 1970), p. 111.

11. For some earlier attempts to apply the territorial perspective to nonspatial dimensions of interpersonal relations or to represent nonspatial aspects of social accessibility in quasi-spatial terms, see, for example, Erving Goffman, *Relations in Public* (New York: Harper Colophon, 1972), pp. 28–61; Kurt Lewin, "Some Social-Psychological Differences between the United States and Germany," in *Resolving Social Conflicts* (London: Souvenir Press, 1973), pp. 18–33; Robert Ezra Park, "The Concept of Social Distance," *Journal of Applied Sociology* 8 (1924): 339–44; Georg Simmel, *The Sociology of Georg Simmel* (New York: Free Press, 1950), pp. 321–22; Eviatar Zerubavel, "What Do They Know about Me?—Social Information in Everyday Life," presented at the annual meeting of the American Sociological Association, New York, August 1980.

12. Goffman, *Behavior in Public Places*, pp. 39–40.

13. Edward T. Hall, *The Silent Language* (New York: Premier, 1959), p. 16.

14. Barry Schwartz, "Deprivation of Privacy as a 'Functional Prerequisite': The Case of the Prison," *Journal of Criminal Law, Criminology, and Police Science* 63 (1972): 229 (italics added).

15. Erving Goffman, "On the Characteristics of Total Institutions," in *Asylums* (Garden City: Anchor Books, 1961), p. 4.

16. L. Coser, *Greedy Institutions*, p. 1. See also Stephen R. Marks, "Multiple Roles and Role Strain: Some Notes on Human Energy, Time, and Commitment," *American Sociological Review* 42 (1977): 921–36.

17. I have borrowed the notions of "sociofugality" and "sociopetality" to characterize the social qualities of different situations and milieus from Osmond's and Sommer's characterization of buildings in particular and spaces in general. See Humphrey Osmond, "Function as the Basis of Psychiatric Ward Design," *Mental Hospitals* 8 (April 1957): 28; Robert Sommer, "Sociofugal Space," *American Journal of Sociology* 72 (1967): 654–60.

18. Edward T. Hall, *The Hidden Dimension* (Garden City: Anchor Books, 1966), pp. 113–29.

19. Murray Melbin, "Night as Frontier," *American Sociological Review* 43 (1978): 12–17. On the relationship between intimacy and exclusivity, see Simmel, *Sociology of Georg Simmel*, pp. 126–27.

20. Hall, *Silent Language*, p. 17.

21. Talcott Parsons, *The Social System* (New York: Free Press, 1951).

22. Chauncey D. Leake, *Percival's Medical Ethics* (Baltimore: Williams & Wilkins, 1927), p. 219 (italics added).

23. Eviatar Zerubavel, *Patterns of Time in Hospital Life* (Chicago and London: University of Chicago Press, 1979), pp. 40–41.

24. Sebastian de Grazia, *Of Time, Work, and Leisure* (Garden City: Anchor Books, 1964); Wilbert E. Moore, *Man, Time, and Society* (New York: John Wiley, 1963), pp. 33–34.

25. Zerubavel, *Patterns of Time in Hospital Life*, pp. 106–13.

26. Schwartz, "Social Psychology of Privacy," p. 743.

27. It is interesting to compare the stratification of social accessibility with that of observability and expected behavioral conformity. See, for example, R. Coser, "Insulation from Observability and Types of Conformity." For more on the relationship between high social status and professional commitments, see Rose Laub Coser and Gerald Rokoff, "Women in the Occupational World: Social Disruption and Conflict," *Social Problems* 18 (1971): 535–54.

28. Zerubavel, *Patterns of Time in Hospital Life,* pp. 41–42.

29. Parsons, *Social System.*

30. Max Weber, *The Theory of Social and Economic Organization* (New York: Free Press, 1964), pp. 329–36.

31. Alexis de Tocqueville, *Democracy in America,* vol. 2 (New York: Vintage, 1945), p. 191 (italics added).

32. Ibid., p. 194 (italics added).

33. On paid time off as an employee's fringe benefit, see Donna Allen, *Fringe Benefits* (Ithaca: Cornell University, 1964); Jane Moonman, *The Effectiveness of Fringe Benefits in Industry* (Epping: Gower Press, 1973), pp. 11–37; G. L. Reid, "Sick Pay," in *Fringe Benefits, Labour Costs, and Social Security,* ed. G. L. Reid and D. J. Robertson (London: George Allen & Unwin, 1965), pp. 200–245; John E. Shea, "Holidays, Vacations, Accidents, Sickness, Long-term Disability, and Other Time off the Job," in *Handbook of Modern Personnel Administration,* ed. Joseph J. Famularo (New York: McGraw-Hill, 1972), pp. 36:1–16; Francis M. Wistert, *Fringe Benefits* (New York: Reinhold, 1959), pp. 27–35, 90–99.

34. George Soule, *What Automation Does to Human Beings* (London: Sidgwick & Jackson, 1956), pp. 86–101.

35. Karl Marx, *Capital,* ed. Frederick Engels, vol. 1 (New York: International Publishers, 1967), pp. 543–50.

36. B. Knickerbocker, "More Workers Balking at Compulsory Overtime," *Christian Science Monitor,* 22 March 1978, p. 7.

37. On overtime pay, see William Goldner, *Hours of Work* (Berkeley: Institute of Industrial Relations, 1952), pp. 47–51.

38. On flexible working hours, see Albert S. Glickman and Zenia H. Brown, *Changing Schedules of Work* (Kalamazoo: W. E. Upjohn Institute for Employment Research, 1974); J. Carroll Swart, *A Flexible Approach to Working Hours* (New York: AMACOM, 1978); Michael

Wade, *Flexible Working Hours in Practice* (Epping, England: Gower Press, 1973).

39. Moore, *Man, Time, and Society,* pp. 25–26 (italics added). See also E. P. Thompson, "Time, Work-Discipline, and Industrial Capitalism," *Past and Present* 38 (1967): 56–97.

40. Jean Hallaire, *Part-Time Employment* (Paris: Organisation for Economic Co-operation and Development, 1968).

41. L. Coser, *Greedy Institutions,* p. 2.

42. Zerubavel, *Patterns of Time in Hospital Life,* pp. 32–34.

43. On this moral imperative, see ibid., pp. 40–41.

44. Ibid., pp. 43–46; Eviatar Zerubavel, "The Bureaucratization of Responsibility: The Case of Informed Consent," *Bulletin of the American Academy of Psychiatry and the Law* (forthcoming).

45. Melbin, "Night as Frontier," p. 10.

46. Emile Durkheim, *The Division of Labor in Society* (New York: Free Press, 1964), pp. 1–31.

47. For a pioneer sociological account of the regulation of concern within the domain of health care, see Harold I. Lief and Renée C. Fox, "Training for 'Detached Concern' in Medical Students," in *The Psychological Basis of Medical Practice,* ed. Harold I. Lief et al. (New York: Harper & Row, 1963).

48. L. Coser, *Greedy Institutions.*

Index of Authors

Index of Subjects

Abstract conception of time, 61–64
Activity cult, 56, 58
Ahistorical time, 112–14
Alienation, 166
Atatürk, Kemal, 99

Background expectancies, 19, 21
Beeper, 149–50, 153, 161, 163
Benedictine monasticism, xvii, 30–42, 49–55, 62, 64–68, 128
Bolshevik Revolution, 46, 73, 99
Book of Jubilees, The, 78–79
Breaks, 8, 63, 155, 159
Bureaucracy, xvi, 45, 140–41, 152, 157–60, 165–66

Calendars, 70–101, 130, 133, 158; and cognition, 14, 17, 28; and group identity, 70–81; and organization of life, xvi, 7, 11, 31, 44, 62, 166; reform of, 75, 81–94, 98; sacred, 108, 112–13; sectarian, 75–76, 78–81; and social control, 45–46, 121; and social solidarity, 67; and symbolism, 82–95
Canonical hours, 35–37, 64
Christianity, 32, 54, 72–73, 98–99; and French Revolu-

tion, 85, 87, 89, 91. *See also* Church
Christians, 33, 71–74, 76, 97–99, 115–16. *See also* Church
Chronological eras, 73, 83, 86–87, 95, 97; Christian Era, 74–75, 86–87, 96–97, 113; Era of the Creation, 73–74; Republican Era, 83, 86, 95–96
Church, Roman Catholic, 72, 75–78, 82, 84–86, 91–92, 97–98. *See also* Christianity; Christians
Cleisthenes, 82
Clock, 60–62, 129; and hospital life, 14, 150, 162, 165; in monasteries, 36–39, 64; regulating life by, 9, 11, 47–48, 158; and time reckoning, 15–17, 26
Clock time, 12, 41, 61–63, 129–30
Clockwork environments, 14, 16
Clothing, 122–24, 132
Cognition, 12–30, 73, 89–90, 102, 111, 114
Collective memory, 74, 92
Commitments, 52, 139, 141–42, 144, 146, 150, 165; bureaucratization of, 146, 157–66; divided, 139; professional, xvii, 56, 144, 146,

195